An in depth look at how an unlikely couple raised thirteen (13) successful children.

YOU'RE GETTING BUMPED

KELLY D. WILSON

YOU'RE GETTING BUMPED.
Copyright 2023-2024 by Kelly D. Wilson.

All rights reserved. No part of this book may be reproduced or transmitted in any form or my any means, electronic or mechanical, including photocopying, recording, or by any means, electronic or mechanical, including photocopying, recording, or by any information storage and retrieval system, without written permission from the author.

PRINTED IN THE UNITED STATES OF AMERICA

First Edition

Paperback ISBN 979-8-35093-881-4
Hardcover ISBN 979-8-35095-394-7
eBook ISBN 979-8-35093-882-1

To The Wilson Family

ACKNOWLEDGMENTS

This work brings to life vividly remembered stories told by the people who lived them. They endured my endless questions with loving patience and a willingness to offer details revealing both the good and bad in their lives. I can only hope that I have been true to their vision of the past.

If I have succeeded in that hope, it is owed to the encouragement of family, friends, neighbors and most importantly to the kindest, most supportive partner possible, Jerry Malach.

CONTENTS

ACKNOWLEDGMENTS		I
INTRODUCTION		VII
PART 1	**THE BEGINNING**	**1**
1	BARBARA'S ROOTS	2
2	ENTER BARBARA	10
3	DALE'S ROOTS	19
4	VIRGIE'S CHOICE	30
5	MARIE	35
6	VIRGIE'S REVENGE	38
7	BARBARA'S FAMILY UPENDED	47
8	DALE LEFT BEHIND	53
9	DALE REMEMBERS	66
10	UPS AND DOWNS	71
PART II	**AN UNLIKELY PAIRING**	**77**
11	THE UNION	78
12	A MARRIAGE IN THE MAKING	88
13	BABY BOOM BEGINS	95
14	THE FUTURE IN DOUBT	101
15	THE WAY HOME	105
16	THE KILL FLOOR	112
17	WAR AND THE KELLY BROTHERS	117

PART III   NEW BEGINNINGS   123

   18   MANOR MAGIC   124
   19   EXPECT THE UNEXPECTED   133
   20   THE FEW WHO KNEW HIM   140
   21   TRANSITION   142
   22   THE ONE-ARMED MAN   151
   23   OVER THE HILL TO CHERRYVILLE   154
   24   NEVER CROSS MOM   160

PART IV   THE FARM YEARS   165

   25   THE GENTLEMAN FARMER   166
   26   LUCKY   178
   27   YOU'RE GETTING BUMPED   182
   28   THE TRUTH WAS FUNNY   192
   29   LAND, KIDS, SHEEP, COWS AND HORSES   194
   30   THANKSGIVING DAY   199
   31   THE ASSEMBLY LINE CONTINUES   202
   32   COUSIN MERLE   211
   33   THE CHICKENS CAME HOME TO ROOST   215
   34   THEY KNEW HOW TO GET THINGS DONE   222
   35   MOM MADE IT WORK   226
   36   THE SHETLAND PONY BUSINESS   234
   37   BABY DUTY   238
   38   THE GROCERY STORE MANAGER & THE LA-Z-BOY   247
   39   A PINHOLE IN THE DIKE   251
   40   THE FARM AUCTION   258

PART V   THE TOWN YEARS   **263**

   41   THE NEW HOUSE   264
   42   COFFEYVILLE   268
   43   CAMELOT LOST   273
   44   THE GREAT ADVENTURE   277
   45   A TRIAL PERIOD   282
   46   ALTAR SOCIETY FRIENDS   286
   47   OFF TO THE RACES   289
   48   MOM THE DISCIPLINARIAN   297
   49   VIRGIE AND SID   304

PART VI   MURALS ON CAROUSELS   **309**

   50   THE MIDDLE YEARS   310
   51   THE CENTER OF THE UNIVERSE   315
   52   STORM CLOUDS GATHER   323
   53   HONORARY MOTHER OF THE YEAR   333
   54   A NEW ERA   337
   55   UNPREPARED   344
   57   AFTER DAD   352
   58   UNTIL LATER   359

PICTURES   364
THE FAMILY   369
LONG MARRIAGES   372
OCCUPATIONS   373
AUTHOR BIOGRAPHY   375

INTRODUCTION

The family history you are about to read spans over 100 years. It tracks the lives of Barbara and Dale Wilson and addresses the question: What prepares two people to raise thirteen successful children and how did they do it? I learned the answer by listening to the stories told by people who knew them best. These are my words giving voice to those storytellers—their memories adding color to faded snapshots resting in untended boxes and drawers.

A conservative estimate, two children per direct descendent, predicts that within ten generations there will be 20,000 men, women and children who owe their existence to Barbara and Dale. Many of them will have their own kids. Along the way they will learn that there is a natural chaos to raising children. It is akin to a sleepy volcano that rarely erupts. Oh, there are the little shudders that rattle the windows and spill the orange juice now and again. But the big one, the one that turns the house into useless splinters, the one that tests our faith, *that* one, typically hides only in our imaginations. It frightens us into becoming the kind of parents we railed against when we were kids.

Like every family, we are a collection of stories, the combination of which paints a picture that is never complete. Imagine a mural painted on a carousel bending away from you to the left and right. To your right, you recognize certain characters like a favorite grandmother, or maybe an eccentric uncle. They represent what came before this moment—the expression of their lives inching away from you and your place in front of the mural. Now, as you look farther away to the right, the mural curves into a past either forgotten or untold. But your history is there, as surely as you are here.

You are reading this because a mother and father, a single parent, grandparents, an aunt, a foster family or adoptive parents raised you to this moment. In the process, they learned a seasoned truth about raising children, and you will learn it too in your time: You champion their dreams and absorb their failures, and in the end, they complete you and deplete you, without a vague notion they have ever done either.

Directly in front of you are the images of my parents Barbara and Dale Wilson and their 13 children, playing out on the mural as their own stories glide into the past. Whether you are of the first generation, the seventh or the tenth, the seeds of your existence were born here.

And so, this family endures.

PART 1

THE BEGINNING

Hope is the cradle of dreams,
Borne of faith
Or willed by conviction.

1

BARBARA'S ROOTS

Told by Madeline - Barbara's Sister

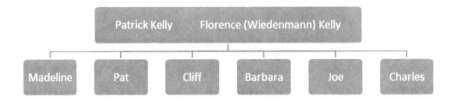

I feel fortunate to tell my sister's story. Her life is a testament to what is good in this world. She had faults, but they were dim shadows compared to the inspired light of her kindness.

Barbara provided some of the happiest moments of my life. She did it by sharing the most precious gift a sibling can offer a barren sister; her children. She humored me when I offered impractical advice, like when I told her she should be a better housekeeper. I had little clue, and she knew it. While she let me pretend I played an important role in her children's success, I was, at best, a cheerleader. I enjoyed all the fun of sharing their lives without the drama of babydom, teenage angst or any other catastrophe that befalls a kid while growing up.

Her 1920s and 30s "struggling class" upbringing—somewhere between a lower class and a middle class yet to exist—foreshadowed the life she chose. I say that while believing it is a rare individual who actually 'chooses' a particular life. It doesn't happen that way for most people. I think we stumble into an existence that is more a surprise than a choice. Take my own life for example. I married Al Lafayette, but it was more out of exasperation than love, and I don't mind admitting it.

I was the Kelly family's first child—ten years older than Barbara. Our mother, Florence and father, Patrick had two girls and four boys. I was considered tall, though I preferred, 'statuesque'. I studied glamor magazines to ensure my hair met the standards of the day, and in that sense, I was clearly trendy. My taste in clothes was another matter. I knew early on that my body was made for classically styled dresses, shoes and accessories. Our family might have been poor, but our circumstances were never revealed through my fashion. I became expert at modifying cheaply designed patterns and sewing them back together into something special.

Some of my girlfriends thought I looked like a movie star. One even said I reminded her of Lauren Bacall. I pretended it was impossible to believe something so outlandish, while letting the words repeat in my brain like a fading echo.

As foreign as it sounds by today's standards, in the 1920s and '30s most young women *aspired* to become housewives and mothers. It was an honorable goal, born of a dream they understood and that was nurtured by near universal experience. It fulfilled their purpose as history and convention defined it. It completed them. Those who felt trapped tended to escape through education. They became teachers and nurses and a few of the brilliant ones, scientists and doctors. Their road was difficult. In 1915, the percentage of women graduating with medical degrees was 2.9%. By 1930 only a single women's medical school existed.

For my part, I was neither brilliant, nor driven. Enter Al Lafayette.

I met Al through a friend. While ok, he was hardly my type. He stood half a head shorter than me, which meant I had to wear flats rather than the high heels I preferred. He slicked down his coal black hair with pomade. It made him look more like a mafia figure than the electrician he had become. In fact, that job was his saving grace. He had a trade and tradesmen were in demand.

We went out a few times with only limited success. He was a bad kisser. His parents emigrated from France, and I think he believed the French kiss was how it was supposed to be done. If I decided to give him a chance, his reeducation would be messy, but I could make him a decent kisser.

On the plus side, he was fun and courted me with enthusiasm and gifts. It became clear however, that he was developing a mad crush before I was ready. Regardless, I continued to accept his offers while making it clear I would be dating other men. He halfheartedly agreed.

Before long, he began showing up on my family's front porch when I came home from a date with someone else. On one occasion, I was with a sweet young man I had seen three times. Three seemed to be Al's limit. My date and I arrived home from dinner and a movie. We climbed the five steps leading to our front porch. When we reached the top, I noticed Al sitting on the ceiling-mounted porch swing, wielding a pipe wrench the size of his arm. He came at my young suitor with a menacing glare, an upraised wrench and a conviction that caused me to shudder. The young man turned so fast he stumbled over his own feet and in a flash, he was off the porch and streaking toward his car.

"And don't come back," Al yelled. "She's gonna marry me."

That was the first time I heard his real intentions, but I had to admit it was a little romantic in a 'freaky side show' kind of way. Al turned to face me, the pipe wrench now resting on his shoulder.

"You're gonna marry me," he said. And with that, he sauntered down the porch steps and into the darkness. He carried away my future that night, along with the pipe wrench and his persistence. Oddly enough, I didn't mind. I was going to be a housewife and hopefully a mother. I would learn to love him—and that's what happened. Did I 'choose' that life? In an odd way, maybe, but I believe it was more the 'surprise' I mentioned earlier.

Enough about me, now back to the world that shaped Barbara. Our parents, Patrick H. Kelly and Florence Wiedenmann, were an unlikely pairing of a gregarious Irishman, and by universal agreement, an understated and dour German lady. They met near Hiatville, Kansas. Patrick was 31, Florence 21. He was tall and broad shouldered with a wide face, distinctly prominent nose and a strong chin. She was slight, with a tiny waist and a sharp face punctuated by small, close features. Family and friends considered her the prettiest of her sisters. Some thought she was quiet and bookish to a fault.

Apparently, Patrick found that trait desirable. He might have reasoned his buoyant charm was a perfect antidote to her natural reserve.

I mentioned that Florence was a teacher. You might wonder how someone with an eighth-grade education was qualified to teach? In the early 1900s a person could take a standardized test covering a wide range of subjects, including— Reading, Writing, Arithmetic, Orthography, English Grammar, Geography, United States History, Physiology and Hygiene and the Constitution of the United States. An applicant was required to score at least 75% in each subject. Florence scored 84%.

Later in life we asked Mom why she married someone so much older (in that era, 10 years was a great deal of time). She thought about it briefly before answering. And then she admitted, "Because he could take care of me." I knew there was a potent precision in that answer, but the greater truth was that he loved her and she loved him. You knew it through the little things they did for one another—simple things whose value came largely from the pleasure of one's giving and the other's receiving.

It seemed odd that Patrick waited to marry so late in life. People found him handsome, fun, kind and loving. A former teacher himself, and later a rural mail carrier, he surely stood out as stable and a good catch. Then again, the odds were low that he would meet an eligible young woman on the sparsely populated prairies of southeast Kansas. Compounding the problem, he lived on the original Kelly family farm with his parents, along with a sister and brother. Plus, he was thirty and beyond middle age. It was 1910 and most men married in their late teens or early twenties as life expectancy for a male was only 48.4 years. It wasn't so much that young people were in a hurry—life itself was the hurry.

Regardless of why Patrick waited so long to marry, or why Florence chose a man considerably older than herself, the die was cast and the Wiedenmann and Kelly families were going to host a fine wedding. Florence's parents were financially comfortable. Her dad, C.A., was a member of the Wiedenmann family that settled Westport Landing, considered the birthplace of Kansas City, Missouri.

Florence was their first child and they intended to give her the grandest ceremony they could afford. Good intentions aside, there were only so many extravagances a person could buy in Hiattville, Kansas. Patrick and Florence had little money at that point, so Patrick contributed to the cause by taking advantage of his perfect cursive penmanship. He wrote each wedding invitation by hand and friends in the printing business said the results were indistinguishable from printing press quality. One was as elegant as the next.

The wedding took place on July 6, 1910. The Society page of the local newspaper provided a thorough recap (The column even included: "Society Editor's Phone No. 128"). The first paragraph read:

> On last Wednesday morning at 9 o'clock at St. Patrick's Catholic Church in Hiattville, Miss Florence E. Wiedenmann, eldest daughter of Mr. and Mrs. C.A. Wiedenmann and Mr. Patrick H. Kelly, eldest son of Mr. and Mrs. T.J. Kelly, were united in marriage by the Rev. Father O'Brien. The young people were attended by Miss Grace Kelly and Mr. John Driscoll.

After the wedding, they mortgaged a small house in Hiattville and set about raising a family. Florence wanted a baby right away. In fact, it took nearly two years before I was born in June of 1912. In short order, Patrick, Cliff, Barbara and Joe arrived. Then, ten years—and a huge surprise later—Charles was born. From the beginning, Patrick felt uneasy about how fast the babies were coming. He needed to make more money. Sugar may have cost only 5 cents a pound, but rent or a mortgage payment could easily consume nearly half of a working man's salary.

Hiattville consisted of little more than two square blocks. Like many of the homes around us, the white frame house we "owned" was mortgaged to the maximum the bank allowed. Florence said it gave Patrick a sense of pride to say the house belonged to us.

As a young girl I often begged mother to show me the few pictures she had of their wedding day. It was an opportunity to see her happy—a chance to watch seriousness melt from her face and hear her speak in long, joyous sentences. She always began by talking about a breakfast held at the Kelly farm shortly after the ceremony. Next, she told of how they gathered the following day for a more formal reception. She described opening presents, and she would point to a bowl, a vase, or the set of painted dishes in the cupboard. Sometimes, when she was in the mood to impress her listener, she moved to the wooden side bar to reveal her rarely unsheathed fine silverware. And finally, with appropriate fanfare, she mentioned the solid oak bedroom furniture her parents gave them.

She told me that in 1910 horse drawn carriages and ice trucks were still common on city streets. She remembered with zero fondness that indoor plumbing and running water were fanciful dreams for most rural people of that era. Dad often sat in a nearby chair, listening to our conversation. He rarely said anything, preferring to enjoy watching Florence trace gently through her memories. She seemed genuinely happy in those moments. And that brought a smile to his face.

When Dad did say something, it was typically off topic and generally about men he considered great by the standards of the time. He loved talking about how Ford introduced the Model T, also known as the Tin Lizzie, in 1908. I think he just enjoyed saying "Tin Lizzie", because he had to tell you where the name originated.

Apparently, in the early 1900s, car dealers created publicity for their new automobiles by hosting car races. In 1922, the year I turned ten, a championship race was held in Pikes Peak, Colorado. One of the contestants was Noel Bullock and his Model T named "Old Liz." Old Liz was unpainted and lacked a hood, which led to spectators comparing her to a tin can. By the time the race began, Old Liz had the new nickname "Tin Lizzie." To everyone's surprise, the ugly duckling won the race.

In 1914 Dad abandoned his mail carrier route, bought a good used Model T Ford, and began selling insurance throughout Bourbon County. His territory included their small town, Hiattville, and the far-flung country that surrounded it. To his advantage, he was selling to people from his old mail route who knew and trusted him. Dad created a small office space in a corner of the parlor just inside the front door. After a day spent traveling the countryside in search of new customers, he devoted evenings to the paperwork that followed. Mom told me she worried every time his great hulk came to rest on the finely spindled, wooden chair sitting in front of his mottled oak desk.

He travelled the countryside over crude roads amounting to little more than a couple of well-worn wagon wheel ruts. The snaking paths wound through grasslands and fields of corn, oats or winter wheat. Patrick called his clients "salt of the earth" people—men, women and children who depended on the land for their survival. Like the crops they coaxed into existence each year, they grew and prospered in furrows of upturned dirt.

Most of his customers were first and second generation descendants of the pioneers who originally settled the land. Many of their parents or grandparents homesteaded 160-acre sections made available by The Homestead Act of 1862. Signed into law by President Abraham Lincoln, The Act allowed settlers to pay a small filing fee and gain title to the property in one of two ways. The first method required that they live on the acreage, build a house and grow crops continuously for five years. At the end of that time, they owned the property.

The second option allowed them to build a residence immediately and begin growing crops. After six months they could pay the government $1.25 per acre and the property was theirs. By 1900, over 80 million acres of public land had been distributed under the Act.

In addition to the Homestead Act, the Federal Government granted various railroad companies millions of acres of public land through Land Grants. Railroad owners were expected to build the transcontinental railroad and telegraph systems. In the process, they would help settle the West. Many land grant owners wielded their power ruthlessly, taking advantage of the very settlers the government intended to help. Adding insult to injury, instead of distributing the property, it became their personal possession to be bought and sold at will.

"*Even today,*" George Draffan states in his 1998 study, Taking Back Our Land: A History of Land Grant Reform, "*the largest land owners in many Western states are still the land grant railroads and their corporate heirs.*"

Pioneers who acquired their property through the Homestead Act, stood at least a reasonable chance of making it in the West. And that's what our grandparents did when they began farming their 160 acres in southeastern Kansas.

It all sounds so simple—claim your land, build a house, often made of sod and the genesis of the term "sod busters," grow a few crops and you're off. The truth, however, was riddled with hardship and death. Drought sometimes destroyed their crops, or harsh winters froze them out. Much of the land was wide open prairie and natural resources were scarce. People used corn husks for fuel and without medical care even relatively minor injuries or illnesses often led to death. The survivors were the hardiest of souls, and these were the men and women Patrick depended on for his living.

Through it all, weak sales and long hours, Patrick remained steady and upbeat. His predictions about our future were always laced with optimism and success. And he meant it. He intended to make it true by his own determination and hard work. Of course, little kids believe anything they're told. Patrick's vision became our own.

I pretended everything was fine, even while carrying the dark secret I shared with my parents. I learned it while listening to late night whispers between Patrick and Florence as they worried across the kitchen table over how they would pay one bill or another, or who should be paid first. And with that secret, I worried too. Would we have to go back to the farm?

2

ENTER BARBARA

Told by Madeline - Barbara's Sister

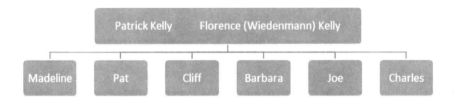

In 1920, Bankers Life Insurance Company approached Dad with an opportunity to open a branch office in Pittsburg, Kansas. Pittsburg's population was 18,000 and to our way of thinking, "The Big City". He jumped at the chance and within months the family moved to a two-story frame house on East 8th Street. It was modern, meaning it had an indoor bathroom and running water in the kitchen. Those were glorious amenities in the 1920s. My brothers Pat and Cliff shared a bedroom and I was given one of my own. We were in a real town now, and it was better than I ever imagined.

Our family's life was typical for our circumstances. Patrick worked hard every day and earned a decent wage, while Florence tended to the house and kids. Her job demanded devotion and a strong back. Modern conveniences were minimal and heavy work the norm. We lived in a quiet neighborhood where everyone around us seemed in pretty much our same shape.

The 1920s marked a turning point in our lives and American innovation spurred its creation. The middle class was born in that age, made up of people just like our family. Urban living blossomed and leisure time eased into a typical day. The consumer age was born. America's industrial giants repurposed themselves as wartime production gave way to the manufacture of new technologies like automobiles, radios, toasters, razors and vacuum cleaners to a name a few. The leisure merchants were everywhere.

A marketing powerhouse emerged in 1888 when Richard Sears used his first printed mailer to advertise watches and jewelry. Aided by the Homestead Act of 1862, and America's westward expansion on the heels of railroad development, Sears, Roebuck & Co.'s first mail order catalogue was introduced in 1893. By 1920 it was widely believed there were more Sear's catalogues in American homes than Bibles. The consumer revolution now had its advocate.

∼

By 1922, our family had clawed its way to the first rung of the evolving middle class ladder.

It was into this world that Barbara's life began. She entered during the same age as some of the greatest writers of all time: Sinclair Lewis, Willa Cather, William Faulkner, F. Scott Fitzgerald, Carl Sandburg and Ernest Hemingway to name a few. What they did for literature, Barbara would do for motherhood.

The Roaring 20s defied description. Some called it the Jazz Age, while others referred to it as the Age of Wonderful Nonsense and still others the Age of Intolerance. A period with that many names was surely up to no good, and the decade that followed proved the point with catastrophic certainty.

I was nine and my brothers Pat and Cliff were eight and four when Barbara arrived. She was an immediate hit and would go on to be the family favorite for the rest of her life. Sweet from the beginning, she rarely cried and was always happiest in Patrick's arms. Meanwhile, Florence treated her like she did all of her children, a serious duty. I think it was in her blood to be—I want to be fair about this—cold. It's the only description that works. She was a good mother without being very motherly. Our house was generally clean and neat, though sterile on some level. An unexceptional cook, her meals were always on time and dinner was more a social function than a gastronomic delight. As we sat around the table, Patrick's jovial and animated manner entirely exposed Florence's quiet reserve. The woman seemed without cheer.

~

As I mentioned earlier, Patrick's daily routine back in Hiatville began before first light. He typically reappeared around supper time. That pattern changed once we moved to Pittsburg. His office nearby, he could enjoy a leisurely breakfast before leaving for work and often came home in the middle of the day, just to be with the kids.

We all cherished him, especially Barbara. I remember the curve of her slim body curled up on his lap, watching her stroke his colorful tie as he read her stories of a beautiful princess or magic frogs. I had outgrown that lap of luxury and it made me jealous of Barbara, jealous of her smallness. I know now that it wasn't about size at all, it had to do with her natural goodness. Patrick adored her because she was worthy of it.

Patrick enjoyed the break from driving so many miles between appointments, even though he continued to work long hours. He was a natural salesman and this new, more populated territory played to his strengths. The only chink in his business armor was an undeniably soft heart. He sold a great deal of insurance, but if his customers couldn't afford their premiums, Patrick often made the payment himself. It was a habit that sat poorly with Florence. How could the rest of society be doing so well, she reasoned, while Patrick's farmers were incapable of paying their bills.

Florence nurtured a broad worldview. It came to her through frequent trips to the local library. There, she could satisfy her passion for reading while perusing the latest editions of The New York Times, Cosmopolitan, McClure's, Time or The Saturday Evening Post. Patrick sometimes saw it as a blessing, often, a curse. It was a blessing because she was aware of what was going on in the world outside of Pittsburg, Kansas. It was a curse for exactly the same reason. Patrick knew that, absent context, Florence was free to imagine whatever she chose. And unfortunately, she imagined that life in Pittsburg should resemble the prosperity taking place in big cities like Chicago and New York. She read about them. She knew.

At least one day per week, somewhere between meals, laundry, ironing and general housekeeping, she donned an ankle length cotton dress, a pair of low-heeled oxford shoes and her black arm purse. She locked the house, and depending on her route, walked the ten to twelve blocks from our home to the library. She travelled brick-paved paths admonishing, "Don't Spit on the Sidewalk", representing an effort begun by Dr. Samuel Crumbine to help control tuberculosis and other infectious diseases. Dr. Crumbine was a contemporary of Bat Masterson and Wyatt Earp.

I often walked beside her as she made her way downtown. She held herself fully erect, a forward gaze trained on the tree lined path in front of us, her gate steady and purposeful. When the Library building came into view, she often stopped for a moment to take in the silhouette of the white limestone and red tile roof cloaking her sanctuary in a permanent embrace. You see, Florence revered the written word and the knowledge that came with it—little surprise she held its house in such high regard.

Florence knew the library's history as if it were part of her own family. In one of her rare moments of extended dialog, she told me how construction of the Art Nouveau building began in 1910 and was completed in 1912. "The year you were born," she added for impact. The Library Board of Trustees had approached steel industrialist Andrew Carnegie who was well known for his philanthropy towards libraries. He agreed to donate $40,000 to the Pittsburg effort. Florence emphasized **$40,000**.

Most Carnegie backed libraries bear his name, but not the Pittsburg building. Local miners were adamant that "Carnegie" should not appear on their library. They, along with many other Pittsburgh residents, were also clear that an elaborate design was unacceptable. The result was an exterior constructed of Cartage limestone in Prairie Style architecture and a listing on the National Register of Historic Places. Pittsburgh residents were wise to set conditions for taking free money.

Florence came alive the moment she entered the library. She soaked in the atmosphere as if the scent of book-lined shelves were rain washed air, and the Arts and Crafts style furnishings were part of her personal living space. The impact of a 1920s library, though clearly affecting fewer people, was to a woman of the word, a woman like Florence, equal to computers and the internet. I enjoyed watching her standing in front of an army of books, finger brushing the bindings of one before allowing her hand to drift effortlessly to another. The books were piano keys, producing a melody that only she could hear. She was happy there.

Until "coming of age" subjects interested me, I typically headed to a tiny corner of the library reserved for children's material. I knew Florence would linger over her choice of new books to take home. Then, she would catch up on current events in the periodicals section. As a child, I was impressed with her penchant for reading, and I wondered just how much she must know. Later, I felt a certain sadness about that part of her life. What was the point of learning so much if you never shared it with anyone? Then again, maybe reading was her escape from a world of sameness—the expression of a journey she would never take.

It was in the periodicals section Florence became aware of the buoyant U.S. economy roaring all around us. The 1920s ushered in a decade of prosperity never before experienced by any generation. While the top one percenters enjoyed dramatically greater wealth appreciation, (consider "The Great Gatsby"), even a typical city dweller benefited handsomely from the age of consumerism. Soldiers returning home from WWI had money to spend at exactly the moment new technologies were challenging our Victorian traditions with affordable automobiles, moving pictures and radios. And those were the facts Florence took home to Patrick. Why couldn't his clients pay when the rest of the country was doing so well?

For all her study and knowledge, she made one critical error in reasoning. She believed the new advances affected everyone equally, or at least to one positive degree or another. She failed to realize that the coming Great Depression of the 1930s began to devastate farming economies as early as 1919 with the end of World War I. During the war, European farming ground to a halt, prompting the rest of the world to call on U.S. farmers to make up the loss. Prices for our crops soared, but prosperity lingered only until Europe turned on the tap again. Over half of the U.S. population was dependent on farming. Small acreages were the norm and these were the same men and women struggling to pay for their insurance coverage. These were Dad's customers.

I was twelve years old the first time I overheard Florence complaining to Patrick about his largesse. We had just finished lunch. Pat and Cliff hurried outside to play, Barbara was put down for her afternoon nap and I, sitting on the living room sofa, pretended to read. Mom and Dad were in the kitchen. Patrick's hulking frame leaned heavily against a counter top as he watched Florence return just washed and dried dishes to their place in the cupboard. It was then she began to speak in her, "quiet way". It started with a question: "Why do you pay other family's bills?" It was simple, straightforward and delivered with a thoughtful calm. That gentle quiet, however, was laced with barbs of prickly disapproval. It moved Patrick to a state of unease.

I peeked around the edges of my opened book to take in the unfolding drama in the next room. I watched Patrick move to the head of the kitchen table and ease his body into a waiting wooden chair. He propped his right elbow on the table top and leaned forward. A restless finger tapped against the side of his nose as he considered her question. Finally, he raised himself up and moved to his desk. He gathered some papers and placed them in a brown leather satchel before heading to the back door.

Just as it looked like he might leave without a word, he turned to Florence and said, "I pay them because they need help."

Quicker than he could open the screen door, she countered, "How do you know they'll ever make it up?"

"They will," is all he said.

She watched him go, dried her hands on a waist apron, then casually returned to whatever she had been doing. How could she be satisfied with his answer? Even I had trouble understanding him and I was just a kid. Patrick was too kind for his own good and these people were just taking advantage of him. I held to that misguided notion until a particular Saturday in late May of 1925.

PART 1   THE BEGINNING

∼

The insurance office was open all day on Saturdays to accommodate Patrick's farming customers. That was the day they typically came to town for shopping and to buy staples. It was also the day I could count on Patrick to slip me a few coins for cleaning the office and emptying the trash cans. I typically rode to the office with him in the morning and walked home after finishing my work.

On that morning, Patrick had just settled into his rolling, curve backed, wooden desk chair when we were both startled by what sounded like small cannon fire. Hurrying to the plate glass window at the front of his office, we glanced up the street in one direction and then the other. With a smile and a chuckle, Patrick said, "It's just the Petersons".

"Did that noise come from their truck?" I asked.

"It's what they can afford," Patrick answered. "I told you about them."

And then I remembered the Peterson's story. They were one of the families Patrick defended to Florence while trying to explain why he paid past-due premiums. The family lived ten miles south of town and a half century behind the times. Patrick told us their land had been homesteaded by Mr. Peterson's grandfather who built their two-story frame home. Water was piped into the house from a cistern and was delivered by a hand pump fastened to the kitchen sink. A two-seat outhouse, framed in white flowering spirea, stood guard some twenty yards from the back door. Beyond that were loafing sheds, a hay barn, pig pen and various sized corrals. Each enclosure was lined in chicken fencing and barbed wire.

Patrick and I watched Mr. Peterson, his wife Louise and their four daughters descend from the truck's cab. The young couple appeared to be in their 30s. Each of the girls was blonde, petite and one was just as pretty as the next. They huddled together in Louise's shadow until Mr. Peterson lined them up and began handing them packages wrapped in old newspapers or stacked neatly in cardboard boxes. Once the truck was emptied, Louise led the girls, shortest to tallest, up the block to the insurance office. Flawless blonde hair and radiantly smiling faces made their shabby, but neat and clean dresses, look almost fashionable.

Louise noticed me and Patrick at the window and tipped her head in acknowledgement. Her eyes were barely visible under the felt cloche hat she wore low on her forehead. Her cotton housedress, likely the best dress she owned, looked neat but dangerously near its final trip to town. Dad moved to sit behind his simple wooden desk. I think he felt more official there. Louise opened the door and pressed her back against it for the girls to pass by. One by one, they paraded through the open door, walked to Patrick's desk and placed their offerings in front of him.

"What's all this?" Patrick asked with outsized amazement.

The tallest girl patted her parcel and answered, "I brought eggs, Mr. Kelly."

"You sure did," he said.

"That ain't all," Mr. Peterson allowed as he stepped into the room. "There's a couple'a fryin hens in the boxes and as much'a our garden vegetables as we could muster this time of year. It's too early for most of it you know, but we'll bring more when she comes in." He hesitated, and then as if suddenly remembering something, added, "That ain't all", his voice lusty with assurance, "I'll have yer money to ya this fall. Almanac says it'll be a wet year awright. We'll git you paid up when the crops come in."

Patrick smiled and nodded his head, but said nothing, as if to indicate it was a given Mr. Peterson would do what he said. He knew how to accept a gift from the heart. The bounty in front of him was no small matter to this family and the right way to handle it was with grace and appreciation. He took time to inspect each box and package, periodically looking up at the girls to register his surprise. As if on cue, they beamed back broad smiles and the smallest among them wiggled with delight.

"This has to be the best gift I ever got," Patrick said. "My family sure can use it. I think it might be the biggest surprise I've had all year." That comment even coaxed a demure smile from Louise. He stood up and shook Mr. Peterson's calloused hand. The farmer looked resolutely into Patrick's eyes, "I mean it," he said. "You'll be gittin that money."

With a tilt of his head, he nodded toward the door, causing the girls to line up and giggle out of the office. Louise followed close behind. "Oh," he said as he turned back while still in the doorway, "sorry bout that backfire, Mr. Kelly."

"Never gave it a thought," Patrick said as he patted Mr. Peterson on the back.

The door closed. Patrick returned to his desk and began to look over the chickens and vegetables. "He'll pay it back," he commented, more to himself than to me.

Even after meeting the Petersons, even after witnessing the power of their gratitude, I had trouble understanding why my father would pay their premiums. It was only later, after the Great Depression had become a reality in our own lives, that I really grasped what Patrick had done for the Petersons. He proved to them, and to himself, that humanity was still alive. He pulled them forward while the rest of the world pushed them back. He offered them hope. You see, they *were* Patrick, and he knew it.

I wish I had told him what a good man he was. I wish I had told him I loved him more often. I would have, if I had only known what was coming.

3

DALE'S ROOTS

Told by Velva - Dale's Sister

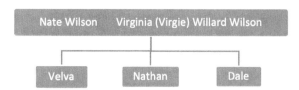

I was Dale's only sister and his oldest sibling by ten years. I helped raise him. Maybe that's why I found it so easy to forgive his shortcomings, fearing I may have had something to do with what brought them to life. Though only a sister, I was like too many mothers, tending to see what made him special and blind to what made him human.

∼

A good friend of mine described me as a cross between Mae West and Annie Oakley—heavy on the Mae West. She commented, "It's in the way she moves."

To set the record straight, unlike Mae West, my clothes were typically a little conservative and my hair was a natural chestnut brown. In the 1940s, I wore A line dresses with padded shoulders and tight, high waist tops because they flattered my full, ample hipped figure. Dresses gave way to pencil skirts in the 1950s and they became my style of choice.

Back to the way I moved. I'm taking some poetic license here, but this is how my second husband, Harold Stith, described me in a letter to one of his friends. We had never met, so I think Harold was trying to paint the most flattering picture possible. After describing my round face, high forehead, intelligent eyes and devious smile, he put it all together by writing with some authority, that I was 'pretty'. And this is how he tried to capture my essence: "Upon rising from a chair, Velva typically uses both hands to smooth her skirt down over her hips. She does this while moving in one direction or another, never standing still, her movements graceful and unhurried. She's confident in her womanhood and knows how to use it to her advantage.

She dominates a moment with undemanding certainty. Never coarse, she simply implies a wilder self tucked neatly away within her private person. Men defer to her and women envy her confidence. Velva gives little notice to any of it.

There are few things typical about Velva, and the least conventional is her voice. When you finally meet her, you'll know you've never heard a tone quite like hers and are unlikely to ever hear it again. It has a nasal quality, laced with a twang and buttressed by a charmingly educated hillbilly character. The twang was passed down from her mother, Virgie, who was originally from the hill country of Tennessee. Virgie makes it sound backward—Velva makes it sound sexy."

He left the letter on a table next to his chair, confident I would read it. I loved him for that. And now, back to my little brother, Dale.

～

Life played an interesting trick on Dale Wilson. I know, because I watched it happen. He was forced to become someone special in spite of his inherited shortcomings and in defiance of a turbulent upbringing. His story is straight out of a Dickens novel. He dealt with poverty, abandonment, unrealized hope and a childhood of disappointment and despair. The fabric of his life, primarily woven with the dull gray threads of want and need, came to colorful life through the love of a faithful wife, and the success of accomplished children.

Dale exhibited few traits expected of a man who would eventually father thirteen kids. In fact, I always thought his nature forbade such a thing. These are just a few of his evident contradictions: He stubbornly asserted his selfishness while being forced to share nearly everything about himself. He brooded in unnatural silence as his growing family demanded more and more of his attention. He spent nearly as much money on personal interests as he did on the family's upkeep. He was a pragmatist and unable to demonstrate affection—even to the hopeless romantic he married. Some may quibble with that assessment, given that thirteen children are living proof to the contrary. I would point out however, that sex and affection are not the same thing. Dale was good at only one of those activities.

~

Our family took root near Joplin, Missouri when our dad, Nathan Wilson, met our mother, Virgie Willard, a recent transplant from Tennessee. Though her first name was actually Virginia, somewhere along the line people began calling her Virgie and the name stuck. It suited her, unsophisticated and country sounding. Virgie was born and raised on a farm where her family's hard core, fundamental religious teachings dominated her upbringing. She owed her simplicity and uncomplicated world view to that cloistered existence.

Before moving to Missouri, her father, J.D. Willard had been a farm hand back in Tennessee. He worked for wages and could see no hope for a better life until President Abraham Lincoln signed the Homestead Act of 1862. The Act resulted in a dramatic expansion of farming in America. The number of farms tripled from 2 million in 1860 to 6 million in 1905. The number of people living on farms grew from about 10 million in 1860, to 22 million in 1880 and to more than 31 million by 1905.

In an effort to further increase property ownership and to expand the nation's footprint to the west, land was dispersed through Federal Land Grants. These grants, provided by both Federal and State governments, amounted to an incentive for railroad investors to expand. The nation became connected by the interlacing construction of trunk lines and linking terminals. In 1850, there were 9,000 rail miles available, by 1885, that number had grown to over 87,000 miles.

Land grants amounted to loans provided per mile of rail construction. In addition, the law granted the rail operators ownership of 20 sections of land

PART 1   THE BEGINNING

(a section is one square mile, or 640 acres) per mile of track. The railroads then used that land to provide low-cost loans to farmers and merchants along their routes, thus insuring future customers for rail service. Premium land and affordable loans were advertised heavily in Europe. The offer included extremely low transportation costs and led to thousands of farmers from Germany, Scandinavia and Britain settling the heartland of America.

Through ingenuity and determination, the Midwest was settled in puzzle piece plots of Homestead or railroad land. One of those parcels was owned by Virgie's dad, JD. Another, only a few miles away, was farmed by Nate's dad, Nathan.

In 1907, like most young people of that era, Nate and Virgie were likely to meet at either school or church. Since school was out of the question for Virgie, church, actually a revival, served as the backdrop for her first encounter with Nate. Nate, handsome and self-confident, was 18—Virgie, petite, cute and shapely, was 16. After dating for only a matter of months, they were married. Their marriage license contains the signatures of both fathers, granting consent for the two to wed. Virgie, then 17, was still a minor. I have always imagined their wedding ceremony with J.D. standing menacingly behind them, a shotgun cradled securely in his arms.

Shortly after the wedding, Nate and Virgie rented a small acreage near Joplin, Missouri. The land, flat and fertile, joined the original Wilson homestead with only dirt roads or tree lined boundaries distinguishing one property from another. They picked up the spade and the hoe exactly as their parents and grandparents had done before them. In fact, I'd be willing to bet if you travelled back to the beginning of organized farming, you would find a Wilson and a Willard ankle deep in just turned dirt. It was the only life they knew, and up to that point, the only life they could have imagined.

Nate and Virgie were married in 1908. I was born in 1909. Two years later, Nathan came along, and after ten years more, Dale arrived. As excited as I was about a new baby, Virgie seemed at cross purposes over the news. The timing was awful. It was 1920 and the U.S. agricultural economy had seen its heyday and now appeared on the verge of collapse. During WWI, American farmers thrived as Europe roiled in turmoil and their crop furrows morphed into strategic trenches. Our goods were needed worldwide and demand consistently swallowed up available supply. And then the war ended and so did our farm life—we just didn't know it.

We were truck farmers, as were most of our neighbors. We grew fruits and vegetables on small plots of land and at harvest, loaded them onto trucks and drove them to the nearest buyers. If you were one of the first producers of the season, the local market was a great option. More often than not, products were sold to a middle man who shipped them by train to the north or east. Our lives flowed to the rhythm of the seasons and we fell into the false comfort of lasting permanence. That is how life tricks us—pretending "now" and "forever" are the same thing.

WWI ended. Dale was born. Our luck began to drift between "not much" and "none at all". And I was trapped. I was taken out of school after 4th grade to care for Dale and tend the house while Virgie helped Nate with the farm. She was only slightly bigger than a race horse jockey, but she could work circles around grown men twice her size. I think it was pure will that drove her. That, and a religious conviction stoked by the certainty "God's will" would see us through our trials and tribulations. Why, she could twist the meaning of any outcome into "God's will". If we succeeded on the farm—it was God's will. If we failed and had to move to town—it was God's will. The woman could win no matter how things turned out. And in that she found great comfort.

In the beginning, taking care of Dale was like playing with a favorite doll. I felt grown up. Plus, getting out of school struck me as a real bargain. Those feelings disappeared with diaper changing, cleaning house and preparing some of the meals. You may wonder who would turn those responsibilities over to a 10-year-old girl. The answer was Virgie, and every other overworked farm woman fighting the same losing battle. Necessity is its own master. That's how children like me became women before we were teenagers. Odd as it sounds, at only ten years old, I was within six years of getting married myself.

Farm life was isolating enough—take away school and the only social events left were at the church. That's where I met other kids just like myself—a place where we could all feel normal. After praying and singing, forgiving and blessing, we were allowed to play on the just mowed grass surrounding the church. Maybe that's why religion was such a vital part of Virgie's life. It was her link to the outside world. It's where we gathered with people like ourselves—people who understood that struggle and survival meant the same thing.

I believe the threads of Nate and Virgie's bindings began to unravel a few years after Dale was born. I remember, because it happened just before they made a life changing decision. They worked the farm together, he behind the mule and plow, she milking the cow, helping plant seeds, feeding the chickens and wringing a neck or two when meat was needed.

They both planted the seeds of their crops and their future. They both weeded the long furrows between rows of budding plants. They both harvested the fruits and vegetables and loaded them onto trucks for their trip to a buyer. They did this while beginning to want different things out of life. It all seemed fine—until it wasn't.

~

I first sensed the ill winds blowing when church gatherings became less festive. The women tried their best to pretend everything was normal. They brought their pies and casseroles to pot luck dinners and placed them on linen covered table tops already heavy with fruits and vegetables and just baked bread cooling beside crocks of recently churned butter. Wooden floors clacked under the restless feet of swirling kids. Virgie said the women did it for the children, but I think it was for the adults. Somehow, the women needed to counter the grave predictions coming from smoke filled corners where husbands and fathers gathered to discuss the end of our way of life.

It was difficult for them to understand why buyers from the north and east quit showing up. No one told them Europe was recovering from the war and their own farmers had returned to the fields. Everything they heard or read talked of the booming U.S. economy taking place all around them. It was the Roaring Twenties after all. Sadly, the only thing roaring in our community was the fire pit before it cooled down and the children were allowed to roast marshmallows over glowing embers.

Nate was one of the first to abandon the plow, and I don't think he minded one bit. He was never a farmer at heart and appeared more himself in town than he ever did in the fields. Whether dumb luck or impeccable timing, Nate talked Virgie into moving to Joplin, Missouri just before the rural exodus. It was there, he reasoned, they would have a shot at a good life. Small family farms were a thing of the past he told her. They would starve if they tried to hold out much longer. She reluctantly gave in, her fear of the unknown less threatening than the certainty of going broke.

There was more to her misgivings than fear of losing the farm. I think she believed city life would change Nate and, in the process, make things worse for her. Looking back, it's clear she was right. Like so many other young couples, their union had prospered during good times, but only *true* love survives when things get tough. They failed to love each other enough. As it turned out, their marriage ended long before it was over. Moving to Joplin was simply a boundary between a life Virgie understood, and one she would never accept.

～

Joplin, Missouri was a prosperous mining community. It sprang to prominence on train loads of zinc and lead lumbering from her rail station every day. Financiers, shop keepers and opportunists rushed to Joplin. Many became wealthy supplying the miners and supporting businesses with the goods and services essential to a booming industry. Thousands of former truck farmers—farmers like Nate and Virgie—flowed into Joplin to fill the new jobs. Virgie began waitressing at a small diner. Nate became a traveling salesman for Delco batteries. With Virgie working full time, I continued to stay home from school to care for Dale.

I loved the city more than Virgie hated it. I knew she enjoyed access to running water in the house and an indoor bathroom. I knew the icebox mattered to her. I knew she considered having fresh milk delivered to the back door a treat. I knew it, and I was sure she would never admit it. It was as if she enjoyed being miserable, complaining to Nate about every imagined ill she faced each day. And most of all, she hated the job Nate had taken, a job that removed him from her influence.

In the early 1920s, and for many years to come, centralized utilities existed only in cities and towns. Farmers on the outskirts were forced to read by candlelight or gas lamps. A radio was their primary contact with the outside world, which was out of the question without electricity. That opportunity spawned an entire industry and Nate's new job selling gas-powered electric battery plants. They consisted of a gas generator that was periodically fired up to charge a series of batteries. The batteries then provided power to whatever appliances or lights a farmer chose.

It was in this environment Nate traveled the Midwest for Delco Light (a division of the Dayton Engineering Laboratories company). Here is a newspaper ad from that period:

> Delco-Light is the complete electric light and power plant. When you install Delco-Light you get bright, clean, safe, electric lights in every room of your house, —in every part of your barn and outbuildings. You get electric power at the house, —to pump the water, to run the washer, wringer, cream separator and churn. You get electric power at the barn, —to turn the cornsheller, the grindstone and the fanning mill, —all of this, bright, safe, electric lights, and dependable electric power, at the touch of a convenient button.

The ad also included an illustration of the generator and storage batteries.

Nate typically left home on Sunday afternoons. He liked settling in early in one of the small towns strategically located in his territory. Farmers were up before sunrise, so he made his cold calls before they began working each Monday morning. A 'cold call' means making an unannounced sales visit. Nate typically chose an inexpensive boarding house serving at least two meals per day. It was an era when many families opened their homes to boarders, especially in financially strapped small towns in Middle America. It has been conservatively estimated that from one third to one half of all households took in boarders at some point in their lives.

Nate, a clean cut, dapper sort was likely a hit with unattached women in the farming communities he visited. He always drove new cars and dressed the role of a prosperous businessman. His good looks, generosity and smooth talk were only a few of his many qualities. He could have been the poster boy for the term, 'City Slicker'. But chances are, if he strayed as Virgie claimed, he was just a small-time player. It was easy for a man from the city to turn a country girl's head. Wearing diamond rings and sitting behind the wheel of a fancy new car was a potent attraction.

Maybe he did what Virgie feared. Maybe he *did* live two lives. It was possible. I've often heard, "A wife knows." But the fact is, at that point, no one ever proved Nate did anything inappropriate. It was simply suspicion and all of it came from Virgie. Oddly, her distrust failed to rub off on the kids. I loved my dad and failed to understand why Virgie was always so upset with him. As for the boys, first son Nathan seemed oblivious to the whole affair, and Dale was too young to notice.

It had to be difficult for a child Dale's age. He was bright and curious and he worshipped Virgie. Meanwhile, instead of returning his devotion, her feelings about Nate wounded the rest of us. It consumed her. No matter how much attention Virgie showed us, there was always something missing— a spark of love, tenderness. Even when she concentrated on a person, her focus waivered. At the time it seemed a harmless flaw. Little did we know it would reveal itself in an unimaginable way.

While Virgie stewed over her plight, Nate continued to come home only on weekends. He rarely had much to do with us to the point I sometimes wondered if he cared. I thought that, knowing full well he would give himself up for any one of his kids. I was told his own father was distant and brooding, as was his father's father before him. It's as if Nate was programed to bewilder his own children. Maybe that made us work harder to earn his love. Maybe we needed to do more.

Divorce—never say the word or you risk bringing it to life. In practice, it typically stumbles into existence, more a threat than an intention. And then, out of carelessness or disregard, it begins to take shape. It presupposes a better life while hiding the destruction it will exact on the people it touches. The players try to appear reasonable at first. They create "evidence" to justify the notion, and the spinning begins.

And so it was for Virgie and Nate. We had lived in Joplin for a little over two years, Virgie waitressing, Nate travelling the country selling battery systems. The new normal claimed both of them, and Virgie hated it. She was used to the rhythms of farm life—the quiet of self-sufficiency. Now, she was forced to sling hash and deliver coffee to crude miners whose only concern was getting through another monotonous day. What she wouldn't have given to wring a plump chicken's neck!

Back home, she and Nate became strangers in the same house. She believed he was cheating, and with varying degrees of insistence, made her suspicions clear. Nate neither denied nor confirmed her charges. Then, in 1922 I heard the first mention of the word divorce.

Had times been different, Virgie might have picked up and left right away. She had settled on all the reasons she needed. Instead, she decided that staying put was easier than breaking up the family. Besides, she was a staunch Christian and Christians just didn't divorce, at least not in her family. She also had no idea how she would support herself. Her experience was in farming and raising kids and there were millions of women just like her. In spite of her instincts, she lingered.

While Virgie scrimped and saved from waitressing, Nate bought nice clothes and new cars. He was the bread winner and the keeper of the keys. As his father had done to his wife before him, Nate gave Virgie what amounted to an allowance to take care of the kids and the home. That's the way it was for most families, a wife left to beg for what should have been hers without asking. I vowed right then it would never happen to me. I would have a say in how my marriage worked, or there would be no marriage at all.

Virgie apparently reached the same conclusion. She began working more hours at the diner, probably in preparation for what she knew was coming. I used to help her count her tip money and noticed steadily rising totals. I wondered why. The answer may have been in the way she began dressing for work. She was no longer wearing the plain, ankle length frocks she brought from the farm. They were still fairly typical waist dresses, but now they were more deeply colored or awash in vibrant prints. She began hiking her hemline from ankle length to mid-calf. It was also clear her general appearance had recovered from the farm harsh damage of country living, revealing a creamy complexion and thick brown hair. Her body, forged into taut, angular lines by physical labor, was now seductively curved, and her 'cute' had turned to 'pretty'. The tips we counted proved she was using her most evident asset to best advantage.

Life has no master, but events do and Virgie was about to prove it.

4

VIRGIE'S CHOICE

Told by Velva - Dale's Sister

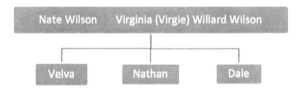

I was 12 years old in 1922. Even then I could see the strain claiming Virgie with each passing day. She needed to make a decision about her marriage. At the same time, she had to figure out how she would raise me, Nathan and Dale on her own. It seemed impossible to a woman like Virgie—limited education, minimal skills and no way to imagine a life different from the one she was living. She was trapped between a loveless marriage and the frightening prospects of surviving as a single mother.

Her world pivoted on a brisk, May morning down at the diner. This is how Virgie said it happened:

> The breakfast shift was real busy that day, like it was every morning. Steam rose up from the sizzling grill that was covered by bacon, eggs, hash browns and pancakes. Biscuits browned in the hot oven and the air hung thick with coffee perfume and blue cigarette smoke that turned grey as it rose up. Men and women, mostly men, claimed the available bar stools. Customers also crowded around the tables for four. All the booths lining the walls were completely filled.

With the bodies, the cooking, the cigarette smoke and me rushing from one table to the next, the whole diner felt humid hot. The second I had a chance, I opened the front door to let in some cool air. While propping it open, I noticed a sharp featured young woman pacing in a circle near the entrance. She appeared upset, while digging at the pockets of a well-worn sweater, her pencil thin fingers searching for something unseen. She looked exhausted and upset so I stepped outside the diner with a coffee pot still in my hand.

"Why don't ya come on in here, Honey," I suggested.

The young woman returned a worried smile, moved to stand next to me and said, "I was just going to get some coffee and maybe some toast on my way home." She tugged at the pocket corners again. "I think I lost that quarter I put in here last night before work."

"Coffee's on me," I said, while looping my arm inside hers. I guided the young woman to a small table with two chairs reserved for waitresses on their infrequent breaks. After pouring a cup of coffee, I slid a piece of apple pie under her nose and placed a fork and spoon on a napkin next to the plate.

"I can't pay for…" the woman started to say.

"You sure can't, Honey," I cut in, "it's on me."

As the breakfast crowd thinned out, I kept an eye on the auburn-haired young woman. I figured maybe she was a hotel maid or janitor's helper. Why else would she be heading home so early in the day? Eventually, the diner was empty except for a couple of retired fellows playing checkers in the back corner. I wiped down all the tables and swept the floor. My new friend had used her fingers to scrape the pie plate clean. It looked like a just-washed dish. I picked it up and invited her to sit with me in a padded booth. I poured myself some coffee and refilled her cup, set the pot on a burner and returned to slide in opposite the wiry young gal.

"What's your name, Honey?" I asked. "Mine's Virgie."

"Ruth", she answered.

"Ruth," I repeated, "like in the Bible story. Where you go, I will go, and where you stay, I will stay. Your people will be my people and your God my God."

Ruth looked confused.

"The Book of Ruth, Honey," I explained, "it's what she said to Naomi. Ruth was the great grandmother of King David."

"O-okay," Ruth said. She looked at me blankly and waited for what would come next.

I don't think she reads her Bible, I thought.

Anyway, I added, "It's a pretty name." And then I asked if she had a family.

"Two kids," she answered, "raising them myself. They have a daddy. Edward is his name."

"How are you raising them yourself," I asked, "if they have a daddy?"

The question caused her to slump forward as if its consequence weighed her down. It was then her story started flowing out like a flooded creek. Ruth said Edward had been killed in the war. She talked fast, like she was running away from the words. Even at that, she told about him in a real tender way.

I rubbed the back of her hand. "I'm so sorry to hear that," I said. "Where was he killed?"

Ruth hesitated before answering—the question seeming to confuse her.

"If you don't feel like talkin' about it, Honey…." I started to say.

"No," she cut in, "it's not that. It just seems crazy to say this, but I don't know whether he's dead for sure or not. I think he is." She paused to take a deep breath and then said, "He is." She twirled a paper napkin tighter and tighter around her finger. "They said he's missing in action. It happened right near the end of the war. How's that for luck?"

"I don't know how you can talk about it without crying," I said. "Do you pray over it?"

"If tears and prayers could bring him back," Ruth said, "he'd be sittin' here right now."

She sipped her coffee.

"Can't nobody help you find him?" I asked. "Surely they have ways."

Ruth reversed our positions and now she was rubbing the back of my hand. "That's what I thought when the letters stopped four years ago," she said. "They make it plain why they can't help. This real nice young fella from Edward's headquarters told me there were over 700,000 casualties in just one battle over there. He said it was in Verdun, or something like that—said it lasted nearly a year and how there was thousands of wives and mothers just like me looking for husbands and sons that won't never be found."

And that was the end of our discussion about Edward. Ruth then went on to talk about raising those kids and how life had taken away, but how because of them, it had given back too. Through them she felt like she still had a piece of Edward to hold on to. Listening to Ruth's story made me realize there are no straight paths in this life. One fork in the road is just as dark as the next. The more she talked, the more my doubts began to mix it up with a new-found courage—the courage Ruth gave me. If she could pick up the pieces of a broken life and move on, so could I.

Each time it felt like Ruth had finished talking, I asked more questions. I was looking for her secrets. What did she have to teach me about the kind of life she was living, and the kind of life I was about to live?

Suddenly, she realized how long we had been talking and said she had to get home to the kids. She went on and on with thanking me to where I almost felt guilty over it. All I could think of was, *I should have given her more.*

As Virgie finished her story, I realized she had found herself. It happened through Ruth. I also knew her mind was made up about divorcing Nate. Part of me was relieved at that moment, it would finally be over. But most of me was just sad.

Virgie followed through with the divorce. It became official on July 31, 1922. At 29 years old, she had been married for 12 years and was now prepared to raise three kids on her own. As frightened as she must have been, I saw a change in her immediately. Apparently, the suspicions about Nate seeing other women took a greater toll than worrying over supporting her family.

As dire as her circumstances sounded, she was never really alone. Nate helped her find a house within eight blocks of his own and agreed to help with expenses. As it turned out, we kids saw him about as much after the divorce as before it—maybe more. We stayed at his house on Saturday afternoons while Virgie did her weekly shopping. It was during those times we actually got a little bit of his attention.

Whenever we were around him Nate complained about slow sales, even though I knew better. I think it was just his way of trying to trick God. If he played poor, maybe he'd get help from a divine source. In fact, I think Nate was just a guy who played the odds. He said he believed in God… but I think it was just in case. Whatever his game, the complaining failed to hide that he was happier than I had ever seen him.

All in all, I liked the changes. I was still taking care of Dale, so my life was pretty much the same. For their part, Nate and Virgie settled on peaceful cooperation. During the next few years, they got along better than when they were married. Divorce suited them.

Then, along came Marie.

5

MARIE

Told by Velva – Dale's Sister

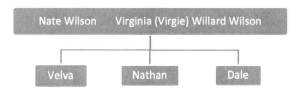

Our lives changed little between the divorce in 1922 and the day I made my surprise announcement in 1926. That was when I told Virgie I wanted to marry my boyfriend, Mark. We had dated for only a few months. Acting so quickly made my plans sound hasty and unwise. Looking back, they were. The most we had in common were lust and immaturity.

In my defense, even though I was only 16, it was fairly common for teenagers to start families early. Virgie, torn between happiness for me and worry over how she would care for Dale, signed her consent. Nate's reaction landed somewhere between politely curious and indifferent. I found out later there was a reason for his scattered attentions. He had become focused on a woman ten years his junior—the spoiled and uncaring, Marie.

Nate began dating Marie sometime in early 1926. I remember he mentioned her name a couple of times, though his comments were unremarkable. Regardless, at that point he kept her away from the family. Then, gradually he began talking about her more often and it was obvious their relationship had changed.

We first met Marie at her 26th birthday party. They shuffled us kids in and out pretty fast. We were there just long enough to size her up a little. She moved about the room with more flair than her presence deserved, though I have to admit she inspired notice. I liked her hair. It was black and cut short, which was all the rage at the time. Squared off bangs covered her forehead and drew a perfect line just above her pencil darkened eyebrows. A small birthmark on her left cheekbone looked like a butterfly. She fluttered her fake eyelashes at me when we were introduced, while presenting a palm-down hand.

It was easy to see why Nate wanted Marie. He was thirty-seven and already showing signs of age. His temples were now peppered with gray hair and lines formed at the corners of his eyes. I think he was trying to hold on to his youth through this shapely young woman. I doubt he considered her immaturity or lack of education a liability. His motives were more primal than that.

I stood at a distance and studied Marie. I knew she had invented the woman Nate now craved. People do that in matters of love. They conceal their true natures just long enough to score their prize. And then life asserts itself and they lose track of the creature they created. In time, traits they professed to find adorable while dating, become fingernails dragged across a chalkboard. And so it was with Marie.

In the beginning she seemed harmless enough, I even liked her a little. She pretended to care for us and offered small gifts to influence our opinions of her. It worked on me and Nathan for a short time. Dale, for his part, would have nothing to do with her. At six years old his affection knew only one target and that was Virgie. Marie's real self began to slip out in unguarded moments. Then, after Nate announced they would be married, she quit coming to any of our events and even spoke ill of Virgie in front of us.

That was the end of Nate and Virgie's amicable divorce. Overnight, whatever goodwill they enjoyed living separate lives, turned into a battleground. I'm confident Virgie believed Marie had been in the background from the very beginning. I'm equally confident she had not. Demanding and self-centered, Marie would never have allowed Nate to put off their union for over five years. She was too manipulative to let him think he exercised that kind of influence over her. No, Marie pulled all the strings—except one, and only Virgie would be pulling that one.

6

VIRGIE'S REVENGE

Told by Velva — Dale's Sister

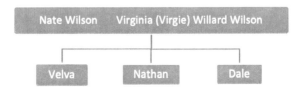

1927 was a watershed year for Virgie.

In October of 1926, I married Mark and moved away from home. In the process, Mom lost her closest confidant. Dad married Marie a year later and from that moment forward, old enough to know better, too self-involved to care, Marie did everything in her power to distance Nate from his past. Virgie was the reason. She sounded country, acted country, breathed country—she *was* country, and it drove Marie to distraction. Virgie reminded the world of who Nate really was. Her existence laid waste to the fantasy Marie tried to construct.

Marie mistakenly believed that once she married Nate his dual life with Virgie would end. The wedding would prove that Nate was *her* prize. Virgie would be put in her place for good, her influence would subside, and her meddling would stop. None of that happened.

Virgie was about to make a move and it was going to shock everyone.

If Virgie had a grand plan, she launched it the day after Nate and Marie returned from their honeymoon. It was in August of 1927. She began raining down complaints on Nate about her circumstances, needling him to fix her problems. Her list of grievances was long, though she tended to focus on two things: She couldn't make it on the meager wages she earned from the diner, and Nate wasn't doing enough to help. She was clearly angling for a larger monthly check, but Nate, practiced in the art of deflecting Virgie's demands, countered that he was now married and with two families to support, was doing all he could. And so, it flowed from one argument to another. In a world bursting with uncertainty, we were sure of only one thing—Virgie would never give up. Dale watched it all with an uneasy quiet.

Virgie's plans began to take shape innocently enough. First, she suggested that Marie begin to look after Dale during the day. That would save both families money. Next, she claimed she needed to work weekends. Dale could stay with Nate and Marie. That's when I knew her strategy had nothing to do with money. She wanted a change. It became obvious when she began talking about living above the diner. Well, we all knew that would never work, where would Nathan and Dale sleep? There had to be more.

The monster under the bed—waited.

~

As Virgie fashioned her future, in 1927 Mark and I were living with his mother in Treece, Kansas. He was a tub hooker at one of the nearby mines and I waited tables at a local diner. We were drawn there by the mining boom in zinc and lead deposits that covered over 2,500 square miles in southeastern Kansas, southwestern Missouri and northeastern Oklahoma. The area was called the Tri-State Mining District and between 1885 and 1970 it yielded about 460 million tons of ore. As early as 1915, there were more than 160 mines and mills within five miles of Picher, Oklahoma and Treece, Kansas. The fallout from those mining operations would eventually make ghost towns of both communities.

In our time, the mines were our salvation and Treece was a community of purpose. We had jobs. We had churches. We were surviving. How could we know that the giant chat hills ascending all around us would eventually bring death and destruction to our descendants? We had turned over the earth, and what was once in the ground now mocked us from on top of it. Wind swept the poison from the hills and people breathed it. Rain washed the poison into the streams and ground water and people drank it. What once lured people to our land would eventually drive them from it. Maybe we should have been more aware of the damage we were doing, but a person can only remember a past and live in a present. The future, that flowing river of possibilities, was more buried than the ore our miners were digging every day.

Like most of my neighbors, I concentrated on work and home. I fixed Mark's breakfast every day, kissed him goodbye and walked to work. The mine's first shift started early, so the diner had to be opened before sunrise. Day in and day out, I carried platefuls of food from the kitchen to hungry miners until my arms ached just to pick up a cup of coffee. It was typically dark when I walked back home.

If you want to know what's going on in a community, spend a little time at a local diner. You'll find out who's sick, who died, who had a baby, who moved away or who moved in. That's where the rhythm of our community pulsed. When I heard, "The mines are hiring," the pace of our lives quickened. With words like, "The mines are letting men go," the tempo slowed.

The mood in Treece had darkened by 1927. I may have been young and uneducated, but I was smart enough to know our lives had turned sour when the miners stopped flirting. My youthful curves were no match for a collapsing economy. Newspaper headlines grew alarming. Zinc and lead production was falling. Men stopped coming to the diner as often. My tips dwindled and everyone seemed on edge.

It was little surprise that I welcomed Virgie's invitation to visit her in Joplin. I would be separated from my worry—if only for a moment. I was excited about going home. Virgie would cook a traditional country meal of chicken and noodles, greens and homemade biscuits.

It all seemed innocent enough.

Virgie met me with a hug and a smile. I asked if Dad was coming to dinner. She said he was working out of town so I would have to see him on my next visit. I debated stopping by to see Marie anyway, just for Nate's sake. Not this trip. Marie would simply complain about Nate's long absences and I would feel less whole the minute I left her. She enjoyed sucking the life out of every moment and rarely missed an opportunity to do it.

I helped Virgie set the table. Even in her own home, she moved like a waitress—efficient and calculating. Practical to a fault, the simple pink dress she wore was called a "hooverette", known for its durability and reasonable price. Made of washable cotton and considered common, it still sported ruffled sleeves, an accentuated tied waist and was cut slim through the hips. Virgie, who wore her conservative religion like a badge of honor, obviously paid attention to fashion on some level.

As I predicted, she laid out a hearty meal of chicken and noodles with cornbread, greens and an apple pie warm from the oven. Virgie knew how to cook. As hard as I tried, I could never measure up to her in the kitchen. Maybe it was just a matter of liking food someone else prepared. There's something special about that. Even a sandwich made by another tastes better than one you make yourself.

Virgie called us to the table. Nathan sat down first, followed by Virgie, then me and finally Dale. He smiled at me. We clasped hands and Virgie told Nathan to offer thanks. He spoke in a hurried, uninspired monotone that earned a scolding hand-squeeze from Virgie. Nathan was now fifteen, handsome and surprisingly polished. The rest of us were half finished when he took his last bite and asked to be excused.

"You'll miss your pie," Virgie pointed out.

"I need to meet a friend," he said, and he was off.

I watched Dale through much of the dinner. He seemed fine for a 7-year-old. I could still sense our connection and knew that, for the most part, he was a happy little boy. In spite of recent changes, his life appeared stable. He rarely saw Nate or received much attention from him when we all lived together, so things were little different since the divorce. It was the darnedest thing—I never understood Nate's distant ways, but I knew he cared about us kids. If our dad's treatment mattered, Dale never showed it, but it surely drove him closer to Virgie. In the end, as long as he was with her, life was good.

Virgie sent Dale to bed early and invited me into the kitchen. She poured us coffee and sat down across a narrow white table from me. There was small talk about her diner and my diner and how things were getting worse every day. Before long, we were discussing things strangers might talk about. It felt awkward, like there was something else she wanted to say. Finally, she did.

"I had a talk with Nate," she said, her eyes locked on the coffee cup cradled between her nervous hands. The kitchen grew smaller and I felt strangely disconnected from my own mother.

"Oh, you did?" I asked.

"Yes."

"And what did you talk about? Has Marie been stirring up trouble again?"

"No, it's not that," Virgie said after pausing to sip her coffee. "I just can't get by on the little money I make, Velva. Things aren't the same. Your dad put me on an allowance and he won't give me any more. I can't afford to live in this house."

"What are you going to do?" I asked.

"I'm moving to that apartment over the diner."

"That tiny place" I countered? "It's barely big enough for one person. Where would…." And then it hit me. She was planning to live there alone.

"What about Dale?" I asked.

She was ready for that question and answered it matter-of-factly, "He'll live with Nate and Marie. So will Nathan."

I stared at her, wide eyed, jaw dropped and feeling numb. It was impossible to imagine she would give Dale up, especially to Marie.

"She hates him," I said. "She would never take him in."

Virgie sat quiet as I stumbled around in my own thoughts. Finally, I realized the truth and asked, "Nate hasn't told her yet, has he? What is she going to think?"

"I don't care what she thinks," Virgie said. "Dale needs to live in a home. I can't take him to a one room apartment, Velva. You know that."

I felt abandoned myself. Dale would be crushed. How could he ever understand what was happening to him? Marie would make his life miserable and he barely knew Nate. Where would Dale find love in that house? There had to be another way.

Virgie knew I was dumbfounded and quickly added, "I'll see him nearly all the time, Velva."

I wondered what "nearly" would come to mean, and I had my doubts about why all of this was happening. It was possible that forcing Dad to take Nathan and Dale was the greatest injury Virgie could cause Marie without actually killing her. Could my mother be that cold and calculating?

Virgie went on with her excuses—in my mind, none of them worth more than a dozen rotten eggs. But she was my mother. A girl stands with her mother. And so, I let my misgivings become stones in my shoes. *Maybe she'll make it up to him in some other way*, I thought. That lie lasted just long enough to settle my nerves. I gathered myself and began to ask more questions.

"What did Dad say about all of this? I'm surprised he didn't offer you more money."

"It wasn't just about the money," Virgie said. "I told him Dale needed a real family. He needed a mother and a father. He needed a home."

"What'd he say to that?" I asked.

"You *are* his family," he half yelled. "A child should be with his mother."

"I turned on him with the truth: Who says a mother is better than a father? He's a boy. He needs a man's hand. I've raised him on my own since the divorce. He needs you now."

She carried on, even though I had stopped listening. I knew Nathan would be fine. He was a teenager and would be happy to go wherever things were easiest for him, and that was with Nate and Marie. It was different for

Dale. He was just seven years old and had only known Nate as a weekend father. He had no relationship with Marie and her maturity level was only marginally greater than his own. All she really wanted was to be free of us. It was hard to imagine that this was the world Virgie had chosen for Dale.

"When are you going to tell Dale?" I asked.

"Nate and I will tell him as soon as he lets Marie know."

"What if she refuses?"

"She won't refuse," Virgie said. "She's not about to give up her meal ticket."

"You're probably right," I agreed.

We sat in silence for a time. I hoped Virgie might have a change of heart. It was possible. A person can recoil from speaking dreadful words that seemed harmless in their quiet mind. But Virgie sat steady and unwavering, her plan unaffected by my grief. And that pained me even more.

With little notice, I rose up and told her I had to go back home.

"I thought you were going to spend the night," Virgie said.

I fumbled for an excuse and finally said, "I borrowed this car. I have to get it back before morning. I forgot to tell you."

I collected my things and headed for the door. Suddenly, I felt weak. My breathing turned shallow and my legs became limp and unsteady. I turned back to Virgie. I wanted to say something, anything that might change her mind. Instead, I walked quietly to the boys' bedroom.

Dale's bed was left of the doorway. I moved to stand next to him. He was asleep, oblivious to the furious pain coming his way. I reached down to stroke his warm cheek. He stirred. My heartbeat quickened. "*He can never think I had anything to do with this,*" I thought. With that, I hurried out of the room, thanked Virgie and left the house.

The twenty-three-mile drive from Joplin to Treece felt like a hundred. I had to go through Galena, Missouri and Baxter Springs, Kansas on a two-lane highway. It felt narrower than I remembered. My mind raced with possibilities. I plotted how Mark and I could raise Dale with our family. That would never work. We lived with Mark's mother in a house so small it felt crowded with only three people. Plus, we had only recently decided to have a baby.

As I pulled into our shabby driveway—two dirt ruts separated by a grassy island—I turned off the motor and began to cry. What was I going to do about Dale? I resolved to visit him more often.

It was all I had.

Virgie followed through with her plan. Dale was sent to live with Nate and Marie. I never asked how he reacted when they broke the news to him. To this day, no one has ever talked about it and that suits me just fine.

It turned out Virgie lived over the diner for only two months before moving in with a family by the name of Green. The Greens, like many of that era, took in boarders to help pay expenses. Virgie continued to work at the diner, a steady presence in the lives of local miners who ate there often. Her days were filled with a sameness that might drive others to despair, but not Virgie. She enjoyed the simplicity of her routine. It played into her sense of deliverance in the hands of hard work and regular church going. She attended Wednesday evening services, Sunday of course, and joined in every revival the area had to offer, as if her soul depended on it. She was the Bible's handmaiden.

If Virgie could dance, only she and her mirror knew about it. Singing in her church was restricted to acapella religious hymns, and I doubt alcohol ever touched her lips. I never heard her utter a curse word, and she hated lying. Considering all that religious grounding, I wondered how giving Dale to Nate and Marie made sense to her. Where was God in that? I tried to be sensitive to her circumstances, but I think a mother finds a way.

While Virgie went on with her life, Dale was in shock over what had happened in his. Nate's house had become little more than a prison and Marie was its warden. Nate traveled most of the week and she resented his absence. She took out her frustrations on Dale. When Nate did get home she started fights—one after another. Early on, their battles were hidden behind closed doors, but eventually Marie began waging them in full view of Dale and many of them were about him. They were figments of her imagination, but fight by fight she drove a wedge between father and son.

To be fair, it must be clear by now that Nate was hardly a Father of the Year contender. Marie's insecurities had nothing to do with his inability to connect with his children. His shortcomings likely came from his own upbringing, coupled with an inherent selfishness. What Marie did however, what her endless fights demanded, was Nate's complete attention. As a result, I think he began to resent Dale. How could he constantly defend him against Marie's charges without eventually believing there was a measure of truth to her attacks?

If Marie had only considered Dale an inconvenience, her indifference might have rendered him invisible. Instead, she made him the embodiment of her failures and the source of her unhappiness. She worked to make his life more difficult and caused him to feel unloved in his own home.

Marie exercised authority over Dale, but she enjoyed little power. Virgie, on the other hand, wielded authority, power and unwarranted influence— influence the rest of us believed she ceded when she abandoned Dale. She robbed him of trust and scarred him through ignorance. And even after all of that, he was incapable of loving her less.

How did Virgie fail to realize Dale would have gladly lived over the diner with her? He would have slept on the floor and eaten only one meal a day if that's what it took. He would have shined shoes or sold apples on a street corner. All he wanted was to be with his mother.

Instead, she was the shiny object he could never quite have. Every time she came to visit him, or he spent time with her, he was sure she would take him back. All he wanted was to hear her say, "Stay." She never did.

7

BARBARA'S FAMILY UPENDED

Told by Madeline – Barbara's Sister

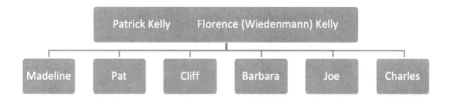

Barbara turned twelve in 1934. By then the Great Depression had swallowed up the world in a couple of mighty gulps. The rich hardly noticed. They continued to indulge themselves with the trappings of privilege. They took comfort in claiming that people should just work harder if they wanted to succeed. I doubt they ever saw us, even when they looked our way. Ethically flexible, they refused to accept that most outcomes are determined by pure chance. Even the recently dispossessed turned a shaded eye to the already humbled.

It was easy to spot those soon-to-be destitute people from the seasoned poor. Their clothes told the tale. As the depression took root, the nearly poor kept up their appearances, hoping a job was just around the corner. Soon, sweat stained shirt collars, fraying cuffs and unshined shoes completed a metamorphosis from butterfly to caterpillar and the differences disappeared. Success was now measured by their place in a bread line.

As disruptive as the depression was for adults, children barely noticed. Games still had to be played. School still had to be attended. They were still with their families. That's what really mattered. And so it was for Barbara. Sweet and gentle, she had what she needed, a mother who saw to her needs, a father who adored her, brothers and a sister who protected her. Ordinary adults became heroes by overcoming hardships that were merely inconveniences to kids like Barbara.

∼

February 27, 1934 started out like most other days. Patrick got up early—a habit from calling on farmers before their day started—ate his breakfast and left for the office. Florence woke the kids and while they finished eating, packed their sack lunches. She then hurried them off to school. After finishing the dishes, she bundled Charles up in warm clothes and a heavy jacket and left for the library. A biting cold wind strafed her uncovered ankles. Florence tilted her head toward the snow filled air and maintained a measured pace.

Her chattering teeth tapped out a steady rhythm as she entered the library. The building appeared near empty except for one librarian at the checkout desk. Even weak sounds raced noisily through the hollow corridors. Florence unwound her neck scarf and moved closer to her bookish friend. The two exchanged smiling nods, as they always did.

"Just look at Charles," the sandy haired woman said. "All I can see is his face." She waited for Florence to unbundle him. "And what brings you out in this cold weather?" she asked. They both laughed.

"The new Saturday Evening Post," Florence answered. "Is it in yet?"

The librarian held up a magazine. The cover was a picture of an attractive couple framed by a heart.

"Do you mean this one?" the librarian asked. "The first installment of the new Scoggins novel is in here. I kept this copy behind my desk just for you."

C.E. Scoggins was one of Florence's favorite authors. The book being serialized was, "*House of Dawn*". Another of his books, "*Tycoon*" was made into a movie starring John Wayne.

"Thank you so much," Florence said. She adjusted Charles higher on her hip and accepted the magazine.

Her preferred reading area was tucked away in a quiet corner toward the back of the building. She found a colorful picture book to occupy Charles and settled into one of the broad, leather backed chairs. Charles became fussy almost immediately. Florence, ever respectful of library etiquette, whisked him up and hurried home.

The rest of the day passed quietly until the kids arrived home from school. They first checked to see if Florence had baked cookies, nothing on the counter. Then, in a boy-induced hurry, they changed out of their school clothes and headed outside to play in the snow, leaving Barbara alone to entertain herself. She was fine with it. Patrick would be home soon enough and he always found interesting things to do.

∼

Barbara may have been riding her bike, or walking aimlessly with a friend. Maybe she was reading a book like Florence wanted her to do. More likely than not, however, she was just sitting at the front door waiting for Patrick to come home from work. No one ever offered those details. It hardly mattered what she was doing when life altering news rained down on her. One moment her father was the joy of her life, the next she was told he had had a heart attack and was in the Girard hospital.

Barbara told me she knew what "heart attack" meant. Her friend Betsy's dad had died of one, which meant danger was nearby. She watched her brothers pace in circles. Their worry made her nervous so she decided to sit on the front stoop, as if her presence there might bring him home. She wanted to ask someone if Patrick would die, but by asking she might be inviting it in. She kept quiet and prayed.

Patrick died at 7:00 p.m. that evening. He was 53 years old.

Death was still an abstraction to Barbara. To comprehend what it meant it had to be reduced to terms she understood. She would never again curl up against his massive frame. She would never again hear his booming Irish laugh or whisper her child secrets into his willing ears. "Never" seemed like an impossibly long time.

Florence, stunned by Patrick's passing, wore a stoic face. If she expressed any profound grief, it was out of sight and no one heard it. I actually wondered if she knew how to cry. Oh, I know she was sad, her body told the truth. Typically soldier erect, her shoulders now slumped forward more heavily and she sometimes stumbled over nothing at all. She was alone. I wondered what would happen to her.

Her mastery of emotions spilled onto the boys as each worked to hold himself in check. Even as they sat silent, I knew they were devastated. Pat was now the man of the family and he took that role seriously. Motivated by grief, a sense of responsibility, or maybe both, he made Florence a promise we would all learn to regret. He assured her she would never have to worry about money. He said the family would take care of her and two-year-old Charles. I guess that's what he thought a man was supposed to do. In the process, we took away whatever incentive she had to pick up the pieces of her life and fashion a new one.

As difficult as it was for all of us, I think Barbara hurt the most. She suffered openly—sorrow come to life. Florence watched in wonderment. I thought she might be envious of Barbara, or simply surprised by her obvious disregard for what anyone else thought. Either way, I worried Barbara might have trouble overcoming the shock of Patrick's death. To my great relief and amazement, she bounced back quickly. That's when I realized how special she was.

Barbara understood that life imagines nothing of the living. It happens and it moves on. She treated sorrow and joy with the same respect, and then she let them go. It was a trait that served her well for the rest of her life and she would call on it often.

~

The family continued to live in Pittsburg, Kansas after Patrick died. Al and I moved to a home near the family. I had become a librarian so we gave Mom whatever money we could afford. Florence took in laundry. Barbara helped with ironing and deliveries. Young Pat stuck to his promise and assumed responsibility for everyone else. As I look back on it now, I'm amazed by what he did. In the very heart of the depression, he, an eighteen-year-old, did whatever it took to keep the family together. He led by example and made decisive moves. Like the time he was offered a manager's job at a grocery store in Joplin, Missouri. He packed the family's belongings, loaded them into an old Packard and they moved within a matter of days.

As each of the kids became old enough to work, a portion of their income went to the family's upkeep. Barbara was no exception. As a teenager she baby sat for neighbors and friends and helped Florence. At 18, having graduated from high school, she became a telephone operator for the local AT&T office. The average salary for an Operator living in New York City in 1938 was $23.63 per week. Barbara was making something less than that in Joplin.

Manual telephone switchboards and switchboard operators were used until the 1960s. A caller heard, "Number Please" and their connection to a desired source was made by a human being. The world's first telephone operator was George Willard Croy who was hired in January of 1878. In September of that year, the first female operator, Emma Nutt, was chosen by Alexander Graham Bell. She represented a sea change as young women began to replace the teenage boys previously employed to do the job. The company reportedly claimed the boy's behavior was unacceptable. The more likely reason was that they paid women from one half to one quarter less than they were paying men.

Chosen women were typically young, attractive and single, appearance standards the company insisted on for many years. Management's purposes were similar to those of the airline industry when it created a glamorous image for stewardesses. The goal was to enhance the public's view of air travel.

It may be difficult to imagine today, but telephone service had to be 'sold' to end users. Attractive women were walking advertisements for the phone company. Barbara fit the mold perfectly. She was young, pretty, shapely and willing to work hard for very little money. In fact, she was thrilled to have a job and held on to her position for a number of years.

Barbara was an exceptional student. Had she been born years later, college might have been in her future. It was different in the late 1930s. Maybe if she had been passionate about a technical field, say, science, healthcare or education, she would have found a way to get an advanced degree. However, like most of her friends, Barbara was a generalist. Millions of young women lived her life, and their prospects grew from events outside their control. Getting married and raising a family was their goal, and Barbara was little different. If she harbored some broader dream, nobody knew about it. She was passionate about being a wife and mother. In her mind there was no higher purpose. A romantic, Barbara wanted a guy to sweep her off her feet. It would take an 'in-charge' type to win her over.

He would soon drive into her life in a shiny new car.

8

DALE LEFT BEHIND

Told by Velva - Dale's Sister

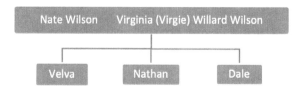

The Great Depression dragged on.

Joplin's mining district began to feel the economic meltdown as early as 1928. Two years later, zinc and lead prices reached all-time lows. Employment in the mines was catastrophic. At its peak in 1924 there were 11,187 miners employed. By June and July of 1930, only 500 part-time workers were needed.

It was no different in Treece, Kansas. Mark and I were still living with Mark's mother in a small, paint starved frame house on the edge of town. Mark was barely holding on at the mine. Layoffs were routine and it was obvious his days were numbered. I continued to work at the café where Mark's mother was the cook. Even with three incomes, we struggled to make ends meet and the stress began to poke at our marriage.

Small mining towns like Treece appeared exhausted even when the economy was good. Add a world-wide depression and what passed for living became unrecognizable. Hope withered along with the mines, and survival replaced ambition.

Even though times were tough, I had been through worse. I knew what it was like to be without. I knew how to make a meal out of potatoes, salt pork and a few vegetables. I never gave a second thought to slipping uneaten food from the café into a tin can and taking it home for super. You get used to living just above nothing—a place where food is a luxury.

I could deal with the hardships in my own life, but I could never get used to seeing whole families living out of old cars. They sprang up like dandelions overnight in an empty lot near my diner. They tended to move often, so it was rarely the same car, or the same family I had seen the day before. Maybe the local sheriff told them to move on, or maybe they found out there were no jobs in Treece and simply left to look elsewhere. Either way, I know I dreaded walking past them on my way to work.

A woman knows another woman at a glance; knows the essence of her without exchanging a word. I felt that way as I crossed the paths of too many mothers squatting next to makeshift campfires, brewing their family's morning coffee. They typically looked up, as mothers do, their instinct to protect a child still honed to a fine edge. In the beginning, before the Great Depression grew "Great", most of them smiled. Over time, the smile disappeared, replaced by a vacant stare—eyes lifeless and defeated. It was haunting. I wanted to help, but by giving away something that mattered, I might become one of them.

I realize my dread was born of fear. Not for what they might do to me, but for the possible future their existence foretold. I had the same feeling when I saw people huddled under old newspapers in drainage pipes, or when teenagers left home by hopping onto moving rail cars. They needed to find jobs and "somewhere else" had to be better than "here". Their mothers suffered to see them go. At the same time, I guessed they felt some relief, knowing there was one less mouth to feed. It was odd to see sorrow and resignation settle on the same troubled face.

Such was our world. And somewhere in all that chaos, Virgie met her future second husband, Sidney Snead. He was 49 years old, ten years Virgie's senior. He had never been married. I learned he lived in a boarding house near Virgie's and ate at her diner several times each week. Sid was about as common as an old shoe. His weathered face and slightly collapsed frame, spoke of a man who had worked in the open air, doing manual labor most of his life. He tended to walk with a shuffle, as if his body had grown too tired to stride out with any confidence. A painfully quiet man, Sid spoke only when spoken to. Maybe he was shy, though I think the truth was he just didn't have much to say.

Virgie rarely mentioned Sid in her letters. The first time I met him in person was the day she revealed her next shocking news.

~

By 1930, Dale had been living with Nate and Marie for a little over 3 years. My vow to visit him, though well intended, became infrequent trips to Joplin around holidays. "The road to hell is paved with good intentions," Virgie always said. The words were tangled thorns in my head.

At least I spent as much time with Dale as possible on those occasions. He was ten years old and I wanted him to know he had an ally. To be honest, I also wanted to find out what it was like living with Marie. Maybe she had turned out less cruel than we all imagined. Maybe time had softened her. If only that had been true. In fact, she was meaner than a dog with a bone, shallower than a pie plate and as jealous as a teenage girl guarding her first boyfriend.

Dale rarely spoke ill of anyone, at least not to me. He had to be poked and prodded for the smallest bit of information about school, Nate, Nathan, Virgie or himself. But he was quick to abandon that secrecy when it came to Marie. The mere mention of her name turned him angry and almost talkative. His resentment was obvious and focused. Most of it had to do with being separated from Virgie. Even though he had a right to find serious fault with what she had done to him, she was still his mother. Whatever blame she deserved, he heaped onto Marie.

I asked Dale if he had talked with Dad about Marie's treatment. He said Nate didn't know anything about it. I knew otherwise. Nate could have been accused of a lot of things, but ignorance wasn't one of them. He had simply decided to avoid the conflict whenever possible.

Clearly, Nate would be of no help, which made me wonder if Dale ever told Virgie about his problems. If he had, she never spoke a word of it to me. Either way, she had to know what was going on. She knew it and apparently chose to ignore what it might be doing to Dale. That's where things stood in Dale's life, his father turning a blind eye to his plight, and his mother failing to care enough to save him.

I stewed and worried and prayed. Then, I fell into the crypt of complacency, that place where you leave well enough alone. You stop asking questions for fear you might find out the truth and have to do something about it.

Early that year Virgie asked that I meet her in Joplin. She said she needed to tell me something. I immediately thought of Dale. She was finally going to take him back from Nate and Marie. It had to be something like that. Why else would she make such a point of my being there? I had almost given up hope for Dale, and now my fondest wish for him might be coming true. I told her I would be there.

As agreed, I met Virgie at her diner following the lunch hour. I assumed we would leave for Nate and Marie's from there. My arrival was announced by tinkling silver bells over the diner's front door. I liked the sounds they made, high pitched and sweet. They reminded me of Christmas.

I wore the only nice dress I owned. It was deep purple, with a high waist, a broad collar and buttons running down the front. As the door latched behind me, I glanced around the narrow room and noticed the counter stools and all the tables sat empty, except for one at the back of the room. There, sitting ridged, but smiling, was Virgie. Across from her, a man I assumed to be Sid, leaned against the table top over crossed arms. Virgie was wearing a decidedly drab dress, something she might throw on any day of the week. Suddenly, it felt like something was wrong. I say that, knowing it is unlikely I felt anything odd at the time. We just say things like that when looking back. We imagine that life changing moments were surely foretold by some kind of instinctual insight, and then we create it.

As I wove my way around the scattered tables, Virgie rose to meet me. Sid also stood up in a shoulder heavy version of respectful attention. I kissed Virgie's cheek and we both sat down. Sid joined us after an appropriate pause. We sipped coffee and exchanged recent news. Much of our conversation centered on the Depression. That same topic dominated nearly every room occupied by more than two adults, and we were no exception. We talked of homeless people and hungry children, of jobs drying up all around us, and of when the nightmare might end. And then an awkward silence disturbed the meaningless noise.

Virgie tickled her spoon with an anxious finger. "Sid and I are moving to Texas," she finally said, her wary eyes considering my reaction.

Sid squirmed. Virgie's announcement had caught him off guard. It was as if an orchestrated plan had suddenly struck a foul note. I failed to understand why either of them would be so uneasy. Virgie's surprise was surely just a prelude to the good news, the news that they would be taking Dale with them. Virgie knew I had helped raise Dale, maybe she thought I would be upset they were moving so far away.

"The mines are down to part time work," Virgie continued. I nodded my understanding. "Sid found a job as a Pumper on an oil lease in Texas." She went on to describe what he would be doing, though I had no interest. "There's a small house on the lease we can live in for free," she said. "Sid was told not to expect much."

Virgie clearly welcomed this change. She had always been a country woman at heart, soil in her veins and all that. So, I was happy for her.

"Where will Dale go to school?" I asked.

An already awkward encounter suddenly turned cold. Virgie leaned back in her chair while smoothing the front of her dress.

With her head turned toward the windows, she said, "We can't take Dale with us," and then she hesitated, as if there might be something more. Instead, she simply took a deep breath and waited for my reaction.

I must have been looking at Sid, because Virgie shot to his defense as if my absent stare implied blame. "It's not Sid's fault," she said.

I considered explaining that the thought never crossed my mind—that all I was thinking about was Dale.

"Why aren't you taking him with you?" I asked.

Virgie began making excuses: There was only one school in the area—it was a long way from the lease, and they had no way to get Dale there—the house had only one bedroom—Sid's $946 yearly salary was barely enough for even two people to live on—the nearest neighbor was miles away, so Dale would have no friends.

I listened, but behind my hearing were thoughts of what it would do to Dale. I wanted to tell Virgie it wasn't right to leave him behind. I wanted to tell her he was just a little boy and he needed his mother. I wanted to cry for him.

Virgie finished with, "He'll be better off with Nate and Marie."

I wish I could remember if more was said, but what would it matter? Virgie's mind was made up. Whatever misgivings she might have considered had been put away and she was ready to move on.

"Why did you want me here?" I asked.

"I want you to be with me when we tell Dale," she said. "He might need you."

No, I thought, *that's not why she called me. She wants it to look like I agree. She wants him to think I was part of the decision.* Nothing could have been further from the truth.

I told her it was impossible. I had to go home soon, that Mark's mother was taking care of the diner by herself. Virgie knew I was lying. I didn't care. I wasn't about to be present when Dale found out his mother was leaving him.

We made small talk for the next half hour or so, all the while, my attention was trained squarely on the wall-clock behind Virgie. I wanted to be gone before Dale got home from school.

"He'll be coming to visit us every summer," Virgie stated over and over again. She said it with more fanfare than the bargain deserved. "He'll like that."

And that's where I left it.

～

Virgie kept her promise every summer thereafter. Sometime during the school break, Nate bought Dale a bus ticket and shipped him off to Texas for as long as Virgie would keep him. At the end of one of those visits, I think it was in 1934, after he turned fourteen, I told Nate I would meet Dale's bus at a nearby town and bring him on to Joplin. I knew it might be the last chance we would spend time alone together. My life felt more complicated by the day, so who could predict where I would be in a year?

I drove to a small town in Oklahoma, just across the border from Kansas and parked across the street from the bus terminal. The driver stopped only long enough to allow a couple of passengers to exit. As I gathered my purse, I saw Dale step down from the bus. He stretched and yawned and straightened his hair with the toss of fanned out fingers. It was clear he had just awakened from a nap. I came up to his back and hugged him from behind. He turned without a word and barely touched his cheek to mine. After collecting his beat-up suitcase and loading it into the car, we headed to Joplin.

He sat silent, so I used my sometimes-successful tactic of making him answer questions. I opened with, "Did Mom do your laundry before you left?"

"No, he said. "Mrs. Snead had enough to do."

After a quick glance his way, I continued on as if nothing had happened. But something *had* happened. Virgie had been demoted. She was now, Mrs. Snead. She was still our mom, and Dale would remain devoted to her for the rest of his life, but he would never again address or refer to her as Mother or Mom. It was always, "Mrs. Snead". I wondered if that was his way of punishing her for leaving him. She surely deserved it, and without ever hearing a word from her, I knew it must have cut deeply.

It was late summer. The two-lane road to Joplin wound through sun bleached pastures, now more golden than green. They gave way to a patchwork of corn fields stretching out in every direction. The corn stalks, tall and regal just a month before, had turned a mottled green with withered tips.

Dale resisted my attempts to engage him. He swatted away my questions with brief answers as quickly as I asked them. I noticed him picking at a blemish on his face.

"Don't do that," I said. "You'll make it worse." Then I felt awful for saying it. I was sure he felt self-conscious about his skin. It had been a problem for some time. Virgie claimed it was because Marie fed him so poorly. Nate said he ate too much candy, while I put my money on the stress of living with Nate and Marie. It could have been any of those things, heck, just being a teenager was enough. Whatever the reason, he looked worse after his trip to Virgie's.

Dale seemed mature beyond his years. It made sense, a person grows more through adversity than privilege, at least that's how I saw it. His grown-up exterior however, concealed a little kid stirring just beneath that practiced facade. I wanted to hear from the little kid. I wanted to know what damage we caused. As we cruised along, I pressed and prodded until finally, he began giving up important parts of himself. It happened when I asked if he would rather be living in Texas or Missouri.

"Texas," he said, and then he went quiet again.

I sensed he was trying to decide whether to tell me more. Maybe he still blamed me for some of his unhappiness. Of course, it didn't matter. I carried enough of that guilt by myself. Regardless, I persisted. From one moment to the next it seemed he had made up his mind and decided to talk. I became cautious, like by moving I might scare away a suspended hummingbird. I wondered if this was the new Dale. Maybe he had reached an age where such an exchange was possible. It would have been nice if that were the case, but it turned out to be the first of only two times he would open up to me. Had I known, I would have listened more closely. I would have savored it. I would have closed the car windows and tried to trap us in that moment. As it was,

I let too many of his words drift away, intent on enjoying the rhythm of a voice I heard so rarely.

He told me about packing more clothes than he needed for his trip to Virgie's— about getting on the bus in Joplin and waving goodbye to Nate. He remembered hoping it would be the last time he had to deal with Marie. And most importantly, he wondered if Virgie would keep him in Texas instead of sending him home at the end of summer. Maybe this would be the year.

As he told his story the details allowed me to imagine him settling into his seat on the bus, a sense of relief mixing easily with anticipation. Each shift of the labored gears, each rotation of the spinning tires moving him farther from the life he wanted to escape in Joplin. It might have taken a bus stop or two, but eventually he would have allowed himself to focus on where he was going instead of where he had been.

I guessed he leaned back and dreamed of living in Texas. I knew his desires were deeper than just being with Virgie. He harbored romantic notions of ranches the size of small countries and great herds of cattle advancing across the prairie to the crack of a cowboy's whip. When the bus crossed the Red River, he must have smiled.

And then my imaginings gave way to his own descriptions. He told me about white-faced cattle dotting the horizon as far as he could see and how a small herd of horses began galloping along a fence bordering the road. He said there were pintos and roans, chestnuts and palominos, a mahogany bay and a dusky buckskin. They ran as one, black hooves chewing up the ground in front of them. Eventually, they curved away in unison, no longer interested in the boxy white bus.

To my surprise, he began offering more details and told his story like it was a movie. While something less than word-for-word, this is what he told me:

The trip took a full twelve hours over two-lane highways with stops in every bus town between Joplin and north central Texas. He knew the route well and checked off the landmarks that told him when they were near his real home. He scooted forward to get a better view through the bus's front windows as they topped a steep hill—his hill. At the bottom, where the land curved higher to meet the next rise, sat a nameless wooden building with a single hitching rail standing guard in front. He mentioned that scene many times for the rest of his life so I know it captured him. Was it because it was within a mile of Sid and Virgie's lease in Young County, TX? Or maybe the setting appealed to his fascination with the old west. Either way, that's where the bus stopped and it's where Sid and Virgie waited.

Sid, sporting a tattered straw hat and oil-stained overalls, stood close to Virgie. She wore a plain cotton dress hemmed about mid-calf. Her short brown hair was curled tight in defiance of the hot wind buffeting their land most days. Just as every other year, the bus ground to a stop to deposit Dale. He quickly collected his faded tan suitcase and wedged it into the bed of Sid's black service truck before assuming his seat next to the passenger door. The truck smelled of oil-soaked rags and gasoline. Dale took in a deep breath.

Sid checked the bag one last time, spit out his chew and mounted the truck. Virgie sat between the man and the boy as they headed south to the oil lease. After about a mile, Sid turned off the main road and onto a dusty trail. Tire tracks marked the path, though they often faded into the sandy soil, only to reappear again as if a fickle mirage. Their sole companions were nodding steel horse heads, widely spaced across the distant landscape and sucking ancient deposits of oil from deep within the earth. Their bottom-hole pumps were anchored in formations with names like Neugent, Henderson, Gloyd or Dees sands.

Sid was responsible for keeping his section of the lease's pumping equipment in working order. Until well into the 1950's, electricity was an urban convenience. Most of the rigs were in isolated locations and powered by diesel motors that had to be refueled every day. Sid's area was part of a greater lease consisting of thousands of acres. The property was just off of what is now called Gun Range Road, directly west of the northern end of Graham Lake. Along with Sid and Virgie, the most common living things out there were rattle snakes, turtles, and mottled green lizards willing to give up a tail if you caught one.

The single lane trail eventually led to Sid and Virgie's rarely painted, slat wood house with a rusty tin roof. It was owned by the oil company and was probably thrown up in a matter of days. Shaped like a box, it had a narrow lean-to porch stretched across the front of the house from corner to corner. Its interior consisted of a tiny parlor, a dining area, a small kitchen and one bedroom. In back, 30 to 40 feet from the rear door, was a two-seater outhouse.

Dale typically stayed for two or three weeks—sometimes up to a month. Each day, he followed Sid around to the pumping units—horse heads nodding constant approval. Dale lubricated their moving parts wherever Sid pointed to a protruding grease zerk. He poured diesel fuel into engine side tanks and watched Sid bleed the lines. Dale was respectful. He minded Sid, found him kind and genuine. They did manly things together. After servicing his units, Sid often took Dale fishing at one of the lease ponds filled with unnatural looking green water.

Dale enjoyed Sid's quiet company, liked that he was a man of few words and the ones that did escape him were spoken softly. That aside, Dale was baffled by how Virgie found Sid attractive in the first place. He moved about with a deliberation that bordered on sluggishness. He nearly always had a chew of tobacco protruding from between his cheek and gum. Invariably, some of its juices would leak from the corners of his mouth. By the end of the day, what with spitting and chewing, the leak had stained his hide right down to the curve of his chin. His face was brown and leathered from the blowing sand and relentless sun. After years of abuse, his skin appeared to melt into gentle folds. Sid was as homely as Nate was handsome.

Virgie on the other hand, was still petite and attractive, though she made every effort through plain dresses and clunky shoes, to blend in to the colorless landscape all around her. She enjoyed her austere life. It brought her closer to the demanding God she worshiped. Every breath she took was offered to his glory. I wondered how Dale fit in to that kind of life. He showed little interest in religion. Regardless of his own doubts, I believe he respected Virgie for her certainty.

Virgie raised chickens for eggs and meat. The flock was turned loose to roam the yard during the day, scratching around in the sandy soil for bugs or hoping to find some undiscovered feed from the morning scattering. Periodically, Virgie would calmly grab an unlucky young rooster for roasting or a couple of hens for frying. She had no sooner snatched them up, when, by a skillful twist of her wrist, they were dispatched to chicken paradise. The head was removed and the body tied upside down to bleed out on the parched sand.

In the meantime, she filled a large pot with water and brought it to a hard boil. She seemed to know instinctively how hot the water had to be to suit her purposes. Next, she submerged the bloodless body into the water, twisted it one way and then another, bobbed it up and down and then repeated the process until a feather could be pulled effortlessly away from the wing. Having reached the perfect condition, she de-feathered the bird in less than a minute.

In the evening, she used chicken feed to lure her flock back into the coup. Next morning, she collected eggs and the play began again—an ageless cycle of destruction and renewal.

Virgie enjoyed the chickens, but her greatest love was working the garden. She laid out an expansive form, tilled it all up with a spade and hoe, designed her planting schedule, decided where to place compatible varieties, planted the seeds, watered when needed (which was most of the time) and stooped to weed every inch of her garden every day. She planted a summer and winter garden and it was a rare occasion when greens failed to show up on her table.

They typically bought hogs from a local farmer and butchered twice a year. The hams were smoked and the rest stored in a salt and spice laced wooden barrel. They enjoyed a thick slice of skillet fried ham every morning, along with eggs, red eye gravy and country fried potatoes. The leftover bones were used to season the pot of beans she almost always had simmering on the gas stove. Her menu wasn't much, but they never went to bed hungry.

"And that's what you did every day?" I asked.

"I did other things outside and we went to church on Wednesday evenings and Sunday mornings and then the late service too," he said.

That was pretty much all he had to tell and Dale's story ended about as quickly as it began. He leaned his head back on the seat and slept. I wondered if he was dreaming about Virgie's lean existence, the tattered house, blowing sand, meager food and the colorless countryside. It really didn't matter how I framed it, that desolation is where Dale willingly visited and ached to live from age 10 through 18.

I think he believed his life could have been made right again, if only Virgie had kept him on one of those trips. I doubt she ever considered it.

9

DALE REMEMBERS

Told by Velva – Dale's Sister

Nate, for all his faults, did the best he could to take care of Dale. To him, "taking care" meant providing what was needed to survive, and in that, he succeeded. What he failed to deliver was affection, attention and moral support. That flaw led to Dale's unceasing efforts to gain Nate's approval. I had been there. I knew what it was like to devote yourself to pleasing a man incapable of pleasing himself.

Dale told me a disturbing story that proved just how serious he was about winning Nate over. We talked about it on Saturday, June 27, 1936. I know because I was in Joplin to celebrate Dale's 16th birthday. Marie was there. She put the whole thing together and bragged about it as if she had stopped a war. The party ended soon after lunch. I wanted to be alone with Dale, so I asked him to go for a drive with me. He accepted in a heartbeat. I think he wanted to get away from Marie just as much as I did.

It turned out to be one of the hottest summers in Joplin's history with forty-three days over one hundred degrees. Even with the windows rolled down, the car felt like an oven. I decided to stop at a community park with swings, a slipper slide and picnic tables painted in different colors. We found a red one under a shade tree and sat down across from one another.

I turned my face to a feeble breeze. Dale picked at a splintered piece of wood on the bench seat. He seemed uneasy.

"What's wrong," I asked.

"Nothing," he said.

I knew otherwise. He had something on his mind. It felt just like when he told me about his trips to Virgie's. We were back in that same moment. He was trying to decide if he could trust me.

"You know you can tell me anything," I said. "I'm good at keeping things to myself."

He shifted on the picnic bench which caused the whole table to move. A quick glance my way proved everything was okay. He leaned forward, his elbows coming to rest on his knees. I smoothed out my dress, pretended to look for something in my purse, smiled for no reason and waited. He looked toward me again.

"Now, you can't say anything about this to anyone," he said.

"Of course not," I answered.

We shifted to look toward one another and he began:

A few weeks ago, Nate told me to get my jacket and come with him. It was hot that day so it didn't make much sense to wear a coat, but I didn't question him. I found one in my closet and headed for the door.

"Put it on," he told me. "And stick this in your pocket."

He took hold of my left wrist, turned my palm face up and placed a short barreled, black pistol into my hand. My whole body jerked back. Nate chuckled.

"It won't bite," he said. "Just don't point it at anybody."

"What's this for?" I asked.

"We're going to collect a bad debt," he answered.

I followed him to the car, surveying his back and wondering if this could be for real. He was wearing his suit, as he always did when it came to business. That surely meant things weren't as bad as I imagined. I continued to convince myself everything was okay, all the while worried that the gun in my pocket might go off at any second.

Nate drove to a parking lot where he stopped at a distance from the local hardware store.

"A guy's going to show up in a few minutes," he told me. "When he does, get behind my car and keep an eye on things."

"What kind of things?" I asked.

"You'll know," he said. "Nothing's going to go wrong." He started to get out of the car, turned back toward me and added, "But if a fight starts and I'm losing, just step out and point the gun at him. He'll take off."

It wasn't long before a dirt-splattered pickup truck eased into the parking lot and stopped nearby. "That's him," Nate said. "Now go."

I did as I was told and moved behind the car. It felt like my whole body would explode. I crouched down with a view of both Nate and the dirty truck. A tall, broad shouldered man in overalls eased out of the cab. He looked like a farmer, probably one of Nate's customers. I could see his face in the shade of a wide brimmed straw hat. Neither his expression nor the attitude of a work-hardened body betrayed his intentions. All I knew was he looked scary. It was clear why Nate had given me the gun.

They moved closer to one another. Nate stopped to let the farmer come forward. The other guy stood nearly a foot taller. They both seemed nervous. Nate reached into his inside breast pocket. I could hardly breathe. My hand strangled the gun's grip. I made sure to avoid the trigger. In an instant, the man seemed angry. I pulled the gun from my pocket and shielded it against my chest. A trickle of sweat dripped down from my forehead and onto the back of my hand. The surprise caused my fist to tighten. *Don't touch the trigger,* I thought.

Nate waved a folded piece of paper like a sign of truce. He handed it over when the farmer drew close enough to take it. The other guy squinted at the document, his eyes scanning it from top to bottom. He raised his head and spoke. Nate answered.

The taller man began to fumble for something in his pocket.

My body jolted to attention. I clutched the gun and got ready to move into the open. Time staggered. Finally, after all that, Nate held out his hand and the farmer filled it with a wad of bills.

I fell against the bumper and finally breathed.

Dale finished telling his story and looked toward the swing set where three little kids were in a shoving match. He turned back to me, his head held high. I could tell he felt proud and was unconcerned about my reaction. He had passed some imagined test. It proved Nate trusted him and that was the point. He also seemed relieved to have told someone. It must have been tough to keep such a thing secret.

"Weren't you scared?" I asked.

"I don't know," he answered. "I had to do it."

I wanted to ask more questions, but knew I shouldn't. Anything I had to say would appear critical of Nate. After all, he put his son in jeopardy for money. The other guy could have been carrying a gun too and Dale, the guy with the gun, would have been his greatest threat. I wondered if Dale thought about that. I wondered if he cared either way.

He had pleased Nate and that was enough.

I was happy he shared that story—happy he trusted me. He took a deep breath, looked my way and I realized there was more. As he began picking at the splintered wood again, he looked straight ahead.

"Did you know Nate and Marie fight most of the time?" he asked.

"I know they fight," I answered.

"Well, it's almost all the time," he said. "When I was little, they tried to hide it from me. Now they just do it right out in the open. I think Marie enjoys me watching them. She smiles at me sometimes when Nate turns away. It's a wicked smile."

A few months ago, she was complaining to him about being gone all the time. Then, she started in on how he needed to give her more money. The yelling went on and on. I tried to tune it out like I always did. I was just happy it wasn't about me. Then Nate turned his back on Marie and said, "Hit her for me, Dale. I can't do it, they'd arrest me. *You* hit her."

"Really, just like that?" I asked.

"Just like that," he answered.

"What'd you do?"

"I left the house. It's not how he raised me."

And that was it. That was the last time he ever spoke with me about anything personal. Our relationship became a casualty of his guarded nature. I always wondered what he had to protect, and why he needed to keep it secret. From that moment on, we typically talked about the weather and such.

10

UPS AND DOWNS

Told by Velva — Dale's Sister

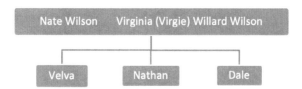

Mark and I delivered a baby girl, Colleen, in 1929. A few years later, we divorced. We had weathered some of the toughest financial times in U.S. history, but we failed to weather each other. I often wondered why things went wrong between us. The truth is, I doubt they were ever right.

As much as I hated the idea of divorce, it paved the way to a future only luck, or divine intervention could create. I met and married Harold Stith, the most wonderful guy I ever knew, in 1936.

In the meantime, a world war, hidden within the pretense of diplomatic resolution, began with the stroke of a pen in March of 1938. It was at that signing that Nazi Germany was allowed to annex Austria. Emboldened by his success, Hitler then turned his attention to Czechoslovakia—to their northern and western borders with Germany. In short order, Britain and France gave in to Hitler and the Sudetenland, formally part of German-Austria, was annexed. Weakened by the loss of some of its most valuable territory, Czechoslovakia was helpless to resist Germany's total occupation. The conquest of Europe had begun.

War happens in the absence of imagination.

Britain and France failed to imagine what Hitler really wanted or what he was willing to do to get it. Germany's citizens failed to imagine that their adoration of Hitler could create a monster—a monster that would be their undoing. Honorable men and women, people who should have known better, failed to imagine that progress of thought, education and industry is an illusion. We only borrow it until madness overcomes reason and the German experience infects some other part of the world.

While war took shape in Europe, the Depression continued to test America's will.

By that time, the "New Deal" had begun to impact the poorest among us. We knew that a paycheck was more than digits on a piece of paper. It represented hope. It proved we had value. But there was something missing—millions of Americans had forgotten how to dream.

Inspiration appears in many forms. In 1938 it came to America through a squat bodied thoroughbred by the name of Seabiscuit. He appeared undistinguished on his best day. His conformation looked all wrong for a real race horse. He was short, close-coupled and unimposing. He ate too much and slept in marathon laydowns. His early form was dismal as he was losing low level claiming races with authority. It was only after being purchased by Charles Howard, a car dealership owner with imagination, trained by Tom Smith, a horseman with unique insights and ridden by a jockey, Red Pollard, as down on his luck as Seabiscuit, that this little horse became a champion.

In that same year, one of the richest men in the world, Samuel Riddle, owned true royalty in the form of a blueblood named War Admiral. He was as regal as Seabiscuit was common. While Seabiscuit was setting track records on the West Coast, "The Admiral" dominated in the East. Whispers began to circulate that only a match race would prove which was the superior runner. Soon, the entire country wanted an answer.

The Admiral's wealthy owner held out for as long as he could—there was nothing to gain from matching his blueblood against what he called "a lowly claimer" from the West. Pressure mounted from every direction. Concessions were made. Purse money was adjusted. Finally, the rich owner agreed. Chances are, he thought of the match as merely a horse race. He failed to realize that most struggling Americans were identifying with Seabiscuit. We needed a win. In spite of everything he had to overcome, maybe Seabiscuit could beat the odds. Maybe he could prove that hope was still alive and that the little guy could succeed again.

Over forty million Americans tuned their radios to the race coverage on November 1, 1938. Businesses closed. People gathered in bars, hardware stores, movie theaters and even churches. Harold and I left work early to listen from home.

The radio coverage began well before the race. It was the first time I had heard that Seabiscuit would be ridden by a substitute jockey. His name was George Wolfe, "The Iceman", one of the best riders to ever mount a horse. I was relieved.

Harold and I kissed for luck. The race caller's voice swelled with anticipation. The jockeys worked to rein their horses into a fair start. After a couple of fruitless efforts, the horses approached the starting line together, the bell rang and they were off. Seabiscuit took an early lead. I set my cup on a table, afraid I might throw coffee everywhere.

Harold looked surprised by the early going. "Seabiscuit is faster," he said. "That wasn't supposed to happen."

Seabiscuit held his lead half way down the backstretch. My heartbeat quickened. It was tough to know when it happened, but the race caller began to announce that War Admiral was closing the gap. Harold took my hand and gripped it like a vise.

And then they were body-to-body, head-to-head, their footfalls churning the track with courageous effort. They remained locked together out of the turn and into the stretch. The moment pulsed with uncertainty. One of them would bend to the pressure. It was then that George Wolfe looked over at War Admiral's jockey, Johnny Longden, and hollered the immortal words: "See you later, Johnny." Seabiscuit hit another gear and won by over three lengths.

The little guy had beaten the rich man's horse. The masses could dream again.

Dad died of a heart attack on Christmas day in 1938. He was only fifty years old.

I was stunned when Marie told me the news. Harold and I were living back in Joplin at the time, so he drove me to Nathan's house. I wanted to tell him in person.

When I broke it to him, Nathan stood silent for a moment, processing news no one prepares to receive.

"Does Dale know?" he asked.

"He knows," I answered.

Dale was still living with Nate and Marie. He was there when Marie found out. Everyone else wondered why he had stayed in that house. I knew. He stayed because it was a place where he felt secure. As much as he hated Marie, he enjoyed the comfort of being near Nate—the one constant in his life. I had a sense it was only in Nate's passing that Dale truly understood how important he had been. He may have given his heart to Virgie, but it was Nate who kept it beating.

Nathan, Dale and I gathered away from Marie. Our father had died and we needed time together; just us. It was interesting how quickly our minds gave up his sins and our hearts filled the space with claims of his virtues. Whatever criticisms we had of him in life, were quickly forgotten now that he was gone. He was just our dad.

I helped Marie plan the funeral. It would amount to little more than a plain coffin in a tiny church, a preacher telling us it was God's will and a small congregation of mourners—listening but not hearing. We hoped Virgie would show up, no matter how unlikely that might be. Sid was a pumper and pumpers rarely took days off. Besides, they were barely getting by and a trip to Joplin in winter was, for them, about as likely as a trip to Paris in spring.

Marie wanted Nate's obituary distributed widely. He was still selling battery systems to farmers all over the state. She said it was only right they should know of his passing. That's the claim she made. What she really wanted was the opportunity to be the center of attention, shamelessly soaking up pity from strangers—the grieving wife set adrift by cruel fate.

∼

The weather at Nate's funeral matched our mood; cold, wet and gloomy. The church's wood siding dripped with mourning. The funeral-goers assembled and Marie led our family down the center aisle. She issued a few sobs and dabbed her eyes beneath the black netting that masked her true feelings. I secretly wondered if she cared at all about Nate's passing. I had heard of the fights and her claims he was seeing other women. If she was serious about even a small part of what she argued, could she really be that sad?

Dale's bottled-up emotions were another matter. His sorrow was as real as Marie's appeared false. But no matter how much he hurt, there was never a moment he seemed on the verge of telling us what he thought or how he felt. That was Dale's way. He was stoic, probably because he was too self-conscious to show emotion— men don't cry after all. Nathan, more handsome than ever, also concealed whatever stirred inside of him. But I knew. They were hurting, just like I was. For all his faults, in our world, Nate's passing was like a boat losing its anchor. Who would we now strive to please?

As we proceeded down the aisle to Nate's unadorned coffin, I noticed an odd assortment of women. I had never seen any of them before that day. They were apparently also strangers to one another. Even in the tiny church, the chasms between them were evident. They dotted the pews in appropriate black garb, eyes downcast, fingers locked, black hats or veils covering their heads.

There was one colorful exception. Planted imposingly in the front row on the left, was a middle aged woman with bleached blonde hair who dazzled in a red, form fitting dress with a flamboyant collar that rose high on her neck and pointed to a garish, wide brimmed hat festooned with colorful, hand sewn flowers and a fake diamond hat pin, that matched the polished glass neckless she wore tight around her throat and was intended to scream "expensive stones" to compliment an assortment of shiny bracelets stacked imposingly up her left arm. She verily rattled when she moved.

I wondered who those women were, and I hoped Marie suspicioned Nate had been with every one of them. Oh, how I hoped it. I caught her lifting up the black web over her face. She wanted a better look at the brazen woman in red who, primping and preening, stood out like a clown at a black-tie dinner. The jewelry-soaked lady intermittently applied fresh coats of red lipstick to her thinning mouth until the preacher delivered his final, "Amen".

The service ended. The unknown women left without saying a word. Only the minister and our family attended Nate's coffin to the burial site. We all watched as his secrets descended into the ground and were buried with the corpse they protected.

Marie inherited everything except for the new, 1939 Ford Coup Nate bought just weeks before he died. He made clear that if anything ever happened to him, the car should go to Dale. Marie honored his wishes. Dale accepted the car and set about relocating himself and Marie to a boarding house. Even though Marie found a job at a department store, and Dale was still working at the leather factory, their combined incomes were too little to pay the mortgage on Nate's house.

I was surprised Dale looked after Marie for even a day after Nate's funeral. Looking back, I'm guessing he did it out of respect for Nate. Marie deserved much less.

PART II

AN UNLIKELY PAIRING

Advice on finding love:
Opposites attract.
Choose your soulmate.
Follow your heart.
Find someone who makes you laugh.

This is how it actually works:
You don't find love—you live it—and love finds you.

11

THE UNION

Told by Madeline - Barbara's Sister and Velva - Dale's Sister

What Things Cost in 1940

Car:	$800
Gasoline:	$0.18 cents/gal
House:	$6,550
Bread:	$0.08 cents/loaf
Milk:	$0.34 cents/gal
Postage Stamp:	$0.03 cents/stamp
Average Annual Salary:	$1,900
Minimum Wage:	$0.30 cents per hour
Stock Market:	131

Madeline – Barbara's Sister

Only two people were inspired by Dale and Barbara's introduction, and they were all that mattered. A mutual friend brought them together at a soda shop. Thankfully, I was visiting Joplin from Pittsburg, KS the day after it happened. Otherwise, their "meeting" story might have been lost on the carousel of life that set all of this in motion.

I first heard of Dale Wilson the day after they met. Barbara was still living in Joplin with Florence, Pat, Joe, Charles and a couple of boarders, John Sears and Kathleen Smith. We found out later that Dale was living with his stepmother in a nearby boarding house. Nothing on that day felt special, until everything about it turned out to be.

We were gathered for a family meal. After coffee and small talk, everyone else scattered and left the dirty dishes to Barbara and I. I washed, she dried. After stacking the plates and salad bowls and putting them back in the cupboard, we decided to have something sweet. Barbara collected a few chocolate chip cookies from a glass jar and arranged them on a small white platter. I poured the coffee. All the while, I considered what I might say. I think things were awkward because I hadn't seen her for over three months. I felt guilty about it.

For her part, Barbara was just happy I was there. Innocent to a fault, she was alone in a house full of boys and welcomed the advice of a woman. Any sound wisdom was unlikely to come through Mom. Since Dad's death, Florence spent most of her time in an isolated world where only she could go.

I knew Barbara wanted to be like me, a married woman living away from home. I had been in her shoes. I too had idolized wives and mothers. Remember, we lived in a time when a typical woman aspired to that purpose. I could have told her the dream was a rosy illusion; that married life had its own thorns. I knew in the end the issue would take care of itself. Her envy would be tempered by experience and she could decide for herself if the fantasy made sense.

She encouraged me to sit at the head of the table, a place typically reserved for Florence. She pulled up a chair nearby, so close our knees bumped from time to time. As our conversation began, we circled one another with meaningless chitchat, searching for an anchor. I told her about my job at the library—Florence's refuge. "In fact," I said, "I'm sure I was hired because of her."

After a few stabs at useful topics, I asked about something more personal, "Are you dating anyone?"

Barbara blushed, smiled, put her cookie on the table and said, "Not really. But I met someone I'd like to date. His name is Dale. I think he likes me."

"Tell me about him," I encouraged.

The floodgates opened. "He's skinny," she said. "He's very handsome," her dancing blue eyes lit up with the memory. "All the girls were looking at him. My friend Alice said he looked like a movie star."

Which one?

"And he's smart," she claimed. (I wondered how he proved that.)

It was obvious Barbara was smitten with this guy. She embraced the smallest detail of that first meeting. Everything about him was valuable.

"He has wavy hair," she continued. "He's taller than me—5'9" I'd guess."

I enjoyed seeing Barbara so happy. She had liked other guys before, but this one was different. Maybe he would live up to her expectations, though it was unlikely. She was still susceptible to puppy love, and this boy sounded way too adorable to be true. Nonetheless, I concentrated on every word as she glided through the list of things she liked about him. Blindness had set in.

"And he wears a Fedora," she said. "He kept running the rim through his fingers while we talked."

"How old is he," I asked.

"Eighteen," she answered. "And he has his own car. A brand-new Ford Coup. Can you imagine?"

I had forgotten about most of her claims just as Barbara ran out of good things to say about him. She finished with how his blue eyes sparkled when he unleashed his perfect smile. I wondered if she would think of a single, unflattering thing to say about him.

"He didn't ask to drive me home," she concluded.

Not much, but there it was.

Barbara got up from the table and poured me a fresh cup of coffee. I was struck by how stylish she looked. It helped that she was slim and shapely, though I had to take credit for part of it. I sewed for her, and I could make common dresses appear fashionable. She returned to the table and refilled my cup. Her smile reminded me of when she was a little girl curled up on Dad's lap. Like so many other times since he died, I wondered what he would say about this new development. He would probably just hope that what she wanted was also good for her. He would point out that life has a way of distorting that equation. And he would ache to hear just one more little girl secret whispered into his ear.

She sat back down and said, "He probably won't even call."

A distant gaze proved she hoped otherwise. In fact, at that very moment, she was busy thinking about *him*. Whatever image now stirred in her head was powerful, whether she ever saw him again or not.

I patted the back of her hand.

"We'll see," I said.

Velva – Dale's Sister

Dad's death set Dale adrift. His uninspiring job at the leather factory did little more than pay the bills. Whatever ambition he felt had been tied up in pleasing Nate, and now that motivation was gone. He spent much of his free time with Harold and I. I needled Harold to find out what was going on in Dale's life. I might as well have asked him to find out Hitler's next move. Dale was the most private person I ever met.

I had no reason to be surprised by his secrecy? Most people lead two lives. The first is on display for everyone to see. The life we create is acted out in broad strokes, no real details—our essence slipping out in drips and drabs. The other is our essential selves—the life playing out in our heads. That one conceals our pettiness, our prejudices and our secret desires. It is rich in truth and poor in revelation. I was always curious about the world inside Dale's head, and confident I would never find it out.

We knew Dale dated. He was a good-looking young man and attracted women with ease, though he never volunteered anything about them.

One evening during dinner, just in passing, I asked Dale if he was dating anyone.

"Met a girl yesterday," he said.

"What's she like?" I asked.

He rolled his eyes at me and reluctantly answered, "Black hair and pretty. Her name is Barbara Kelly."

"Oh, Irish," I commented.

"I guess," Dale said.

And that was it. That was the first time we knew Barbara existed. I wish I could say I sensed something significant about his answer, but I would be lying. There was nothing to suggest his life would change forever because of that meeting.

Madeline – Barbara's Sister

Dale began visiting the family soon after their introduction. I felt sorry for him. Our brothers, Pat, Cliff and Joe were strong and handsome, more like our outgoing Irish father than dour German mother. Facing three young, virile men bent on protecting their sister was no easy task. It had to be intimidating. As imposing as they might have been, however, they were equally friendly and accepting. We were still living in hard times and they refused to make life more difficult for anyone. Besides, it was early in the relationship. No matter how much he liked Barbara, he seemed the type who would cut and run if things got tough.

It was only after he became a regular face at the Kelly dinner table that my brothers and I grew wary. Barbara had clearly fallen for this skinny young man with few prospects. What if things became serious? What would we do then? What *could* we do? Ultimately, we decided to give it time. Maybe it would just burn itself out. If it didn't, we would try to understand what Barbara saw in Dale. We owed her that.

～

We had dinners with Dale. We probed. He resisted. The brothers took him to the front porch for conversations over beer. They talked. He listened. In the end, he knew a lot about us and we knew next to nothing about him. What we did know with certainty however, was that he and Barbara were a frenzy of contrasts. He was quiet and sullen—she, engaging and ebullient. He was closed off—she, an open book. He practiced no religion—she was a staunch Catholic. He was raised by uneducated parents—she, by a former school teacher and a professional business man. He harbored a natural distrust for mankind—she was a beacon of acceptance for all. None of it mattered. Their differences were glue, binding them together instead of forcing them apart. We sensed the inevitability of their union, but secretly hoped time might be on the side of a break up. Barbara and Dale were about to lay waste to that notion.

∼

Their courtship lasted a number of months. They each worked low paying jobs, so dates rarely involved much money. The exception was going to a movie. In 1940, it cost them twenty-four cents apiece and occupied an entire evening. The entertainment started with a variety program, typically trailers. Then a newsreel filled the screen and it was followed by a cartoon or short film. Next, a low-budget (B movie) played. The curtains closed for a short interlude and reopened in anticipation of the high-budget film—the A movie.

Some theaters sold popcorn on site. If they didn't, you could purchase it for five or ten cents a bag at one of the popcorn stands near the movie house. The Encyclopedia Popcornica stated, "During the Depression, popcorn at 5 or 10 cents a bag was one of the few luxuries down-and-out families could afford. While other businesses failed, the popcorn business thrived. I even read of an Oklahoma banker who went broke when his bank failed. He bought a popcorn machine and started a business in a small store near a theater. After a couple years, his popcorn business made him enough money to buy back three of the farms he'd lost."

Besides the movies, their favorite activity was driving around in the fancy car Dale inherited from Nate. It was rare for someone Dale's age to own such a nice vehicle. It might have even played a role in turning Barbara's head in the first place. Whenever she talked about meeting him, she always mentioned the car. It makes complete sense. She was accustomed to walking or taking a bus. Riding around in a new Ford, sitting next to a handsome young man with her head resting on his shoulder, must have felt exhilarating. Make no mistake, Barbara was hopelessly in love—maybe with the man, maybe with love itself. Either way, it was enough.

Dale was no less captured by the moment. He found Barbara's attention intoxicating. There was an inescapable goodness about her that made him feel better about himself. She believed in him, had faith in what he would accomplish. She imagined a successful future for them, one he wanted to trust. She must have seemed wondrous compared to a mother who gave him up as a child and a step mother who worked so hard to make his life miserable. Barbara turned out to be the one woman in his life he could trust without reservation.

~

Their courtship continued at a leisurely pace until the United States imposed a draft on September 16, 1940. A war with Japan and Germany lurked somewhere in an uncertain future. America prepared for the possibility by registering eligible young men before they were needed. Single males were selected first. Married men received a deferment until required. I found out later that it was only weeks after the draft announcement that Barbara and Dale began discussing marriage in earnest. Marrying right away made complete sense to both of them. It was going to happen anyway, so why wait and risk being drafted? Only a couple of problems stood in their way.

Barbara was still a telephone operator. The Bell Telephone company continued to demonstrate clear preferences for the type of woman they would hire and retain. For instance, even height was an issue. Operators had to sit in front of the company's equipment for long periods, so women were chosen within very narrow height and weight boundaries. As silly as it sounds, women less than five feet tall were considered too short to be operators. Anyone with an accent was rejected. Even English-speaking Americans were given elocution training. They wanted to ensure speech patterns matched the image the company intended to project.

By the 1940s, what started out as preferences became arbitrary standards by which women were judged and hired. Barbara was keenly aware the company preferred single women. She knew of friends who had been let go soon after they married and she was unwilling to take that risk herself. Florence and the family depended on her income. As a result, Dale and Barbara decided their marriage should remain hidden for some undetermined period. The wedding would also have to be kept secret.

A clandestine wedding suited Dale perfectly. He hated being the center of attention and might have skipped the whole event had Barbara suggested a grand show. In fact, some hinted later that he may have convinced her to keep their marriage a secret to escape a spectacle. Others thought he was just avoiding the embarrassment of being too poor to support her. Only the two of them knew the truth.

A secret wedding required that their daily lives continue on unchanged. The Kelly house was small enough that Barbara slept with Florence. She did so long after her wedding day. Dale held on to his room in the boarding house. Meanwhile, they appeared to date, just as they always had.

Barbara told me later that Dale's one concession to romance came in the form of an awkward, but formal proposal. He presented her with a silver engagement band capped by tiny diamonds over the top edge. That same band became her wedding ring. She kept it hidden for months and it rarely saw the light of day. Whenever possible, she pulled it from her purse, cupped it in her palm and stroked it tenderly. In her hand, she held the future.

～

November 9, 1940 was a Saturday. Dale arrived at the house early that morning. Barbara was still in her room getting ready. While waiting, Dale listened to eight-year-old Charles talk about school, or friends or whatever else was on his mind. The older boys went about their Saturday rhythms, completely oblivious to the life changing event about to take place. Barbara finally came into the entrance hall. She gathered up her purse, hat and gloves and kissed Florence good bye. No one noticed that her hair was dolled up in a particularly stylish fashion.

She nearly reached the front door when Florence asked, "Why are you wearing your best dress?"

Dale had rehearsed Barbara for this moment, "We might be going to a dance," she said, and the subject was dropped.

The day was cool, grey and overcast. A classic low-pressure weather system was developing in the Texas Panhandle and had already spilled over into the Midwest. In just days, it would create one of the deadliest snowstorms in Minnesota history. Temperatures dropped 50 degrees in an hour while 60-80 mph winds drove snow into monstrous drifts up to 20 feet deep. But that would happen the following day. Saturday, November 9, was Barb and Dale's wedding day.

They drove to Columbus, Kansas, roughly 30 miles from Joplin, where a Probate Judge would marry them. Missouri required a waiting period between applying for a marriage license and the actual ceremony. Kansas allowed you to get married on the same day. Again, a simple technicality suited Dale's purpose. The last thing he wanted was for any of us to open the Joplin Globe or the Joplin News Herald and see a record of their marriage license.

Barbara told me they were in and out of the courtroom in a matter of minutes. I felt crushed by the thought. No family members were present to see Barbara begin her new life. Not a single flower hung in her honor. No music sounded her entrance. She stood before a judge she had never met and swore fidelity to a man she was yet to know. She probably felt differently about the whole thing. Love is a fog of acceptance.

Dale rented a motel room in Kansas for the day. They returned to Joplin late in the evening and slipped back into the life they left that morning. He drove to our house, parked, and walked her to the door. They kissed goodnight, as if nothing had happened. He returned to the boarding house—alone. Barbara watched him leave, took a deep breath and then tiptoed to the bedroom where she slid under the covers next to Mom.

In that same month Franklin D. Roosevelt became President of the United States for a third term. In preparation for world dominance, Russian Foreign Minister Molotov met Hitler and Ribbentrop in Berlin to discuss the form of a New World Order that would include spheres of influence headed by Germany, Italy, Russia and Japan. Warsaw's Jewish ghetto was cordoned off from the rest of the city by a 3-meter-high stone wall. Everyone knew the world was inching closer to war. What would tip the balance?

It was into that fragile reality Barbara and Dale began life together. After they married (still unknown to us), he came by the house every day after work. My brothers wondered why Dale was suddenly so ever present. He spoke sparingly, though he appeared to make an effort to improve his image. All the while, each of us still harbored hope that he and Barbara would break up. We actually liked Dale. We just felt he was wrong for Barbara.

12

A MARRIAGE IN THE MAKING

Told by Madeline

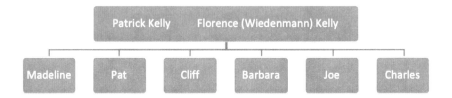

As I think back on it now, it's hard to believe Barbara and Dale were able to hide their marriage from all of us. Dale continued stitching wallets at the leather factory and visited Barbara as he always had. For her part, Barbara completed the ruse by staying on at the phone company and giving most of her money to Florence. She began withholding a little extra cash by skipping lunches and working overtime hours when the company offered them. Dale also began working overtime. He controlled expenses by ruling out movies and drove his treasured car only when absolutely necessary.

After many weeks of subterfuge, they finally saved enough to get a place of their own. In short order; they sheepishly told us about their secret marriage; assured Florence they would continue sending her money every month; acknowledged our best wishes; packed Barbara's few belongings into the back seat of Dale's shiny Ford and drove away. I felt an odd mixture of happiness and apprehension as we waved goodbye. I knew two things for certain; Barbara had what she wanted, and what we want is often the opposite of what we need.

They settled into their new life with few prospects and only marginal skills. It was early in 1941 and Joplin was still riding the mineral mining wave; the engine of the city's growth. So, why didn't Dale work at the mines? Well, like his father Nate, he was more suited to a white shirt than overalls and work boots. He knew he needed to make a change. Just as surely, the thought of interviewing for another job absolutely froze him in place. He apparently decided they could save their way to prosperity

Initially, they lived in a two-room flat. It was cheap enough, but the walls were paper thin and Dale was a glutton for privacy. Next, they moved to a small house; not cheap enough. On it went. Dale's obsession with saving money led to one move after another. It became almost comical. "Does anyone know where Barb and Dale are living today?" was a common joke. We made excuses for them; they were young, they had no experience, they were just finding it difficult to settle. That's what we said in public. In private, we believed Dale would never amount to much.

His most frugal choice was both instructive and curious. We heard he found a landlord willing to let them live in a house for free, as long as they kept the lawn mowed. It sounded like a really good deal. At the same time, we could only imagine the kind of house given up so cheaply. The reality proved our suspicions optimistic. It was a ramshackle place lacking a single benefit beyond the free rent. Few women would have put up with such a house, but times were tough and Barbara could make a home out of a cardboard box if necessary.

Dale agreed to the deal in late winter before the grass began to grow. Around mid-spring, the tide had turned and the grass clearly gained the advantage. Dale came home each evening and said, "I'd better get on that grass." But it was just a passing thought and he figured he would knock it out the next day. Finally, his bargain with the landlord came due. Barbara swore me to secrecy and told the whole story.

"One Saturday morning, Dale decided to mow the lawn. I heard the back-porch screen door slam shut. In an odd way, it was exciting. I hurried to our tiny kitchen window to watch. Dale walked to a small wooden shed snuggled up against the back fence. It was Dale versus the matted green grass and weeds. Our immediate future hung in the balance. He manhandled an old rotary mower out of the shed. After oiling it in a couple of places, he tightened a bolt here and there. I wondered if he was being determined or avoiding the inevitable. He began by trying to push the mower straight through the center of the yard; no deal. Next, he tackled the edges, first with just half the mower, then a fourth and finally with so little being cut the difference existed only in my imagination.

He gave up, returned the mower to the shed and headed for the house. The back door slammed again. "We have to move," he said. "I can't mow it. It's too high." And so, we did."

Barbara, the ever-dutiful wife, picked up the pieces of Dale's last experiment and took her optimism to the next house. Those frequent moves had to test her notion of what a wife should be, and do and say. She had read the novels about life and love and knew most of them ended "happily ever after". She intended to do the same with her own life.

After house hopping for a time, they finally found a two bedroom, one bath home on 6th street. They lived there for the next few years. Barbara continued working as an operator for the phone company, while Dale, even though dissatisfied, remained at Meeker. We mistakenly believed he was lazy or dull. Time proved he was neither. Dale was just painfully shy and unsure of himself. We expected him to excel while he was just doing the best he could to survive. I know now he wanted more, he just couldn't imagine what "more" was or how to get it.

Though quiet and reserved, Dale was a commanding presence at every gathering. People exhausted themselves trying to please him. They never understood why. The harder we attempted to get to know him, the deeper his secrets tunneled away from us. He was something like Greta Garbo who lamented, "I never said, 'I want to be alone.' I only said, 'I want to be left alone.' There is all the difference." It was the same with Dale. He could be witty and charming, though rarely engaging. He could speak volumes without uttering a word. He could cause happiness with the smallest gesture of approval, or gloom with even a hint of displeasure. He wielded these traits unwittingly; a matter of instinct as opposed to manipulation. Singularly self-centered,

Dale's world was the sphere around which all others circled in anticipation of his needs.

Dale's consistent, though often maddening behavior implied a philosophy of sorts. He appeared to know what he was doing and what he wanted. Neither thing was true. Like most of us, he made choices through blind hope. He rode the wave of the unknown to whatever end fate, or God or circumstances took him.

Barbara also struggled to find her way. She had practiced her Catholic faith with certainty for over 18 years. Then, Dale's ambiguous feelings about religion caused her to waiver. Shortly after they married, she became a closeted church goer. Up at 5:30 a.m. every Sunday morning, she attended 6 o'clock mass. She wanted to be home in time to start Dale's breakfast before he got up.

Her fellow parishioners had to wonder about the pretty young woman kneeling alone in an otherwise empty pew. She wore a wedding ring. Her head was properly covered by a black lace veil. Her husband was missing. Over time, the veil and her commitment began to unravel and both slipped away through neglect.

I often wondered how Barbara let such a thing happen. It was so unlike her. Maybe she wanted to please Virgie, who bore a serious disaffection for Catholics. Barbara explained it by saying she thought Dale was a believer, but that he refused to choose between her and Virgie's religion. His best option, she said, was to avoid the subject altogether. What she left out was how perfectly that solution suited Dale's preference. Church-going was a social affair and Dale was anything but social; except when he was drinking.

∼

Dale and Barbara partied infrequently, but when they did it typically included his sister, Velva, and her second husband Harold Stith. Nathan and his first wife Ethyl often joined them. Dale needed the comfort of familiar faces; people who shared his history. In their presence, and with the help of a couple of stiff drinks and one cigarette after another, he could relax and breathe in the pleasure of a fun moment.

In stark contrast, few human beings were ever more devoted to a good time than Velva. She was a flame on water. She attracted others without effort or design. It took only her sexy, joyous nature to pull them in. Shapely stout, Velva stood 5'7" and carried her 140 curvy pounds with seductive grace. She was all woman. Hidden beneath those curves was a worker's hardened body, honed to a fine edge by the farm and the diner. She could carry more plates on one arm than most could manage on a tray.

Al and I joined the Wilsons whenever we were in town visiting Florence and the family. We often met at Dale's favorite local bar that featured dark wooden floors, a couple of pool tables, dart boards and loud music blaring from a juke box trimmed in faux silver. Each gathering was much like the last; small talk about our work, questions about the family, complaints about the economy.

Sometimes on his own, but often prodded by a few of the regulars, Harold would stand; demand the bar's attention and announce he had a challenge for anyone who cared to take it. The first time I watched it happen, I believed he was about to challenge the bar patrons to a game of darts or pool. Much to my surprise, the instrument of the dare was Velva. We could hear her raspy laugh from behind Harold. He asked her to stand. She did. She was anything but muscularly intimidating.

"Barkeep," Harold barked, "bring me your broom." The bartender, Earl, who was completely familiar with the routine, immediately produced a long, wooden handled straw headed broom and handed it to Harold.

Holding it above his head for everyone to see, Harold announced, "If you can twist this wooden handle in Velva's hands, before she twists it in yours, I'll buy you and your table drinks. If you lose, you buy our drinks."

It sounded simple enough to the uninitiated and always enticed people bigger than Velva to accept the challenge. They lined up to take her on. Velva took the broom from Harold with both hands and held it out in front of her. She waited. The first person in line was a bleached blonde woman considerably larger than Velva. She stepped forward confidently, gripped the wooden shaft with both hands and waited for someone to say, "Go". Harold obliged.

The match began with an aggressive assault by the bigger woman. She tried to twist one way and then the other. Both attempts failed. Velva simply stood her ground, seemingly disinterested in forcing the issue. After her initial disappointment, the blonde tried to act nonchalant, as if she hadn't really been trying; a lie revealed by her strained red face. Next, she decided to use her height advantage by rising above Velva and pushing down while attempting to turn the handle. The orientation of the broom's straw head failed to move in either direction. Velva smiled. The cat had played with the unsuspecting mouse long enough. Velva calmly twisted the wooden handle forward. The blonde let loose her grip, shrugged her shoulders and told her husband to buy us a round of drinks.

And on it went, Velva vanquishing one challenger after another. We consumed considerably more free drinks than we ever paid for.

Al and I noticed that as Barbara drank, she became sweeter and more talkative; her tipsy behavior consistent with the warm person we all knew. Harold and Ethyl were equally kind and easy going. Nathan, Velva and Dale; The Wilsons, were often the opposite. On most occasions they just had fun, their clever minds plying each moment for its most humorous effect. On those nights, they were the three funnest people in the room. And then there were the episodes when liquor apparently released their inner demons. During those bouts, they quickly drank themselves through their jolly phases and fell head first into a widening cesspool of antagonism. They chided each other, and all of us too, for imagined transgressions, misguided suspicions and unprovable certainties. In other words, they were mean drunks.

There were the break ups and make ups, followed by debilitating hangovers. And then there was the pretense that a thing didn't happen or a rationalization for why it did. Each was accompanied by the inevitable excuses; they had just had too much to drink, or they should have eaten first. They carried on like that for just over a year and a half. Then, suddenly, Velva, Harold, Nathan and Ethyl found religion. It was the hell fire and damnation kind of faith Virgie brought with her from the hill country of Tennessee. It was practiced on Sunday morning, Sunday night and just for good measure, an extra dose on Wednesday evenings. It was just like Nathan and Velva remembered from their truck farming days when sacrifice was peddled as a virtue. As far as any of us knew, they never drank again.

Dale believed they had to quit drinking to save their marriages, and I tend to agree. I know they enjoyed the making up part of a fight; drinkers tend to like that. Inevitably, the intensity has to escalate to exact the same satisfaction. And then someone crosses the line and there is no path to salvation. We all knew they were heading in that direction. To their credit, they stepped back just before the fall.

Dale respected their decision, though he had no intention of joining that particular club. In deference to their commitment, he became almost obsessive about hiding his liquor whenever Virgie or the siblings visited. While he drank for the rest of his life, he never again did it in front of his side of the family.

As fate would have it, the timing was perfect.

13

BABY BOOM BEGINS

Told by Madeline - Barbara's Sister

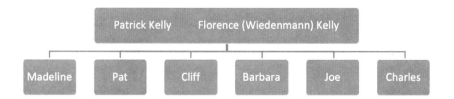

I had been waiting for the call. It came exactly one year to the month after Dale and Barbara were married. As soon as I heard her voice, I knew what it was about. Long distance calls were charged by the minute in those days, so folks like us tended to keep things brief.

"I think I'm pregnant," she squealed.

"Are you sure?" I asked.

"I missed a period," she answered, "and I'm like clockwork. So yeah, I'm pretty sure."

"Have you told Dale?" I asked.

"Not yet," she said. "He's not home from work. I have to go, Madeline. I just had to tell you. He's going to be so excited. Bye."

I hung up thinking, *I sure hope that's true.*

Barbara told me later he was happy when she told him.

"What'd he say?" I asked.

"He smiled at first. Then he became serious and said we were going to have to cut back."

Cut back from what? I wondered. *How do you subtract nothing from nothing?*

I let it go. We would find out soon enough what kind of father Dale would be. All Barbara needed at that moment was my support and I gave it.

~

On the evening of December 7, 1941, Dale drove Barbara to a bluff overlooking Joplin. The weather was unseasonably warm, though the night air was still crisp and cool. They wrapped themselves in a blanket and sat on the hood of his Ford coup with their backs leaned up against the windshield.

The bluff was a popular site. That evening was typical with cars lined up along the rim. Joplin's lights spread out like stars in the night sky. Suddenly, a speeding car veered off the road and ground to a stop in the crunching gravel. The driver, lights still on and the motor running, jumped from the car and hollered, "The Japs just bombed Pearl Harbor." People cautiously left their cars and began circulating.

Barbara and Dale knew, we all knew, the United States would now be drawn into the war. Dale, shaken, eased off of the car's hood and helped Barbara to the ground. He leaned her against the driver's door and began to mill about. They both knew a marriage deferment amounted to little more than a temporary reprieve.

"I'm pregnant," she reassured. "You would be one of the last to go."

Japan's bombing of Pearl Harbor was in response to the U.S. and Europe's blockade of the island nation. Everyone knew Japan intended to become a world power through conquest and occupation. They had already colonized Korea, Taiwan, Manchuria and various Asian islands. They occupied land in China, confiscated in battles with them and Russia. The blockade would deprive them of basic necessities like oil and steel. Japan's miscalculation brought the U.S. into the war and in response, Germany was forced to honor its pact with Japan.

The next day, December 8, 1941, the U.S. declared war on Japan following President Roosevelt's famous "Day of Infamy" speech to Congress. Then, on December 9, 1941, Hitler ordered that US ships should be torpedoed. That same day, China declared war on the Axis Powers, Japan, Germany and Italy. The following day, December 10, 1941, the Japanese overran Guam. A day later, December 11, 1941, the U.S. declared war on Germany while Germany and Italy declared war on the U.S. In just four days the entire world was at war.

Hitler had what he wanted.

∼

Long before WWII began, the Nazi regime began its terror against the Jewish population in Germany. As they advanced across Europe, their evil spread with them. Jews became a splinter in Hitler's eye. He first marginalized them, then demonized them and ultimately plucked them from his vision. Over 6 million Jews were murdered by the Nazis.

Back home, war was about patriotism—the nobility of fighting the good fight. Our brother Pat joined the Army almost immediately and Cliff signed up for the Army Air Corp not long after. We cheered their bravery while forgetting the lessons of World War I—war and death are the same thing. There is no glory in dying—there is only dying.

We heard politicians and commentators promote the notion that we were engaged in a just war. We learned afterward, there is no such thing as a just war. There is, however, such a thing as a "just defense." We were willing to sacrifice a million lives to defend against insanity or tyranny, but not a single soul to gain advantage.

By the end of the carnage in 1945, over fifty million American men between the ages of eighteen and forty-five had registered for the draft. Ten million were inducted into the military. Over 405,000 were killed. Approximately 400,000 American women served during that same period with over 460 deaths.

Worldwide, more than sixty million (60,000,000) people lost their lives.

∼

Even a world war failed to dampen Barbara's excitement over being pregnant. She was as happy as I had ever seen her. I was a little jealous—maybe, a lot jealous. I was ten years older than her and had been married seven years longer and here she was having a baby before me. As much as I loved her, as thrilled as I was for her, it forced me to wonder if I would ever get pregnant myself and the thought unsettled me.

Barbara and Dale agreed she should continue working at the phone company for as long as possible. She lasted eight months. In the meantime, preparations for the baby shifted into high gear. Barbara began buying diapers with whatever extra money she could earn. She borrowed a bassinet and cradle from a neighbor long before they were needed. The rest of us brought her blankets and tiny white baby outfits. White, because a baby's sex was only revealed at birth.

A week before the baby was due, I moved in with Barbara and Dale. I planned to stay in Joplin for as long as she needed me. One morning, I found her sitting on the edge of her bed admiring a small white box she held in one hand. She opened it and ran her fingers over a line of variously colored safety pins.

"You just can't wait, can you?" I asked.

Barbara looked up. I saw love smiling back at me.

∽

Barbara and I timed her contractions until they were three to four minutes apart and lasted at least 45 seconds. I then called Dale and he rushed home to drive us to the hospital. Dale and I hurried and fretted while Barbara remained perfectly calm. She approached the delivery just as she did life, with wonder and acceptance.

MICHAEL DALE (MIKE) - JULY 1942
Number One

Mike was a healthy little kid and performed his baby duties with precision. Barbara was delighted that he nursed almost immediately. She spent five days in the hospital at a cost of around $20.

The following rates appeared in an actual hospital pamphlet in 1942:

Room Prices

Following is listed the daily rate of Private, Semi-Private and Ward Rooms.

This rate covers Room, Board, Floor Nursing, House Physician service and Surgical Dressings.

Ward beds (four beds and over) $3.50

Two and three-bed rooms - $4.00 and $4.50

Private rooms - $6.00, $7.00 and $8.50. (A limited number at $5.00. Subject to price change without notice.)

Deluxe rooms (private bath), $10.00 and $15.00

A two room suite (beautifully furnished) -$25.00. This provides a patient's room with private bath and a sitting room for guest and nurses' quarters.

These rates seem incredibly low until considered against the average family income of $1,885 per year.

~

Around the same time, our brother Pat was assigned to Camp Bowie, TX. He wrote to tell me about a recent letter from Barbara. She let him know that Cliff's wife, Annie, had delivered a baby boy about the same time as Mike's birth. In a letter dated July, 1942, he wrote, "So Cliff and Annie's baby is cuter? Somehow I hoped it would be otherwise as some way or other I have a real soft spot in my hard heart for Barb, she is one sweet kid…"

He went on to comment about how hard it must have been for a mother to admit another child was cuter than her own. I knew better. In my mind it spoke to Barbara's comfort with reality. She had a purity about her that refused to lie about even that sensitive issue. And she knew a cute baby when she saw one.

Only a month later Pat, stationed somewhere in Louisiana, the location a secret, wrote, "Well Sis I always knew Barbara got the worst of the deal, anyway I thought so." He must have been responding to a letter from someone else as I had resolved to keep bad news from him. I suppose he was talking about how little Barbara had to take care of the baby. Dale was still working at the leather factory and his income just wouldn't stretch far enough. Barbara had taken to doing other people's laundry to make ends meet.

Little did Pat know the news was about to get worse.

14

THE FUTURE IN DOUBT

Told by Madeline - Barbara's Sister

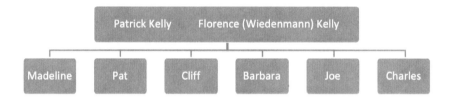

Barbara called me in mid-July of 1943. She sounded distraught and wondered if I could come to Joplin.

"What's wrong?" I asked.

I could hear her sobbing as she answered, "I can't talk about it over the phone. Can you come?"

I assured her I would, packed a couple of things, told Al what little I knew and left right away.

Barbara's street was lined with an arching canopy of oaks and elms, a tunnel of shade against the summer heat. As I entered it, I felt a rush of cooler air through my open window. Moments later, I pulled into Barbara and Dale's driveway, curious and afraid.

I had always thought their small white house with a gabled front porch was cute. Today, and I know this was just my imagination, it looked sad. I opened the screen and knocked on the white wooden entry door. What would I find beyond?

I heard Barbara say, "Come in."

The living room was dark, the shades shut and the curtains pulled tight. Barbara sat in a brown striped rocking chair nursing Mike. A clean white diaper was draped over her chest and the baby's head. She was using one end to blot her swollen eyes. Her nose was red and her black hair uncharacteristically disheveled.

"What in the world happened?" I asked. "Are you alright?"

Barbara inhaled two quick gulps of air and said, "Let me put Mike down."

I opened the curtains and shades of one window. "No wonder you're depressed," I said, hoping that was the extent of the matter and knowing better.

"Would you like some coffee?" Barbara asked as she walked back through the living room on her way to the kitchen. Her voice broke and she moved slowly as if weighed down by something unseen.

"Sure," I answered, and followed close behind her. "Are you going to tell me what happened?"

Barbara remained quiet while pouring what was left from a drip coffee pot into a large cup. I knew what she was doing. Many items were being regulated for the war effort and coffee rations had been cut from one pound per person every five weeks to one pound every six. She left the morning's spent grounds in the basket and added a few fresh ones before starting the next pot.

My stomach churned. This wasn't like Barbara at all. I heard a couple of sobs and watched her wipe her nose and try to dry her eyes. I left her alone. She needed time to collect herself, time to come to terms with whatever she was about to tell me. She stood with her hip against the counter and watched the coffee pot with a blank stare. When it was done, she removed the strainer full of grounds and placed it in a waiting bowl. I knew she would double drip that batch later too. The thought gave me hope. She was still living life, planning, adapting.

I sat at a narrow table next to a window overlooking the back yard. Without thinking, I absently said, "Dale needs to mow the lawn." I intended it as small talk, but the words seemed to cut her to the core. She began crying in earnest now.

"I'm sorry," I said, "I'm so sorry. I didn't mean anything by it. Show me the mower. I'll do it myself."

That offer caused her to laugh and cry at the same time. She took a deep breath and said, "I can just see you out there in your expensive blouse and white skirt trying to mow that grass. Wouldn't the neighbors get a charge out of that?"

I wanted to hug her, but was afraid it would drag her back into whatever despair had claimed her. Instead, I used the lighter moment to ask, "So, why so blue, Barbara? It can't be that bad."

She got up from the table to retrieve a fresh hanky. "Yes, it can," she said.

"Just tell me," I encouraged. "We can fix it. Now what happened?"

Barbara headed out of the room, "Let me check on Mike first," she said. She returned shortly and sat down. "Would you like more coffee?" she asked.

"Barbara, I don't want more coffee. Mike is fine and you're going to tell me eventually, so why not just get it over with?"

She gave up her reluctance and said, "I know none of you like Dale, and I know he can be difficult."

"That's not true," I countered.

"You don't need to pretend with me, Madeline. I know how you all feel." She rubbed the table top with the handkerchief and began to tell her story.

"Yesterday morning I was making the bed when I heard a knock. I checked on Mike and headed to the living room. The front door was open to let in some cool air. I could see a woman through the latched screen. She was carrying something against her chest. *It's a baby*, I thought.

As I drew closer, I recognized the woman and asked what she wanted.

"This is your husband's," she said, while propping the baby up so I could see him under the blue blanket. "I want you to divorce Dale so he can marry me."

I stared at her—maybe a minute or two—maybe seconds. I didn't know what to say. She kept holding the baby away from her chest, I guess to make a point. Finally, I closed the door. I thought I was going to vomit. She kept knocking. I told her to go away."

Barbara hesitated to gage my reaction. When I sat silent, she said, "So that's it. That's the story. That's why I'm crying. You were right all along."

I was stunned. I had always thought Dale was insecure and lazy. I never thought he would do something like this. "So, what happened," I asked.

She told me about confronting Dale and how he admitted it. He said he wasn't sure what he would do and moved out right away.

"What are you going to do?" I asked. "You could stay with me and Al."

"I thought about that," she said, "but I'll stay here for now."

~

Our brother Pat was in Hawaii preparing to ship out to New Guinea at a moment's notice. As I mentioned, I avoided giving Pat bad news, but someone must have told him what happened. In one of his letters, he wrote: "Say Sis I heard that Dale and Barb had separated is it true? I hope not, however I won't be the least surprised if I receive an affirmative answer. I feel sorry for Barb she is so damned sweet, much too good for…." He failed to end the sentence.

It's odd how circumstances cloud a person's judgement. I thought Barbara was too good for Dale too. I thought it right up to the second I found out my sister's heart was broken. And then I wanted him back, flaws and all.

15

THE WAY HOME

Told by Madeline - Barbara's Sister & Velva - Dale's Sister

Madeline

I stayed with Barbara and Mike for two more days. I wanted to know she felt safe; that she had her wits about her. We talked about how she would make ends meet, whether she would take Dale back, if she planned to tell others about what happened and a million other things. She was unsure about all of it. I knew she loved Dale and was caught between those feelings and the thought of losing him. It had to be unbearable trying to negotiate between her heart and mind. I was fine with all of it until she began wondering aloud about whether she had done something wrong.

"Don't you dare say that," I demanded. "You aren't responsible for someone else's decisions. *He* failed you. It's not the other way around."

She heard me. She knew I was right. And none of what I said mattered. Only time would uncover her destiny, and unpredictable circumstances would shape it.

I left her with all the money in my purse, except for what I needed for gas. We cried together and I went home.

I called her every day. I learned she and Dale had little contact in the beginning. I also learned Barbara was capable of something that shocked me. She told me about it a week after Dale left. I have to admit, it was a side of her none of us had ever imagined—and I liked it.

"I called the draft board," she said. "I let them know Dale moved out and I gave them his new address. I also told them what he had done. I think they felt sorry for me."

"What did they say?" I asked.

"They just said they'd take care of it," Barbara answered. "But I doubt that anything will happen."

Velva

After moving out of his house Dale began using our address to get his mail.

All we knew was that Dale and Barb separated. Rumors claimed it was because of another woman. We were also told there was a baby involved. I prayed it wasn't true. I found it hard to believe Dale would do such a thing. Barb was such a sweet young girl. And they had a baby together. How could something like this happen?

Of course, none of our information came through Dale. He was as jaw locked as a snapping turtle on a stick. Nobody was going to pry the truth out of him under any circumstances. And no one was dumb enough to try.

I avoided thinking about where Dale might be living. When I did, my mind saw him with the other woman. Curious or not, I would never find out. He rarely picked up his mail, and when he did he stayed only minutes. It was the strangest thing, the way he disappeared into a life none of us ever knew.

I felt protective of Dale, even though he was far from the child I helped raise. Whether I was being nosey, curious or hopeful, I had to glance at any mail he received. I wanted to find something from Barb. She had beautiful penmanship and an envelope addressed by her would stand out. There was nothing.

We understood why Dale seldom picked up his mail. Most of the time there was nothing to give him, until one day I was stopped cold when I saw a return address from the Selective Service Board. I immediately called Dale at work and told him he needed to stop by.

"What's the rush?" he asked.

"Just come and get your mail," I answered.

He came that evening. It was in early August, 1943. I handed him two letters—the government notice was on top. He froze when he saw "Selective Service". It was no wonder those words unnerved him. By now, the war had become personal to most Americans. Many of us knew soldiers who had been killed, and it was impossible to escape the daily news stories of the latest Japanese or German atrocities. Each one deserved its own offending place in our memories, but soon the images became blurred by sheer numbers. We lost the ability to single out just one event. That is, except in the case of eleven Roman Catholic nuns in Poland. Led by their Mother Superior, they volunteered to take the place of local men who German troops were about to execute by firing squad. The nuns were accommodated. And then the men were killed anyway.

I protected Dale as a child, and even though he created the problems he and Barb now faced, I wanted to protect him again. I knew it was impossible in the case of the letter, so all I could do was ask, "What does it say?"

His face turned beet red. He handed me the document and leaned against the wall.

It looked very official with a prominent seal featuring an eagle at its center. Under that was printed, **ORDER TO REPORT FOR INDUCTION**. Dale's name and an Order number were shown on the next line. And then, in the most unthreatening way I could imagine, this letter, a letter that could change a person's life and end many of them, began: GREETINGS.

I was frightened. I tried to think of something to say. The silence felt ominous.

I was about to utter something useless when Dale mumbled, "She told them."

"She told who, what?" I asked.

He ignored my question. As far as I know, Dale never lied. He hated lying. When trapped between a truth that made him look bad and a lie, he simply said nothing. He left it to the listener to decide what his silence meant. I knew.

He had ten days to get his affairs in order before reporting to his local Selective Service Board. They would then assign him to an Induction Station where he would stay for less than 24 hours. From there, he would be sent to a Reception Center for records assembly, receipt of equipment, occupation classification, immunizations, assignment and forwarding to a tactical unit or a Replacement Center.

"Can I move in with you and Harold?" he asked.

That question told me something important. He was moving out of the other woman's house. Maybe he could patch things up with Barb before he left.

"Of course you can," I said.

∼

I know Dale visited Barb and Mike 10 days in a row, and I know he failed to get what he wanted. She refused to take him back.

He said nothing about what was going on between them. Though he tried to hide his emotions, I felt him seething beneath a labored calm. When it came time to leave for the military, he gave me what little money he had stashed away. It was in cash, as he distrusted the banks.

"Shouldn't this go to….?" I started to ask. I quickly shut up when he glared at me.

Dale still controlled the family car. We walked him to the driveway where he placed his small bag in the passenger seat. Harold gave him a pat on the back and I hugged him from behind. Just then, a guy in a fairly new Chevy pulled up. They nodded to one another before Dale got into his own car and they both drove away.

We found out later that he had parked on the side of a highway, flattened all four tires and left with his buddy.

∼

Madeline

Barbara lived her truth in plain sight. Whatever she felt, whatever she imagined or decided was revealed uncensored. She had someone repair the car's tires and deliver it to her house. She understood when Velva told her about the money Dale left behind. While she thought Velva should have given it up, she knew the Wilson code and that Velva would stick to her word.

A few weeks after Dale was drafted, I asked, "Are you making it okay? You know Al and I can send you money."

"The laundry work is paying our bills," she answered.

"Have you heard from Dale lately?"

"Every day," she said. And then, an awkward pause. "I'm wondering if I did the right thing, Madeline. I don't even know that baby was his."

"But you know he cheated on you," I reminded her.

"People make mistakes," she said, with less conviction than certainty deserves. "You don't think I should take him back, do you?"

My answer wove its way through everything I knew or felt about Dale. It accounted for his difficult upbringing and the betrayal of his mother. It acknowledged his typical quiet and painful shyness. It suspected he would never amount to much and it doubted his willingness to try. Most of all, it remembered he broke my little sister's heart. All of that was true and none of it mattered.

"You're asking the wrong question," I said. "What you should be asking is, *Do I love him enough?*"

Silence. And then, "I don't know what you mean. Love him enough for what?"

"Love him enough to forgive this hurt," I answered. "Love him enough that when you look into his eyes, you see him instead of the woman on the porch."

"Are you saying I *should* love him enough?" she asked.

I wanted to be next to Barbara in that moment. I wanted to hold her hand. I wanted to touch her gentle face and stroke her hair. "I don't think anything *should* happen," I told her. "You're being asked to choose a life with Dale or without him. It's as simple as that. Do you love him enough to forgive him?"

"I think I do," she said softly. "I think I do."

∼

Much of the world had been brought to its knees by 1943. The outcome of WWII was still in doubt. Then, in February of that year, the Axis powers lost their air of invincibility when German forces surrendered at Stalingrad. It was the first major defeat of a German Army since the war began.

Back home, shoes were added to the ration list.

In March, the Germans began to withdraw from Tunisia. By April, the US and British forces met in North Africa, paving the way for an invasion of Sicily and then Italy. In the South Pacific, the Japanese advance had been halted and the Allies were preparing to retake the Western Aleutians. That same month, food rationing was greatly expanded in the U.S. Ration stamps were required to buy meats, cheese, canned milk, butter and other fats along with canned and processed foods.

Our brother Pat was appointed to the recently created Officer Candidate School. By June of 1943 he had completed the program and was a commissioned Lieutenant. Brother Cliff was also a 1st Lt. in the Army Air Corp, the precursor of the US Air Force. In due time, each would distinguish himself in service to the Allied cause—Pat in the Pacific theatre; Cliff in Europe.

On Aug 5, 1943, my husband Al Lafayette was drafted into the US Navy. Only weeks later, Dale was also drafted into the Navy. They had hardly made it through boot camp when both of them were diagnosed with ulcers and were sent to the same military hospital. The joke among their ward mates was that they must have married 'some hell on wheels sisters' for each of them to get such a bad case of ulcers.

Barbara told me again that Dale was writing every day, begging to be taken back. Eventually, his persistence paid off and she relented. She never told me what particular argument swayed her, or how she ultimately decided to forgive him. Regardless, Dale moved in with Barbara as soon as he was released from the Navy and their life began anew. Despite my misgivings, I was happy for them.

16

THE KILL FLOOR

Told by Madeline – Barbara's Sister

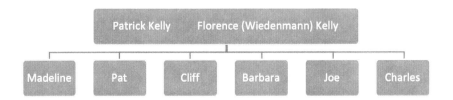

Dale returned from his short military experience and moved back in with Barbara. All appeared forgiven—though I was confident none of it would be forgotten. That said, Barbara enjoyed a unique quality that allowed her to bundle up the past, set it aside and move forward. Her very existence was life affirming. "What good does it do to fret over things you can't change," she asked me, "or to worry about things that haven't happened?"

Dale's progress, or lack of it, was a lively topic in letters from our brother Pat. He was then a Lieutenant stationed in New Guinea. He found out Dale had gone to work for one of the local mines and lasted only six months. In June of 1944 Pat wrote, "I was sorry to hear that Dale quit his job, he doesn't seem to be able to settle down to working and assuming the responsibilities of a husband and father, does he? It will be hard to get another job after quitting an essential industry."

By the following month, Dale was working for a meat packing plant and Pat had become a Captain. In a letter dated July 22, 1944, he wrote, "Am glad to hear that Barb is getting settled and likes it. Dale just doesn't seem to be able to get settled. I used to excuse him as I thought he was just young; however I sometimes doubt if he will ever settle down to his responsibilities."

One month later, after hearing that Dale had been moved to a traveling sales job, Pat wrote, "I hope Dale makes a go of it, however as you say he has an inferiority complex and likewise he hasn't enough backbone to make a good man on the road. He hasn't enough will power or common sense to stay away from liquor and bad company. There are numerous opportunities for footloose men on the road and I am afraid Dale is in this class."

Pat's letter gave voice to what most of us believed. To be fair, I wondered if we disliked Dale or were just being protective of Barbara. I'm pretty sure it was some of both. I knew for certain Dale was a mystery. Contradictions were in his nature and a clear picture would take years to materialize. By then, it was becoming tiresome trying to decide who he really was. Besides, how was he different from anyone else in that regard. Most of us have an unseen current pulsing just below our evident facade. So what if *his* surface perplexed us?

Even his parenting style, such as it was early on, ricocheted between hyper vigilance and hands off. For instance, he demanded that someone hold Mike's hand going up and down stairs until he was five years old—seriously, five years old. Otherwise, he was totally absent from Mike's day-to-day care.

∼

Dale's career in the meat processing business began and ended much as we expected, though it did happen sooner than we thought and for reasons we failed to imagine. Our entire family had high hopes for that job. We wanted Dale to like it for his own sake, but especially for Barbara's. We guessed it paid well and might finally add some stability to their lives. I know Dale felt the pressure from everyone. He needed to finally make something work. To compound his stress, Barbara was pregnant again.

As I remember it, Dale lasted six months; six months of anxiety according to Barbara. As much as it must have pained her, she called to tell me he had quit.

"He was fine with sales," she said, "but he didn't like the paperwork."

"Enough to quit?" I asked. "Is that why he's leaving?"

"No, no," Barbara answered, "it was more than that. He saw something that gave him nightmares."

That explanation sounded a little far-fetched until I heard the whole story.

This is how Barbara said Dale described it:

> I was expected to spend time in every department before beginning to sell the product. It was all straight forward from the start. I spent a few days in the office, where they taught me about paperwork and why details were important. Those jobs looked boring and way too confining. I was glad I'd be in outside sales.
>
> Then they taught me a little about buying cattle and how costs were calculated. They drilled in the importance of maintaining a profitable selling margin. "You better not be giving this shit away," a gruff, seasoned sales manager cautioned.
>
> Next, I spent a few days in the feed lots. It was a barren piece of land, just dirt and manure. A person could smell it from miles away. The cows showed up in stock trucks, mooing and swirling around like fishing worms in a tin can. The truck backed up to a platform where the cattle were prodded down a narrow ramp with stockade panels on either side. As they moved through the chute they were tagged and inspected. Once released, they spread out over a vast lot where long troughs formed aisles nearly the length of the property. The cattle milled around waiting for their next feeding.
>
> Most were nearly a year old and weighed in between seven and eight hundred pounds. We started them on a high-forage diet and gradually added concentrates of grain and grain by-products. I liked that part of the training. I had always wanted to own cattle and now I was in the middle of a vast herd of them. It all seemed ok until my next lesson… *The Kill Floor*.

16 THE KILL FLOOR

My education started around 6:00 a.m. one morning. I was guided into what could only be described as a concrete bunker. Even the ceiling was made of the stuff. Light was sparse. A few hanging fixtures created islands of brightness surrounded by shadows. The air felt cool and damp. The first thing I saw was a skinned cow, strung up by hooks on chains and being pushed along an overhead trolley through open sliding doors. Blood dripped from the limp carcass. The sight of it jarred me for a minute. As I watched the body swaying away from us, the sliding doors closed with a thud.

In quick succession, I heard another sliding door open on the other side of the room. A gold-colored steer entered a pipe chute. He was wide-eyed and on edge. A man on either side of the chute, each wearing knee high, black rubber boots, prodded the animal forward. The channel narrowed until the steer was stopped by a chest high steel pipe. The two men pulled a stock panel tight against his rear end to keep him from backing up. Now, his head was locked in place, unable to move in any direction but forward. He bellowed twice.

As if on cue, the muscled frame of a massive black man rose up to command our attention. He had been sitting in the shadows on the top rail of the pipe enclosure and out of our view. His shaved head glistened as he eased into the light. With practiced calm, he straddled the chute. The cow squirmed between his legs. It was then I saw the sledge hammer. He held it at his side for just a few seconds as he glanced down to measure his target by the yardstick of experience. And then he rocked the hammer forward and back like a pendulum, the momentum leading to a long arc over his head. He looked graceful; his entire body conditioned to the rhythm of death.

I'm sure they thought I watched the whole thing. It felt like a test of some sort—like I was being judged. So, I kept my head fixed forward, my eyes out of sight of anyone around me. In fact, I only *heard* the sickening thud that ended the drama. The trolley clattered down its rails and was positioned over the fallen cow. I opened my eyes when the clanging chains came to rest. Hooks were lowered to hoist the animal up by the back legs. The choreographed slaughter continued with the two men pushing the body until it hung over a grate on the floor. With an experienced swipe of a curved knife, the steer's throat was cut. He bled out while the two men skinned him.

The sliding doors that had clanked shut when I first entered the room now rumbled open. The cow's spent body swung forward and back as it was dispatched to the next room and disappeared forever.

I looked toward the towering black man. "He has to have the worst job in this business," I said to the supervisor standing next to me.

"Save your sympathy," he said. "You're lookin at the highest paid guy in the plant."

Barbara told me Dale was expected to stay in the room for a few more cycles; "…that's what they called it." She also said he watched the entire spectacle only once and that he never got over the sick feeling it caused.

"Well, hell," I said, "that's horrible. Did he quit that day?"

"No," she answered. "He worked there for a few months."

I secretly wanted to tell her Dale was never going to amount to anything and this was just one more example of why. But I dropped it, Barbara had enough to worry about without my judgement piled on.

I changed the subject to her pregnancy, a topic she could discuss for hours. That was the last time any of us heard about the meat packing business.

17

WAR AND THE KELLY BROTHERS

Told by Madeline — Barbara's Sister

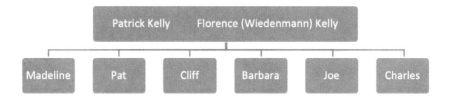

While Dale fought his inner battles at the meat packing plant, the course of World War II began to favor the allies. No one knew it then, but the Battle of Normandy sealed Germany's fate and the Battle of the Philippine Sea marked the end of Japan's dominance of the Asian Pacific. Those events were the climax of the war; that moment when an outcome is inevitable, yet unknowable. War, at its core, is tragedy brought to life. And there was no greater tragedy than the fact that, even though the German/Italian/Japanese gambit had failed, millions more would die before it was all over.

In June of 1944, three of our brothers were still serving in the military. Pat was a Captain and Company Commander stationed in New Guinea. Cliff and Joe were serving in Europe. Cliff was a navigator on one of the Army Air Corp's long-range bombers and Joe served in a MASH unit near the front.

I was closest to Pat, so we exchanged letters routinely. I did my best to keep him up-to-date about what was happening back home. He told me little of his day-to-day life and except for casual mentions, his letters were poor measures of the carnage all around him. Had I known what he was going through I would have tidied up my stories a bit.

I'm struck now by how little we knew about the war. Clearly, it was big—the entire world after all. We knew people were being killed. But it was revealed to most Americans in summary. It came to us through syndicated reporting in newspapers and periodicals and by MOVIETONE NEWS, broadcast between double features at our local theatres. Whether by accident or design, the attempted annihilation of entire populations was masked by the anesthesia of distance. We were coddled by the U.S. government and by our loved ones fighting to preserve our way of life. Even though we entered the war in December of 1941, the first published photograph of a dead American soldier didn't appear until shown in a LIFE magazine article in September 1943.

Pat and my letters overlapped throughout the war years. In all that time, Pat mentioned the war only in passing. I realized later that those letters were a way to separate himself from an existence he needed to forget. He could, at least in the time it took to write me, be connected to a different reality.

It is impossible to remember what I thought about Pat's life at the time. I think I just imagined him safe and secure on some base. We heard about Iwo Jima where over 3,000 Americans were killed. "Okinawa" exploded into our awareness because of the deaths of 12,000 men and women. Big stories, like those and a few others, became immortal by the force of their numbers. They deserved that attention and more, their sacrifices eloquent testimonies to courage. But the war was also fought and won in small battles where ordinary soldiers became heroes in their own right. Our brother Pat was one of those men.

Though he never told a soul about the circumstances that earned it, Pat was awarded the Silver Star, considered the United States Armed Force's third highest personal decoration for valor in combat. His citation states, "For gallantry in action in northern Luzon, Philippine Islands, from 25 February 1945 to 15 April 1945." That meant that for over 45 days, Pat was involved in pitched battles designed to retake land the Japanese had seized early in the war.

Excerpts from the citation read:

> "On 25 February 1945, Captain Kelly, commander of a rifle company, personally led his men in the attack on hill 1802 in the vicinity of Alibeng and wrested it from the well-entrenched enemy with a minimum of casualties. On 8 and 19 March 1945, Captain Kelly, by his gallant leadership and skillful tactics, routed the enemy from …"

It goes on to say:

> "On 21 April 1945, Captain Kelly directed his company in the seizure of tunnels and emplacements…"

> "On 13 April 1945 at Hill "X" near Bilbil Mountain, where the enemy had successfully repulsed seven previous attacks by other organizations, Captain Kelly, despite the danger, continually went forward and probed the strongpoint and caused the enemy to disclose his positions.

> On the following day, Captain Kelly, utilizing every favorable terrain feature and his excellent tactical skill, brilliantly and courageously led his men in an assault which destroyed six enemy machine gun nests and annihilated the enemy force on the shoulder of the hill. In the face of intense enemy mortar, machine gun and rifle fire and numerous counter attacks, Captain Kelly held this ground for five days until reinforcements were available to assist in complete seizure of the hill."

We also learned he received three Purple Hearts for wounds suffered during those battles. None of us realized how amazing his sacrifices were and what his leadership meant to a band of brothers engaged in life-or-death struggles. How could we have known? Pat kept it to himself. He came home content to leave the horror in the place that suffered it.

Oddly enough, the one thing we did know, and something Pat willingly talked about, was when he and his company discovered a cache of money consisting of US dollars, gold, silver pesos and Chinese currency. The Japanese had buried the treasure before surrendering the territory to US troops. They had hoped to retake the position and recover the loot later. In all, more than half a million dollars was recovered. It had to be a relief to report something so unexpected, while keeping secret the real cost of that war.

∼

Meanwhile, in Europe, Cliff, a First Lieutenant and navigator of a Fifteenth air force Liberator, was flying his thirtieth (30) mission in the war on Germany. The squadron's planes were to bomb railroad yards at Linz, Austria. Linz was a German stronghold and the site of a number of deplorable concentration camps. Cliff's Liberator was the deputy lead.

In a newspaper interview, Cliff stated, "We'd been airborne about two hours and having aligned our group with the rest of the air force, the big parade was under way. I was in the nose of the plane working on my logs and instruments when I heard the tail gunner call over interphone that there was a fire on the left side of the wing. I looked out and saw No. 2 engine burning furiously. A sheet of flame was batting out all sides of the cowling.

The pilot pushed the bail-out alarm and I forgot about my maps and charts. The other navigator was in the nose turret. He was banging on the door and I couldn't find my throat mike to let him know I was trying to help him. I finally got the doors open and as I turned around, I saw our bombardier go through the nose wheel door. I went right after him. The last I remember we were at 10,000 feet and my only thought, as I tumbled through space, was to grab that rip cord. I pulled it about six inches and nothing happened. Then I yanked it almost out of its socket. I was in an upright position, but the jolt of that chute opening was as rough as it was reassuring. It was like being stopped in mid-air.

As I floated down, the crosswinds spilled my chute one way and then another. It was mountainous terrain so an easy landing looked unlikely. As luck would have it, I landed about a yard from a rock wall and lay wondering if I was all in one piece. Some Italians came running and picked me up," he continued. "They led me out to a road and took me by donkey cart into a little town where I found our bombardier and another gunner. A bomber from our base flew up that afternoon and picked us up."

WWII reminded the world of just how primitive human beings were still. It taught that blind faith in cult leaders was the work of gullible minds. It was the reflection in a mirror of collective madness.

WWII cost us 60 million people. If you discovered that your next-door neighbors, a family of four, were all killed in a house fire, the loss would be personal and devastating. Four people, people you knew and talked to nearly every day. Four people, the number is dramatic and soul wrenching. So how does a person relate to the loss of 60 million neighbors?

60 million people is the combined populations of Arizona, Massachusetts, Tennessee, Indiana, Missouri, Maryland, Wisconsin, Colorado, Minnesota and South Carolina—every person—man, woman and child.

PART III
NEW BEGINNINGS

*New beginnings
are a second chance at getting things right.*

18

MANOR MAGIC

Told by Madeline – Barbara's sister

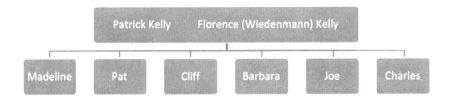

Barbara's second delivery was much like the first. I was there when her contractions started, called Dale and he took her to the hospital while I stayed with Mike. I spent the next week taking care of Dale and Mike. It was easy compared to what was coming

CAROL JEAN – FEBRUARY 1945
Number Two
Mike - 3

Carol's birth focused Dale. He began searching for work in earnest the day after she arrived.

He met a salesman for Manor Baking Company who told him the company was hiring. Manor provided a variety of baked goods delivered door-to-door on a prearranged schedule. Dale knew he could make it in sales and Manor offered a cut on everything ordered and delivered. He tracked down the District Manager and agreed to take whatever they had to offer.

"All I need is a chance to show you what I can do," he told the manager. "I don't care if we have to move."

"We're starting a new territory in Junction City, Kansas," the manager said. "You can take that if you want it." Dale agreed immediately.

Changing jobs again, we all complained. By then, we were convinced Dale would never become the husband Barbara deserved.

Dale knew how we felt. No one had to tell him. To his credit, he made good use of our doubts. They fueled his resolve to make it work with Manor. He drove to Junction City and rented a house, while Barbara began packing their belongings. She lived her life as it unfolded, respectful of the challenges and loyal to a fault.

Junction City, Kansas was so named because of its place at the confluence of the Smoky Hill and Republican rivers. Combined, they become the Kansas River. The city owed much of its prosperity to nearby Fort Riley, a major U.S. military post. Fort Riley was originally named Camp Center, because it was believed to be the geographical center of the United States.

Soon after Dale started with Manor, on April 12, 1945, President Franklin D. Roosevelt died while serving his fourth term as U.S. President. He was succeeded by Harry S. Truman of Missouri, Dale and Barbara's home state. The news staggered the nation. Roosevelt had been the only leader many people could remember. The shock of his death was blunted by the news that Germany signed an unconditional surrender on May 8, 1945. World War II in Europe was over.

In a controversial move, President Truman authorized the military to drop an atomic bomb on two Japanese cities. Within days of this new weapon's devastating impact, Japan conceded and surrendered to the Allies. V-J Day, September 2, 1945 marked the total end of WWII. More than 12 million American men and women were serving in the armed forces by the end of the war. 7.6 million of them were stationed abroad. It would take until June of 1947 to bring them all home and Fort Riley was a common destination.

Fort Riley personnel were from all over the country, earned reliable wages and were eager to accept the convenience Dale and Manor had to offer. Though a portion of the town was rowdy, bawdy and open for fun, the majority of its space was taken up by single family homes. It was a perfect place for Dale to make a name for himself. He felt lucky to have been assigned a completely new territory, especially now that the war was over. Whatever he made of it would be at his own hand.

Sales and delivery proved to be the most consequential change in Dale's work life. Through Manor, he discovered his real strengths, along with a sense of dedication and permanence. Manor was a bakery at heart, but their door-to-door delivery service made them totally unique. In the beginning, goods were delivered on a horse drawn wagon. Up and down the block, young children would line their front windows, waiting to see "The Manor Man" make his way to their door. A former employee said, "Kids would come out and buy something off my wagon, but I'm sure they just wanted to pet my horse, old Dusty. And he loved it."

All the salesmen wore uniforms consisting of buttoned down, tan shirts and pressed, blue/grey slacks. Their caps resembled dress formal, military issue hats of the time with a broad black bill across the front and "Manor Baking Company" prominently stitched into the crest. When the weather turned cool, they added a waist length coat similar to a bomber jacket. The jackets were the same grey/blue color as their slacks.

The Manor Man typically carried large orders to the house on wire racks, balanced on one upturned hand and braced against a shoulder. They called this rack their "bread basket." The basket was filled with whatever goods the housewife had ordered, along with other products the Manor Man believed she might like. Arriving at the door, he called out, "Manor Man" as he knocked. He would unload the prearranged order and then tempt the customer with the extras he carried with him. Bills were paid in cash, unless a credit arrangement had been made earlier. The Manor wage structure was simple; the more you sell, the more you make. It was that arrangement Dale found perfect to his taste. The harder he worked, the more he was rewarded. His income would prove his value to the company, and to anyone else who doubted him.

Established Manor Men typically provided coverage on four, sometimes five days per week in town, and once per week in the country. Their delivery schedules generally amounted to seven, and up to ten-hour work days. Slower days and Saturdays were reserved for cold calling for new customers. In the first few months, Dale had very little delivery business, but he was still out of the house every morning by 5:30 a.m. and rarely returned home before 7:00 p.m. each night.

His pattern was always the same, he finished his deliveries by 10:00 a.m. and immediately began canvassing door to door to sign up new customers. He excelled at cold calls. His first advantage was an unrelenting tenaciousness. Day in and day out, he knocked on doors. Eventually, his knuckles became blistered from the relentless tap, tap, tap on unforgiving wood.

He knocked with his index and middle fingers until they became too sore with blisters. He then switched to the ring and little finger while the first two healed. Each evening, Barbara applied new Band Aids to the resting fingers until the blisters became permanent calluses. A lifetime of hardened and raised knuckles on his left hand bore abundant evidence of his perseverance.

Dale's second advantage was an uncanny ability to charm anyone, especially women, when it suited him. He greeted each housewife at the door with a boyish, blushing grin. Then, on cue, he presented a confident spiel that nearly always resulted in a sale. Barbara said she understood why women responded to Dale the way they did. "He's sexy" was her explanation, "and women say he looks like a movie star." He used those traits to spirited effect. His sales began to grow with surprising speed.

When he took over the route in Junction City, his orders for the day could be delivered from the trunk of the family car. Soon, his business warranted the purchase of a standard company delivery vehicle. It was a Chevrolet panel truck; 196 inches long and weighing 3,425 pounds. It had an enclosed truck body, neatly painted and bearing the name, 'Manor Baking Company'.

A new hire's business typically required one or two shipments per week. Drivers of over-the-road delivery trucks would meet the Manor Man at a prearranged location. His products were then unloaded onto racks in the order he planned to drop them off to customers. In Dale's case, after only three months on the job, they were sending one of the big trucks every day.

A few months after Carol's first birthday, Barbara announced she was pregnant again. Instead of groans and rolling eyes, the news prompted smiles and acceptance. Dale was doing well and Barbara was happy.

LINDA JANE – SEPTEMBER 1946
Number Three
Mike - 4   Carol - 1

Barbara talked about their lives settling into a comfortable rhythm after Linda's birth. Dale was consistently praised for his work. His manager often placed new hires with him for a week or so to learn how to become a successful Manor Man. Dale basked in the glow of the attention, though he never lost sight of what really mattered—sales. There was also talk of a promotion to management where his earning power could significantly improve. Dale discouraged the idea. He had trouble seeing himself supervising other people, though he kept that doubt to himself.

Meanwhile, Barbara was learning how to manage the combination of a 4-year-old, a 1½ year old, and with the addition of Linda, a newborn baby. Oddly, she said she felt more in control with three kids than she ever had with just two. She wisely began to understand the value of training older children to help manage younger ones. She taught Mike how to keep Carol busy while she went about other responsibilities. It was a lesson that served her well throughout her life, and made having thirteen children possible. She felt blessed, regardless of all she had to do. She knew Dale was happier than he had ever been, and that made her happy too.

While Dale built his territory into a juggernaut, he won every sales contest the company sponsored and his income continued to rise. In September of 1947, Barbara announced she was pregnant again. This time, we were surprised. It all seemed to be happening so fast and I wondered how Dale really felt about it. But Barbara told me they were happy, so I left well enough alone. Apparently, they just accepted the idea and went on about their business.

In late 1947, Dale's District manager came to him with a proposition. Management was well aware of his sales numbers and wanted him to interview for a District manager's slot. He was to drive to Kansas City where Manor's headquarters and bakery were combined in the Westport Landing subdivision.

Westport Landing was once Kansas City's main rival for preeminence in that area. The port became the outfitting and starting point for traders, trappers and emigrants heading west on the Santa Fe and Oregon trails. In fact, our family, through Florence's Wiedenmann roots, was one of the original founders of the town. The oldest building in Kansas City/Westport Landing is now occupied by the famous Kelly's Bar. It was once the Wiedenmann Bros. grocery store, providing supplies to settlers heading west. The brothers were siblings of the 10 Wiedenmann children who migrated with their parents from Germany in the 1800s.

Supremacy in the Kansas City – Westport Landing contest ended when railroad tycoons made Kansas City their destination of choice.

Dale, reluctant and insecure, was to meet with Mr. Gene Shine, a longtime employee and sales manager at Manor. Mr. Shine was a clever, hands-on supervisor and intimately familiar with every territory in the company. It was he who ordered the interview to size up his rising young star.

Dale became sick with anxiety over the meeting. He waffled about whether he would go at all. Barbara encouraged him to at least find out why they wanted to see him. He knew, and he was doubtful he could handle the job. How would he manage other men when he could barely find the courage to meet Mr. Shine? He eventually overcame his apprehension and drove to Kansas City.

Barbara told me how it happened:

> Dale sat in the outer office of Mr. Shine's suite. He began to think about all the stories Manor men told about Mr. Shine. Most of them centered on his demanding nature. He was known to be tough, critical and knowledgeable about route sales.

Dale, waiting in the secretary's office, locked his fingers together on his lap so no one could see they were shaking.

Mr. Shine's door opened at the prearranged moment. Shorter than his reputation suggested, he was decked out in a tailored brown suit. Dale immediately noticed the neatly folded points of a cloth handkerchief raised just above the rim of his suit's breast pocket. He considered his own poorly fitted jacket and wondered what "the boss" must be thinking. At least their hair was similar, parted on the left side and a little wavy. Mr. Shine's wire rimmed glasses made him look dignified and professorial.

He reached out his hand. Dale could barely pull his strangled fingers apart. Finally, his grip loosened and he was able to return the gesture.

Dale sensed that Shine (as Dale nearly always referred to him), went out of his way to make the meeting casual and unthreatening. Shine directed him to a chair in front of an impressive oak desk. Dale sat down immediately and grabbed the curved arms to keep his hands still. He sat as stoically upright as he could. He noticed Shine's eyes fixed on his calloused knuckles.

"Where'd those come from," Shine asked, pointing to Dale's hands.

Dale, embarrassed at first, quickly tried to cover up the offending bumps.

"Knocked on a few doors lately," he answered.

Mr. Shine smiled. They chatted casually at first—Shine probing Dale about his past, his family and how many kids he eventually wanted. Dale doubted he really cared about the answer, but since he knew Barbara was pregnant again, he said, "Four ought to be about right."

Shine chuckled, "I'd think so," he allowed.

He quickly dropped the personal questions and began speaking about his respect for hard work. He speculated that Dale had to be putting in a lot of hours to reach the sales figures he was producing. He said he liked how Dale presented himself and that he thought they could teach him how to manage other men. He talked about a large territory in Kansas City that would be perfect for Dale's talents. And then Dale realized Shine had already made up his mind. The job was his if he wanted it.

Dale knew working in Kansas City would create an unwelcome focus. But, if he were as successful as Shine predicted, his income would rise sharply and other promotions might follow.

Dale listened to Shine detail the reasons he should accept the offer; more money, prepare him for other promotions, an expense account and better benefits. He mentioned other inducements, but Dale had tuned him out after, "more money". His mind was made up. Shine's pitch ended with, "So, can we count on you?"

Dale stood up and shook Shine's hand, "I'll take the job," he said.

"How soon can you be here?" Shine asked.

"Barb will want to have the baby in Junction City, and it'll take me a while to train a new man on my route," Dale said. "But I figure I can be moved to Kansas City by April."

Shine agreed to the schedule.

KELLY DEAN – MARCH 1948
Number Four
Mike - 5   Carol - 3   Linda - 2

Barbara needed only a few weeks to recover from Kelly's birth before beginning to pack for a move to Kansas City. Moving had become second nature to her by now, but this one was more daunting. She had to deal with a little boy, a toddler and essentially two babies. On top of that, none of her regular work went away.

Al and I came to help. We had moved to Kansas City in 1945 and were able to steer them to a comfortable house in a stable neighborhood. The home they picked had more than enough room for their family.

What seemed like a great deal of space at the time, would soon be tested by new arrivals.

19

EXPECT THE UNEXPECTED

Told by Madeline — Barbara's Sister

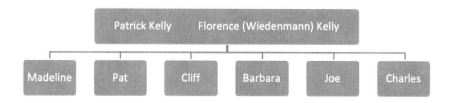

In 1948, Florence, our mother and book enthusiast, was still living in Joplin and raising Charles. They had lived there since the family moved from Pittsburg, Kansas in 1939. During those nine years, one by one, her three older sons volunteered to fight in the war. In between those sad goodbyes, she moved from one house to another, always searching for something cheaper, something she could afford.

Most of Florence's income came from Joe, who had assumed the major role in taking care of her and Charles. For Mom's part, rather than taking in laundry as she had done early in widowhood, she began cleaning houses with a friend. She was surviving as best she could. Regardless, whatever prosperity the rest of the world enjoyed had passed her by and hard times were growing harder.

Florence had become matronly. Her appearance was closer to an elderly grandmother than the mother of a teenage son. Her hair, gray and peppered with strands of black, was braided tight and curled up in a flat ball on top of her head. I asked others if they saw what I did, that her eyes had sunken deeper into their sockets and dark shadows rimmed her cheek bones just behind her glasses. Other things about her had also changed. She moved sluggishly, as if carefully considering movements that had once been instinctive.

Most of us thought she had just aged beyond her years. A difficult life can do that to a person. Others believed she might even be imagining her ailments. I would have gladly accepted either of those explanations compared to the bad news we were given—Parkinson's was taking over her life.

We learned it was the reason for her uncertain movements, her difficulty holding things and the general change in her disposition. We were told her muscles would eventually become rigid and she would be prone to falls, have difficulty talking and might even struggle to swallow. The prospects sounded dismal.

The news actually buoyed Florence. At least now everyone had to admit her complaints were legitimate. At the same time, it made her even more dependent on others. Just after Dad died, brother Pat assumed the role of 'man of the house'. He continued on as the primary breadwinner until joining the army in 1942. Then, as each of the boys entered the military, a portion of their checks went to Florence as a dependent. WWII actually provided her a stable livelihood.

After the war ended and the boys returned home, Pat and Cliff had their own families to support. That left Joe to shoulder the upkeep for Florence and Charles. Handsome, illegible and hard-working, Joe took a job with Safeway and worked tirelessly to make Mom's life livable. He was content with his lot until the day the beautiful and vivacious Mary Lou entered his life. Her mother had spotted Joe while grocery shopping. She immediately returned home to tell Mary Lou to go see the handsome young man she had just met.

Mary Lou, armed with a hurriedly manufactured shopping list, headed to Safeway and what turned out to be her future. She met Joe, they flirted, he asked her to the company picnic and within nine months they were married.

Soon after the wedding in 1948, Joe wrote a letter to Al and I, Cliff and Annie, Barbara and Dale and suggested everyone should begin chipping in to support Florence. He excluded Pat, believing he had done enough for the family already. I knew it was going to be difficult for everyone, and surely

Barbara would be spared the expense. She and Dale now had four kids, had just moved to Kansas City and Dale had assumed a new position. Given his history, the prospects were slim that this job would be his last.

I suggested the rest of us should forgive Barbara the responsibility. Before we could agree however, Barbara sent a check along with a note saying that they would be sending money every month. She told me later it was Dale who insisted they carry their load. From that month forward, they never missed a payment and it forced us to reconsider our attitudes about Dale. We were now dealing with expanding contradictions—contradictions that would play out in new and confounding ways.

As much as we tried to help financially, Florence was always strapped. The money we sent failed to offset her rising costs. Eventually, she was forced to give up her last home and move to Tacoma, Washington to live with Pat, Betty and their three girls. That move meant she had to sell all of her worldly possessions. Rather than allow us to help with the sale, she struck a bargain with a used furniture dealer to take the whole lot. The total sales price was $350. The man knew he had bested a desperate widow and quickly organized a crew to pick up her belongings. Before he arrived, a friend of Florence told her the table and chairs alone were worth more than she was getting for the whole parcel.

When the dealer arrived, Florence tried to back out of the agreement. The man would have none of it.

"I've hired all these men and this trailer based on your word," he said. He acted angry and threatening. "Our time is worth as much as this furniture."

Florence relented.

Through all of the instability Mom faced, mixed with the problems she created herself, Charles was always at her side. Only two years old when Dad died, he grew up in a confusing world where brothers took turns fathering him and moving from one house to another became the norm. Once all the brothers were gone, Florence basically became *his* dependent instead of the other way around.

Chuck remembered the day it all became clear:

> We were waiting in the kitchen of our last real home. All of the furniture was gone and the remainder of our lives were packed into a few cardboard boxes. Florence was sitting on a box holding all of the money we had to our names. She stared down at the bills in her small hands. I pretended to make sure the boxes were taped shut. I heard her sobs leak out as whispers and then build to a restrained moan. I wanted to cry for her, but what good would that have done? She needed support, so I rubbed her back and told her everything would be ok. I said it, having little faith those words were true.

~

Dale turned out to be a natural manager just as Shine predicted. His district in Kansas City grew quickly and there was even talk of him becoming a Division Manager over a broad territory. Dale enjoyed a new-found confidence and loved Kansas City. He was fond of saying, "Early on, I hated it here, but after a year I never wanted to leave. Knowing how he felt, I was surprised when he began talking about buying land and a few farm animals.

Meanwhile, out in Tacoma, Florence found one reason after another to create conflicts with Pat's wife, Betty, an unlikely source of frustration. Betty, a black haired, Mediterranean beauty, was about as laid back as a person could be. And maybe that was the problem. Florence embraced order, while Betty shunned it. Whatever the reason, Florence left Tacoma and moved in with friends in California. Charles was left with Pat and Betty to complete his junior year in high school.

In a series of letters to Pat between April 16 and June 8, 1949, her penmanship proved Parkinson's was working to claim her completely. A very clear and precise writing style gradually slipped into disrepair. Her letters became larger, lines took a downward turn and words appeared slightly disjointed. She began to complain about a thumping in her head and bemoaned the state of her frayed nerves.

The family decided Mom should come back to live in the Midwest. She and Charles needed to be near the family where we could look after them. A discussion of where they would live took place in a few letters and phone calls—no one eager to take them in. To this day I'm unsure how it happened, but Barbara and Dale drew the short straw. Looking back on it today, I have to wonder what sense it made to add two more people to a home with four kids and two adults.

Dale's graciousness threw us another curve. He welcomed Florence and Charles to live with them knowing they would stay a full year until Charles graduated from high school. I think he did it for a couple of reasons. He respected mothers like no man I had ever met, even in the face of being left by his own. And in the case of Charles, he knew what it was like to live where you were unwelcome. He refused to do that to another kid. As it turned out, maybe Dale was the good one among us.

In an April letter to Pat, Mom wrote, "Barbara is going to have another baby in November, seems to be happy about it. Dale is fed up with his job, is away from home too much, is going to try to get a job on a retail milk route. They traded their Pontiac in on a new Ford, which they like fine."

Dale made a habit of trading cars roughly every two years, a pattern he continued for the rest of his life. He liked new cars, liked how they made him feel.

In her June 8th follow-up letter, Florence wrote, "I know you really wanted me there, Pat, but because of my nerves I was to blame that Betty and I couldn't get along, for, Pat, I'm not too happy here either.

Charles got here about 1 p.m. Sat, had a nice trip...

Barbara has a lovely home, her kiddies are all very sweet, they mind pretty good, though Mike is a little bit spoiled but when Barbara tells him to do something, he does it or gets spanked."

Everything appeared to be going smoothly, at least as far as we could see from the outside. Mom and Charles settled in and whether she was happy about it or not, she knew they had to stay until Charles graduated. What she failed to realize was that someone else in that house was miserable.

Barbara shouldered a secret for as long as she could stand it. I think she was embarrassed by what happened and wanted to protect Dale. Or maybe she was just having trouble figuring out what to say. Either way, she told me the whole story one morning at her house when we sat down to talk over coffee.

"I want to tell you something, Madeline," she began. "And don't tell Al about it." She moved her cup around in a nervous circle and tried to warm up to the topic. I remained patient and waited. Finally, she said, "I think Dale had a nervous breakdown a few weeks ago."

"A nervous breakdown!" I repeated. "What makes you think that? I just saw him. He was fine."

Barbara said, "I know. I know. It's like nothing happened, except it did and it was scary."

"Ok, Barbara," I said, "now calm down and tell me what happened." This is how she told it:

> Dale came home early on Friday a couple of weeks ago. And you know that's unusual for him. He never takes time off.
>
> Well, that afternoon he had a few drinks and became very agitated. He talked about the pressures of his job and taking care of our four kids and here I was pregnant again and we're taking care of Florence and Charles too. He said there were others who should be shouldering more of the load. He was working up a head of steam and seemed helpless to stop it.
>
> Between smoking and drinking, he wondered around the house mumbling to himself. I was afraid. Dale's temper could flare up in a heartbeat. I learned to keep my mouth shut and avoid any comment that could set him off. You know how it is, Madeline."

"I understand," I lied, as Al had never raised his voice to me.

"Well, anyway, out of the blue, he said, "Pack up your things and the kids. We're going to Denver."

It felt like we were little kids running away from home.

"What should I tell Florence and Charles?" I asked.

"Tell them we're going to Texas to see Mrs. Sneed," he said.

"When will we be coming back?"

He continued pacing, drinking and smoking, and in between started loading things into the car. Dale never lied to me, even about the girl with the baby. I'm guessing he had no idea where all of it was leading, so he just kept quiet.

We drove all night and finally reached Denver at 9:00 a.m. the next morning. Thank goodness the kids slept almost the whole trip. No telling what he would have done if they had been fussy. We found a motel and after settling in for an hour or so, Dale seemed better. As quickly as he had become someone else, he returned to his familiar self.

"Rest up," he said. "We have to head back tonight."

"Didn't you ask him what happened?" I asked.

"What good would it do to ask him why? I knew he was as much in the dark as I was."

Anyway, we drove home, he went to work on Monday morning and nothing has been said about it since."

"Well," I said, "I don't think it was a nervous breakdown, Barbara. He had a panic attack. I've had a few myself."

"Oh, Madeline!" she said. "When did you ever have a panic attack?"

"Every time you go to the hospital to have a baby," I answered. "And I have to live your life for a week. If you have many more I'll be committed for sure."

We both laughed and left it at that.

20

THE FEW WHO KNEW HIM

Told By — Dale's Trusted Friend

Dale Wilson gave me a start after the war. I was just a regular guy with black wavy hair, a square jaw, a dimple right in the middle of my chin—and no prospects. WWII had taken me to all kinds of famous places, including Paris and London. I remember how the song, "How Ya Gonna Keep 'em Down on the Farm (After They've Seen Paree?)", a WWI hit, found new legs during and after WWII. People thought American soldiers would be changed by the magic of Paris when, in fact, we were changed by the insanity of war. We just wanted to come home. In my case, I hurried back to Kansas City, and that's when Dale hired me for Manor Baking Company.

I learned early on that Dale meant business. He was like many of the tough soldiers I served under during the war, heroes who led men into battles knowing only some of them would return. Those guys were hard with knowing. I had heard Dale was released from the navy for medical reasons, so it was not war that stiffened him. It was simply in his nature to lead.

Dale was a Division Manager for the door-to-door bakery delivery business headquartered in Kansas City. He traveled his territories hiring, training and establishing routes for guys just like me. Route sales and delivery for Manor was a good job and a guy could make serious money if he was willing to work. We earned a percentage of everything we sold, and Dale took a small cut of that. He never said so, but he had to be making really good money for those times.

When it came to his business, Dale found it easy to talk with total strangers. They were potential customers, and that made the effort tolerable. He was also comfortable with people who reported to him. They respected what he knew about the business; knew what it took to make a profit.

He had to be the hardest worker I ever met, and it was evident in how he trained a new hire. Anyone could *tell* you what it took to be a successful Manor Man—Dale *showed* you how to do it.

During my first interview, I remember being curious about the callouses on Dale's left hand knuckles. *What caused that?* I wondered. My first day of training cleared it up right away.

"This is a door-to-door business," he said. "The more doors you knock on, the faster you're going to build your route."

He said this while moving from one house to the next at a pace I could barely sustain. The only time he slowed down was while writing up an order. It was then he became engaging. Women loved him, and women placed the orders. He had a way with them. I could never figure out exactly what drew them to him, but the attraction was obvious and he could turn it on and off at will.

He stayed with me block after block on that first day. When he felt I could make calls on my own, he took one side of the street and I took the other. On it went, one neighborhood after another. He rarely finished before I did, because he was writing more orders. It was something to see.

I knew Dale about as well as anyone, and even I was at a loss to understand him. His rule book was pretty basic—don't lie, don't cheat in business, work hard and your word has to mean something. Beyond that, he revealed very little about himself. If you did learn something, it was just a surface detail. It might disclose a trait or a tendency, but it never helped explain who he was. I just know we all tried our best to please him.

21

TRANSITION

Told by Madeline — Barbara's sister & Velva — Dale's sister

Cost of Living – 1949

New house:	$7,450
Average Wages per Year:	$2,950
Gallon of Gas:	$ .17
New Car:	$1,420
Minimum Wage:	$ .70 per hour
Pound of Bacon:	$ .50
Coffee:	$ .85 for 2-pound bag

Madeline

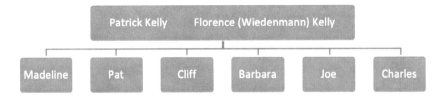

Barbara dealt with pregnancy like most of us react to a sudden cool breeze at the end of summer: Awareness gave way to delight, and the change strengthened her. Graceful and relaxed, she wore her status like a badge of honor. She was a marvel of reproductive efficiency. Even late in her last month she continued to buy and stock groceries, cook three meals a day, clean the house and do her wash by hand. She hung clothes outside during clear weather and inside when it turned bad. She ironed all of Dale's shirts, slacks and even his underwear and was still able to show each child personal attention, all the while, growing a human being inside her. I became exhausted just watching it.

Barbara enjoyed few time-saving devises in 1949. Most electrical conveniences were still relatively new and too expensive for her family. On top of that, Dale had just begun to make decent money and tended to hold on to it as if there may never be more. He saddled her with a miserly allowance—a pattern that continued throughout their lives. She was expected to pay all the bills on a budget established nine years earlier and four kids fewer.

Her typical week went something like this:

- Mondays - Launder clothes, (though she had to wash the cloth diapers more than once a week). She used a tub and scrub board with a wringer attachment. Wash by hand in sudsy water, wring it, rinse it, wring it again and hang it outside to dry. This took most of the day. In between, she prepared breakfast, lunch and dinner and did the dishes after each meal.

- Tuesdays - Iron anything that required it, and that was nearly everything they wore. Permanent press was yet to be invented. She ironed Dale's boxer underwear, T-shirts, handkerchiefs, dress shirts and slacks, plus casual shirts and slacks. Dale never owned a pair of jeans. She also ironed the kid's clothes, I think they each had two outfits, though the babies had many. Sheets and pillow cases were pressed, along with T-towels. Like always, breakfast, lunch and dinner were thrown in for good measure.

- Wednesdays - mending and sewing…breakfast, lunch and dinner.

- Thursdays - house cleaning – every room, with special attention to bathrooms and the kitchen. Breakfast, lunch and dinner.

- Friday - baking – bread, rolls, pies, cakes. She planned meals with leftovers in mind. For instance, by preparing a roast for one meal, she could use the leftovers for a stew the next day. She was a marvel at stretching a dollar and was still able to provide filling and nutritious meals. If a kid turned up his nose at the food she provided, he went

- to bed hungry. She asked no quarter and gave none when it came to food. Breakfast, lunch and dinner.
- Saturday – grocery shopping, unplanned laundry, extra house cleaning, preparation for Sunday dinner. By cooking it on Saturday, she could get a small break one day per week. Sunday meals were a grand affair and typically included a sheet cake she baked on Saturday. Breakfast, lunch and dinner.
- Sunday – a day of rest. Church, breakfast, lunch and dinner.

That was Barb's life and I never heard a single word of complaint. Keep in mind, she was dealing with only half the family she would eventually raise. It was beyond me how she did it week after week. And I saw it with my own eyes.

In a letter to Pat dated November, 1949, Florence offered some interesting insights into how Barbara mothered. Mom was trying to make a point about how the rest of us should worry less. These are her exact words, in this case, referring to her and Betty, Pat's wife:

"Both of us should take a lesson from Barbara, she doesn't seem to worry a bit and goodness knows she has enough to do it. She just got through redecorating the children's bedroom, she and Charles took off all the old paper, plastered all the cracks and holes and painted all the woodwork. She worked till midnight several nights. She works like a trooper and it doesn't seem to hurt her though she looks sort of fagged out, to me, at times. The three youngest, (Carol, Linda and Kelly), are put to bed right after lunch every day for their naps and if they play and talk, she spanks them, but that seldom happens as the two girls generally go to bed without being told and of course Kelly has to be put in his bed, he can't get into it by himself. They generally sleep 1 ½ to 2 hours. At night they are all in bed by 8 o'clock, and if they cut up too much again, they get spanked. That way she has her evenings free from their care, which is a relaxation to her. And they all love her as much as any children can, in spite of the spankings."

STANLEY KEITH (STAN) – NOVEMBER 1949
Number Five
Mike – 7   Carol – 4   Linda – 3   Kelly – 1

Soon after Stan's birth, Dale was promoted to Division Manager of Route Sales over most of Kansas and Missouri. It was clear he would be staying with Manor. His supervisor, Shine, suggested he move to whatever part of the territory suited him. Within months, he bought a farm in Parsons, Kansas. They would move there as soon as the house was upgraded.

Barbara originally balked at the idea. She struggled to imagine a life on the farm, isolated and remote from friends and family. She relented only after Dale agreed to build an addition across the back of the house. The new space would include a mud porch on one end and a laundry room and full bath on the other. More importantly, it came with the promise of a new automatic washer and dryer. That assurance won the day. Even though the house was small, Barbara had worked with much less. I think she knew a family's love made a home—space was just a convenience.

At roughly the same time, Al and I had purchased our own first home on 37th and Troost in Kansas City. It had an upstairs apartment where we planned to eventually move Florence and Chuck following our own upgrades. We hoped Dale and Barbara would stay in Kansas City until we were finished. With little notice, that plan was scuttled. Dale wanted to be near their new farm construction. He decided they would move to Parsons right away, first to a rented house in town and later to the farm when it was ready. I personally believe he wanted his life back and moving away made that happen.

∼

The 1950's were just around the corner and Americans were tired of war. World War I, "The War to End All Wars", was quickly eclipsed by WWII and 60 million deaths. Surely the world had learned its lesson and proved that war is not an answer. Maybe educated, thoughtful people would decide that seeking the common good leaves no room for war. But then a new kind of war emerged, *The Cold War*. I always thought that was a silly label as it created a deception. War is war; hot or cold, it will eventually lead to disaster.

The first major incident of the Cold War began with the Soviet Union's blockade of West Berlin on June 24, 1948. In response, the Allies broke the blockade by initiating a sustained airlift of essential supplies and food. Five to eight thousand tons of supplies were delivered daily. By May 12, 1949 the Soviet Union ended the blockade.

That same year, on October 1, 1949, communist leader Mao Zedong established the People's Republic of China. It brought an end to the on again, off again civil war that had lasted since the late 1920's. Mao eventually caused the deaths of over 40 million of his own people.

Also in 1949, the Soviet Union tested its first atomic bomb, joining the U.S in the Nuclear Age. The North Atlantic Treaty Organization (NATO) was formed. The Federal Republic of Germany was officially founded. The first Polaroid camera was sold for $89.95. RCA perfected a system to broadcast color television. The first Volkswagen Beetle was sold in the US, and the National Basketball Association (NBA) was established.

Velva

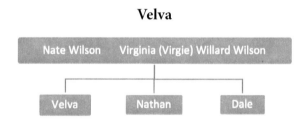

After Dale returned from the military hospital and rejoined Barb and Mike, Harold and I saw very little of them for a number of years. It's possible we were all just too busy with life. Possible, and unlikely. I feared Barb resented me for keeping Dale's money when he went into the military. *I* would have resented it. In my defense, I had to be loyal to one of them, and since I helped raise Dale, that's who I stood behind. I feel guilty about it now, but at the time, I thought I was doing the right thing. Maybe my guilt is why we saw less of them. It certainly had nothing to do with how Barb treated me. She was incapable of holding a grudge.

We visited on a few holidays and were around enough to know about the kids, the house moves and Dale's promotions. It was obvious to us that everything was going well for them until Barb's mother and brother moved in. After that I could see a strain on Dale's face. His frustrations were hidden to the outside world, but I knew he was only pretending. I also knew Barb was paying a price for it. She had to. It was *her* family they were supporting. Whatever complaining she took from Dale was worth it. She felt an obligation and she intended to fulfill it. That's when I realized she could handle whatever life threw her way. She never had to rise, because nothing made her fall.

In May, just after Dale announced they were moving to Parsons, Charles graduated from high school and left to sell magazine subscriptions. He was a member of a state-roving band of young solicitors. Madeline had found a small apartment for Florence and Chuck just a couple of blocks from her and Al. Soon after Chuck left to sell magazines, Florence decided on an extended stay with her sister-in-law Alice and her husband Dick Rader.

I have to write something about Alice. I met her only once, and once was all it took to remember her from that moment forward. She was Patrick Kelly's sister and had continued to stay close to Florence after his death. She was a large presence in both stature and nature. She wrapped her cold white hair in a bun and always wore ankle length cotton dresses with a full fronted apron. She lived on the original Kelly homestead and cared for her mother, father and brother until each of them died.

All-the-while, Dick Rader, a wiry wisp of a man, had been the family's hired hand for as long as anyone could remember. He worked for room, board and small wages. After everyone else died, Alice told him he would have to move. "It ain't fittin' for just the two of us to be livin' together alone on this place."

Now keep in mind, both Alice and Dick were in their sixties, so a scandal seemed unlikely. Nevertheless, Dick said, "Then we'll jest hafta git hitched." He paused for effect, scratched his temple and added, "Guess we'll have to build a fence around the yard to keep our kids in."

∽

We were happy to hear Dale and Barb were moving to the country. Dale had always dreamed of owning land and cattle and now it was possible. Around the time of that news, Barb announced she was pregnant again, their sixth. Surely that would be the end of it.

They first moved to a rental property on Main Street in Parsons, Kansas. It was a two story, frame house with more than enough space for their growing family. They planned to live there until the farm home was renovated. Barb liked the house in town. It was just a mile from their best friends, Bob and Evelyn and close to everything she needed.

Construction work on the farmhouse addition inched along. It would have been finished in a couple of months if not for Dale's condition that the work be paid for as it was completed. When funds were short, construction stopped. That caused scheduling problems for the remodelers. They had to quit, go to another job and wait for Dale to rebuild cash reserves. Only then could they be worked back into the schedule.

In the meantime, Dale, deathly afraid of fire, talked Al into helping him rewire the entire, barely modern farmhouse. Al was a licensed electrician. He was also devoted to the kids, so he happily obliged. Little did Dale know he was creating a debt he could never fully repay.

Al and Madeline made the five-plus hour drive from Kansas City to Parsons at least once per month—more often in summer. Barb told me they were like a second set of parents. Al taught the kids how to build kites from flexible twigs and newspapers with tails of old rags. He showed them how to eat a raw egg right out of the shell (he was the only one who ever did it). They worked together on projects in the barnyard or the chicken house. He took them fishing and hunting for quail.

While Al was playing outside, Madeline helped Barb prepare meals and take care of the babies. When the girls were old enough, she showed them how to apply and remove makeup. She taught them how to sew with a machine and mend with a needle and thread. I realized early on that she and Al were a buffer between Dale and everyone else. Madeline had a way of working him out of his sour moods and wasn't beyond giving him guff if he deserved it. The kids loved watching her stand up to him.

Dale was my brother, and I loved him, but I wondered how Barb put up with his detachment. My uncertainty deepened with each new kid. I doubt he ever changed a diaper, and I know for a fact he never washed one. If he could cook as much as an egg, it was news to me. I think he knew where the grocery store was, but I doubt he was ever in one. He was an island unto himself.

To be fair, Barb helped create her own prison. She did everything for Dale— spoiled him until he was rotten. Taking care of others was in her nature. She was helpless to do less and eager to do more. Dale should have protected her from herself and from his own selfishness. Instead, he relished the attention and assumed his Kingship with vigor. Where the kids were concerned, he was in charge. He was the enforcer. He drew the lines and dared anyone to step over them. Maybe that was enough for Barb.

WWI and II should have taught us enough about war to banish it from our existence forever. War is the failure of reason. But conflict seems to be part of our nature, at least our experience says it is. On June 25, 1950, North Korea invaded South Korea and a new conflict sprang to life.

The seeds of the new war grew from Japan's occupation of Korea between 1910 and the final days of WWII. Their total defeat imminent, Japan withdrew from Korea and other former occupied territories. The Allies demanded unconditional surrender. Japan rejected that ultimatum. They relied on a Neutrality Pact with the Soviet Union to protect them. Their goal was to sue for terms.

Unknown to the Japanese, the Soviet Union, through the Tehran Conference in 1943, had agreed to enter the war against Japan three months after the war in Europe ended. By securing Russia's commitment, the Allies intended to remove Japan's only hope for a negotiated settlement. In the process, they returned land to Russia that was lost to Japan in the Russo-Japanese War—land none of them had a right to bargain over.

Russia was granted control of north Korea, while the U.S. assumed stewardship of the south. During that same period, Stalin extracted huge concessions from an ailing President Roosevelt and an increasingly less relevant Great Britain. The arrangement provided a new arena for the corruption called The Cold War.

On June 25, 1950, North Korea invaded the south. President Truman adopted the "domino effect" international policy philosophy and the U.S. joined the battle. Basically, the notion was that the U.S. had to defend any democratic nation against communist incursion. Otherwise, neighboring countries might begin to fall like dominos to communism. Eisenhower and Kennedy perpetuated the notion and that led us into the Viet Nam war years later.

The U.S., its readiness depleted by years of warfare, unprepared and undermanned, enlisted the UN's intervention against North Korea's attack. By doing so, they declared that the international community was allied against the invasion. Meanwhile, the Soviet Union pretended to have nothing to do with North Korea's aggression, even as their tanks, planes and heavy artillery were clearly being used by the north. Eventually, China entered the fray. After over two years and 33,696 American soldiers killed, the conflict ended in a stalemate. In all, over 1.2 million people lost their lives.

1,200,000 people died for nothing. Our collective humanity murdered again by the hubris of small minds and ineffective leaders.

22

THE ONE-ARMED MAN

Told by Mike #1

I thought living in Parsons, Kansas in 1952 was pretty great. The house was roomy—a two story with a broad landing at the top of a wooden staircase. It was the nicest house we ever lived in. The really neat thing is that we lived right across the street from the Roller Rink on the main road through town and got to use it often.

There were five kids by then, with another scheduled to arrive any day. Dad had started his new job and was gone most of the week. Along with his absence came more worry on his part. He lived in fear of how we could get hurt. Danger was everywhere—water, fire, cars, bullies, falls from high places or bicycle accidents to name just a few. I became sick of the story everyone used as an example of his dread. They never tired of telling how he demanded someone hold my hand going up and down steps until I was five; it was embarrassing. In his defense, I was the first, and as far as he knew, the only kid he would have to keep alive. He was determined to succeed.

He was also hyper watchful when Carol, number two, arrived. Okay, so he would be responsible for a couple of kids. He could do that. Now they had their boy and girl, who could want more? Surprise! The kids kept coming and vigilance gave way to broader strategies.

Based on his actions, and possibly without any real plan, he decided the only power he had over the unknown was physical resolve. He taught us what mattered to him by degrees of punishment. He apparently believed that if you want a kid to remember something, attach shock or pain to it and the association becomes permanent. It's the only thing he and Mom knew. It was how *they* were raised. Even if he were aware of something called "time outs" or "reasoning", it required time he could only wish for, and with a small army to protect, he opted for expedience.

Along the way, once in a great while, he made his point through clever manipulation of circumstances. One of those opportunities surfaced when I was nine years old. Of the many fears Dad imagined, probably the oddest involved the kids sticking their arms out of car windows. He was convinced that an oncoming car would veer too close and one of us would lose an arm. He railed against the tendency. He threatened spankings and even followed through a few times. In the end, his demands were no match for the thrill of an outstretched hand wind surfing through cool air.

He decided to make a dramatic point on a late summer evening in 1951. We heard Dad answer a knock on the front door, which was about as rare as a cat chasing a dog—it just didn't happen. Carol, Linda, Kelly and I gathered about half way down the staircase to see who came calling. Stan was only two, so he was in bed at the time. A young man slightly taller than Dad, 5'10" I'd say, and around 165 pounds, stepped into the vestibule carrying a hat in his right hand. We learned later that Dad hired him a few months earlier and that he was turning out to be one of his top salesmen. The man turned to face us. We all gasped in unison. His left arm was missing from just below the elbow. It had what looked like a small knot where his arm ended. None of us had ever seen such a thing.

Dad knew we were staring and told us to come down and introduce ourselves. I became suspicious. He typically chased us away when adults were present. He believed children should be seen and not heard and practiced the philosophy ruthlessly. But not this time. This time he invited us into the moment.

I knew the little ones were afraid. I took Kelly's hand and led him down the stairs. The others followed and one-by-one, we said our hellos. The gentleman was gracious. He placed the hat under his left arm and shook hands with each of us. He made sure we had a clear view of his stub.

Mom came in from the kitchen, smiling. She was pregnant again.

"Congratulations," the man said. "I heard you were going to have another baby."

"Thank you," she answered, and then asked Dad if she could bring them anything.

"He's just leaving," Dad allowed, and after a short discussion the one-armed man was gone.

We all followed Dad into the kitchen, waiting for an explanation. He said nothing.

Finally, I asked, "What happened to his arm?"

Dad took on a serious tone and said, "He was driving down a highway this side of town. He had his arm outside the window to catch some cooler air. All of a sudden, a truck came by too close and took that arm off right below his elbow." He paused. "Well, you saw it," he said. "Took it right off. That's why I tell you kids to keep your arms inside the car." He emphasized the point with a quick nod of his head.

And that was the last time Dad talked about the one-armed man. Many years later I heard the real story. Mom said he lost his arm in a machinery accident and until that day, she had never seen him without his prosthetic. She guessed Dad was just trying to make a point and had used the perfect prop to do it. Regardless, the lesson stuck. Some of us forgot meeting the one-armed man, but the moral of his story itched in our memories like a chigger bite. Any time one of the little kids tried to stick an arm out the window, someone would snatch him up with the compelling question, "Do you want to lose an arm?"

23

OVER THE HILL TO CHERRYVILLE

(Just for the record, it's CherryVALE, but that wouldn't rhyme.)

Told by — Madeline

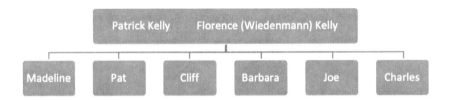

By 1952, Dale and Barbara had owned the farm for roughly two years, though they still hadn't moved in. They were comfortable living on main street in Parsons and in no hurry to make a change. The remodeling work on their country house was moving along as funds allowed. On a personal level, they seemed fine.

At the same time, the Korean War, originally supported by over 80% of the American public, had fallen out of favor. It was creating enormous debt and costing more lives than anyone thought possible. After China intervened, and captured the South Korean capital of Seoul, it spawned a massive change in public opinion.

Dale, along with 49% of the US population, believed it was possible the Korean conflict might lead to WWIII. And why wouldn't he believe it? In only a 40-year span, our planet had experienced the devastation of two world wars. He reasoned it was no time to be making big decisions and began dragging his feet about moving to the country.

HAROLD EUGENE (HAL) – FEB 1952
Number Six
Mike – 9   Carol – 6   Linda – 5   Kelly – 3   Stan – 2

Barbara was fine with the delay. She had just delivered her sixth baby and needed time to adjust. She enjoyed neighbors and the conveniences of town life. She also liked the house. It had more than enough room to support her growing family. What could go wrong? Enter Dale's ego.

It turned out that Dale had negotiated a month-to-month arrangement with the landlord. They agreed on the rent and how many days' notice required before moving out. A handshake sealed the deal.

Everything was fine until the landlord informed Dale the rent was going up in thirty days. Dale was livid. Even though the farmhouse remodel was only months from completion, and he could easily afford the increase, Dale threatened to move if the landlord stuck to his demand. It was the principle of the thing. The landlord refused. Dale gave notice then and there that they would be moving.

He promptly found a small house in Cherryvale, Kansas and told Barbara to pack up. She was shocked. Al and I were visiting the weekend before they moved and Barbara was already packing. I let her know what I thought of the whole thing. "It's crazy," I said. "You'll be there less than three months. And why did he pick Cherryvale? Why not find a place here in Parsons?"

"I don't know," Barbara answered. "He's stubborn. You know that, Madeline."

"But this makes no sense," I said. "Why don't you stand up to him?"

"And say what?" Barbara asked. "I don't have a choice. Besides, he wants me to get back into the church and I'm not going to mess that up. I need to get these kids baptized."

"Why did he agree to that?" I asked.

Barbara continued to wrap dishes in old newspapers and place them in cardboard boxes. "It was his idea," she said. "He wants the kids to go to the Catholic school. The nuns are as strict as he is. It's one of the reasons he picked Parsons in the first place. St. Patrick's goes from first grade through high school."

"At least he has that much sense," I had to admit.

Our conversation highlighted a curious chapter in Barbara's past. One of the biggest shocks I ever experienced was when she dropped out of the church to marry Dale. She had always been a good Catholic, believed in everything about it. Why would she fall away? Since it was such a personal issue, I never brought it up and neither did she.

I think I figured it out though. Dale and Barbara were married by a Justice of the Peace and not a Priest. In 1940, by the standards of the Catholic church, there would have been no question Barbara was living in sin—a mortal sin. The rule was clear, canon 108.1 states that marriage between a Catholic and an unbaptized person is invalid. To the best of my knowledge, Dale had never been baptized. She could not take communion under those circumstances.

⁓

Cherryvale, Kansas was roughly a 25-minute drive from Parsons. By the time Dale signed a month-to-month rental agreement for a tiny house on 2nd St., its population had been in decline since 1920. For all its ordinariness, Cherryvale was a town with a checkered past.

In October of 1870, two members of the Bender family and four additional 'spiritualist' families settled on land just seven miles from Cherryvale. John Bender Sr. and John Jr. registered one hundred sixty acres of land near the Great Osage Trail, which, at the time, was the only open road for travelers moving further west. The two Johns built a cabin, barn, corral, dug a well and then sent for Elvira Bender and her daughter Kate. Once they arrived, a wagon cover was used to divide the house into two equal sections. The family lived in the back half, while the front portion was turned into a general store.

Though they bore the same last name, there is ample doubt whether the Benders were a family at all. John Sr. was sixty years old and spoke little English. His addle-brained son, John Jr. (he laughed for no particular reason at all) was twenty-five, passably handsome with a mustache and auburn hair. Elvira, fifty-five, spoke broken English and was generally considered a hateful shrew. She was also suspected of murdering several husbands. The star of this freak show was Kate. Eye-catching and cultured, Kate insisted she was a healer and psychic and distributed flyers proclaiming her many powers. Her advertised seances acted as an enticement for bringing in potential customers…or should I say…victims.

The body of a man named Jones was discovered in nearby Drum Creek in May 1871—his skull crushed and his throat cut. Over the next two years the area became a black hole of missing persons. Vigilance committees were formed to root out the killers. Their good intentions became its own scourge. Innocent people were arrested and eventually released. Honest, hardworking men who came under suspicion were run out of the county.

Eventually, the Osage community, including the Benders, became the prime target. During a township meeting attended by John Sr. and Jr., the community agreed they would secure a search warrant to inspect every homestead in the area—the Bender property included. Before the end of the next week, the Benders had disappeared. A search of their property turned up nine bodies in addition to the three already discovered. It was generally believed the body count was likely much higher.

Those gathered for the search milled about, angry and lustful for retribution. Their wrath poured onto a poor man named Brockman, known to be a friend of the Benders. First, they hung him until he blacked out. They doused him with water, questioned him, and then hung him again. Kicking, and professing his innocence, Brockman was pulled down and interrogated a second time. The unsatisfied mob then hung him once more for good measure. After he was brought to from the third hanging, they questioned him a final time, but he still had nothing to tell them. He was finally turned loose.

The Bloody Benders were never found.

On a more pleasant note, Cherryvale was also the home of Vivian Vance, Lucille Ball's sidekick, Ethel Mertz, on the long running "I Love Lucy" series.

Cherryvale also produced Frank Bellamy who, at sixteen, wrote the "Pledge of Allegiance".

~

The house in Cherryvale was little more than a small box of a place. It had three tiny bedrooms and one bath. The boys slept in one of those rooms, the girls in another and Dale and Barbara, along with Hal's baby bed, in the third. The tiny kitchen made Barbara's life more difficult, as meals for eight people were prepared with less than a few feet of counter space.

I felt guilty over complaining so much about Barbara's circumstances. I was angry with Dale and felt sorry for her and the kids. What I had to admit however, was that they never seemed to care one way or another about it. It was just life moving along. Barbara knew it was temporary and the kids were too young to give it much notice. Each new house was an adventure, and as long as they were with their mother, life was good. They loved saying, "Over the Hill to Cherryville," and never missed an opportunity to chant it while crossing the overpass on the way into town.

Barbara was as happy as I had ever seen her. She would soon be reunited with her church, and all six kids were about to be baptized at the same time. Father O'Flynn, the parish priest at St. Francis Xavier Catholic church in Cherryvale, began making the arrangements. In the process, he spent considerable time with the family, and he and Dale formed a close bond—as close as Dale was capable.

Early discussions centered around the possibility that Dale might join the church, along with the rest of the family. He even went so far as taking instructions for becoming a Catholic. Barbara was thrilled and believed it would happen. Then, up jumped Virgie. She was a staunch fundamentalist Christian, though she likely had no idea what that meant. What she *did* know was that her son could never become a Catholic. Barbara told me Virgie had been depressed to find out he married one. On this occasion, she wrote him letters and said it would kill her if he decided to go through with a conversion. He abandoned the idea completely.

Al and I were thrilled when Barbara asked us to be godparents to all six kids. At the same time, she told us she was pregnant again. *Why not?* I thought.

The baptism was scheduled for Sunday, April 19, 1953. Al and I reached Cherryvale two hours early. The day was sunny and cool. The kids were dressed as fancy as we had ever seen them. They buzzed with excitement and seemed very proud of their fine appearances.

We piled into our car and Al drove us to the church. Barbara carried Hal, now a one-year-old, while the rest of the family followed behind her in single file like a row of ducks. Father O'Flynn met us at the front doors of the church and led us to a baptismal font. He lined the children up in order of age. He said a few words over the group and then blessed them one at a time. After each blessing, Al and I promised to help the parents attend to the child's spiritual needs.

Dale stood in the background, quiet and solemn.

Dwight Eisenhower was elected President of the United States in November, 1952. A cornerstone of the Republican party platform was a pledge to end the Korean War. America had had its fill of death and dying. Now, with a retired five-star general leading the nation, there was consensus he would keep his promise. As a counterbalance to Eisenhower's aims, the Communist leader, Joseph Stalin, wanted the war to continue. To the relief of peace warriors, Stalin died in March of 1953.

The war threat averted; Dale decided it was time to move to the farm. They only needed to wait until the kids were out of school for summer.

24

NEVER CROSS MOM

Told by Kelly #4

	Dale	Barbara		
Mike	Carol	Linda	Kelly	Stan	Hal

I had just turned five in March of 1953. Dad and Mom were waiting for the school year to end in Cherryvale before moving to the farm in Parsons.

On a bright spring day in April, Mom was washing clothes under an open-faced lean-to in the backyard. I had probably watched the same scene many times before, but until that day it was only a recollection in my child memory—that time before memories become permanent. It was around then that my lifelong recall began to kick in and everything was new again.

I watched her bent over a soap and water filled white porcelain tub, raking dirty clothes over a wooden scrub board. She did this two or three times, pressing the garments into the sudsy water and then back to the slotted plank. Next, she ran the clothes through a wringer, poised on a pivot between the soapy mixture and a tub of clear water. After rinsing and one more pass through the wringer, they were dropped into a wicker basket and then hung on a clothes line three tracks deep.

Whatever fascination the activity inspired, it lasted for only one cycle and I was off to the front yard to watch cars go by. I liked to wave at the drivers and see if I could get them to wave back. After a few minutes into my routine, I saw a black man walking down the sidewalk on the opposite side of the street. His squared off shoulders and straight-backed stride spoke of a man with dignity and self-respect. Of course, my five-year-old mind was incapable of drawing those inferences. It was only in reflection I appreciated the implied qualities of that man.

When he reached a spot directly across from me, I began waving, and in the most welcoming voice I could muster, called out, "Hi, Ni—er."

He did a double take, but ignored me, even as his gait appeared to slow and falter slightly. My mind registered the shift. He stopped, turned in my direction and asked, "Is your father home?"

As if a button had been pushed, a sense of doom settled over me like an early morning fog, thick and damp. I knew I was in trouble. I knew it, and I had no idea why. He wanted to tell on me. But what had I done? My mind gave up trying to figure it out. It was time to focus on discouraging this man's interest. "He's at work," I answered back.

"How about your mother?" he asked.

And now self-preservation kicked in and I lied. "She works too," I said.

He paused and then turned back to his original direction. His gait became confident again and I stupidly believed I had won the day. I watched him for a few seconds more and then hurried to the backyard. I wanted to be as far away from the perceived danger as possible.

Mom had finished hanging out the laundry and was nowhere in sight. That somehow gave me comfort. If she were in the house, I felt safer.

A few minutes later, I heard voices. They were coming from the side of the house. The encounter in the front yard had already left my mind, so I felt no sense of alarm. And then I saw Mom, followed close behind by the man on the sidewalk. She was carrying a switch cut from a nearby budding bush, it was green and flexible. I only glanced at the man as my attention was fixed on how angry Mom appeared. I had never seen her look that way. Her face was red and her body stiff with resolve. She moved directly toward me with giant strides, quick and unwavering.

By the time she grabbed my left arm I was already crying. Even that failed to temper her aggression as she began to rain down carefully aimed swats. I was wearing shorts so the sting of each wallop felt crisp and cutting.

"Don't you *ever* use that word again," she yelled as her switch chased me around in circles. "Now apologize to this man for calling him that."

And then I knew. But where had I heard that word in the first place? I don't remember Dad ever using it, though I'm guessing he had. It probably came from Uncle Al. As much as I loved him, later in life I was embarrassed and ashamed of his racist attitudes.

Mom gave me time to collect myself, though I was still sucking quick gulps of air while saying, "I-I-I'm sorry."

"You're sorry, *what*?" Mom demanded.

"I'm sorry, Sir," I said. He had a stunned look on his face. Maybe he expected a less vicious response from Mom. He nodded his head. "Thank you for that," he said.

I was sent to bed. The boy's room was at the back of the house with a clear view of the yard. I cried and watched Mom talking with the gentleman I had offended. They stood near one another, Mom shaking her head and I'm sure apologizing profusely for my behavior. She took his hand in hers and patted it with her free hand. And now, as if stinging welts on the back of my legs weren't enough, I felt terrible for causing her so much pain. Mom's profound shame branded me with the certainty I had done a wicked thing.

Looking back, I'm surprised I didn't get a second whipping from Dad once he was told about it. I may not have remembered him using the word, but his lack of action proved he had. I think it came down to this: How could he whip me for saying something that came through him?

Soon after that day, Mom must have told Dad and Uncle Al she never wanted to hear that word used around her kids again. As far as I know, Dad obeyed her without exception. Surprisingly, Uncle Al did too. I'm guessing she threatened to keep the kids away from him if it ever happened again. Uncle Al would never let that happen. He loved the kids, and I think it would have killed him to be without us.

That said, he continued to harbor his prejudices in some dark corner of a misguided mind. He waited until we grew up before letting his racism reemerge. Our feelings about him became disturbing contradictions. We loved him because he was an integral part of our lives. And we despised his ignorance about people different from himself. On some level, he was a living lesson of what not to become.

I often think about the man I maligned that day. I wish I could apologize to him now. I wish I could ask his forgiveness as an adult instead of the little kid motivated by pain to say words lacking heart or soul.

Mom would have wanted that too.

PART IV

THE FARM YEARS

The "gentleman farmer" knows
He's an approximation of the real thing.
He plays the field a true farmer has married.

25

THE GENTLEMAN FARMER

Told by Madeline

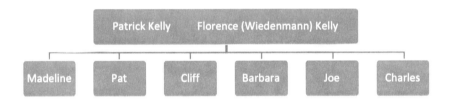

The farmhouse remodel was completed in the spring of 1953. Within weeks, the school year ended in Cherryvale and Mike, Carol and Linda were out for the summer. The move back to Parsons took place in late May. Over a long weekend, Al and I, along with their good friends Bob and Evelyn, helped Barbara and Dale finish the move.

Barbara and I set off to deliver the first load of clothes, kitchen wares and any food supplies we could save from the house in Cherryvale. During the forty-minute drive, we talked of nothing important—our sister selves just happy being together. I enjoyed Barbara's company. She practiced a practical optimism that came across as genuine and sensible, and she delivered it with spirited kindness.

I had taken the three mile drive out of Parsons to the Wilson farm only once before. That's all it took to prepare for the oppressive odor of cow patties and bovine gas we were about to pass through. It was there, on Highway 59, about half way between the edge of town and the Union Gas turn off, that the Parsons stockyards spread out on both sides of the two-lane highway. The bare dirt pens teamed with cattle circling around long metal feed troughs, waiting for their next meal.

Beyond the stench of those cattle laden lots, the land became a mixture of pastures, green with springtime, or tilled and ready for planting. Just past a huge propane tank and small white building, we left the concrete highway and turned down a mud-colored gravel road. The rocks came alive with a crunching chorus of skids and tire raised dust. We traveled one mile before turning north. The Wilson farm, in the shape of a rectangle with the narrower end facing the road, sat at the bottom of 'Siefert's hill and about three quarters of a mile from the turn.

We made a right, onto a pea-graveled entrance that marked the beginning of a circle driveway. Actually, it was more in the shape of an "A" with blooming Spiraea bushes marking its contours. We pulled to a stop where the recently remodeled two story, white frame house with red trim was to our right. Further up the drive, a two-car garage, probably the sturdiest building on the place, sat about 20 feet from the rounded tip of the "A" in the driveway. The bottom half was built of cinder block, while white-painted wood siding enclosed the second level. Its gambrel roof was trimmed in red to match the house.

As much as I disliked the idea of them moving to the country, I felt a sense of peace when we entered that driveway. Thick-trunked Oaks, arching Elms and shimmering Maples, mingled overhead to form a light-diffusing canopy. The shaded air felt cool on my bare arms. A windbreak of five massive cedar trees stood to our left, just north of the drive—guardians against the biting winds of winter.

Barbara parked and we exited the car in unison. I moved around to her side while checking out the surroundings. I pointed to a long, grey building with a flat roof. It sat twenty yards north of the garage.

"What's that used for?" I asked.

"It's a chicken house," Barbara answered.

"Are you going to raise chickens?

"Of course," Barbara said. "What's a farm without chickens?"

"How about all those buildings behind the garage? What are you going to do with those?" I asked.

"It's called a barnyard, Madeline. Dale wants to buy sheep and maybe a calf we can butcher later. Eventually we'll get a milk cow."

"A milk cow," I said, "who's going to milk the cow, and where?"

"We'll wait for a couple of years until Mike is old enough to help me. And the milk shed is right there," she said, pointing to a small building inside a fenced lot. "It has a concrete floor and built-in stanchions."

"I don't even want to know what that means," I said.

She pulled me forward a few steps and pointed to two train railcars sitting parallel to one another, about twenty feet apart. They were perched on four-foot high concrete slabs under each end.

"Those will be used to store hay or feed," she said. "At least that's Dale's plan. And we can stack hay over the garage too."

I considered asking about some of the other buildings, but I was sure Barbara had caught on that my interest was fading. I looked beyond the barnyard and found something I really *did* care about. Out in the distance, across the barnyard's bare earth and eccentric collection of buildings, was an apple orchard bursting with new life.

"Oh, Barbara," I said, "just look at that orchard. Have you ever seen so many white blossoms? Let's get closer."

I wanted Barbara to take a break from the stress of moving. She was five months along and already wearing her familiar pregnant clothes. She preferred skirts with cut outs of stretchable elastic, capable of expanding with the growing baby. The hems had risen over time from just above her ankles with Mike, to now about mid-calf. Smock tops, full and expandable by pleats, hung to just below her hips.

 She hesitated, looked back to the jam-packed car, then to me again. She smiled. We locked arms and walked past the two-story garage, through a small gate and into the barnyard. On the opposite side stood two giant Oak trees, their branches creating an arc over a gated entrance to the orchard.

As we walked between the Oaks, our senses came alive with sight, smell and taste. Apple trees, the most I had ever seen in one spot, were lined up like soldiers in formation and their lines stretched away until an end was out of view. Barbara and I smiled at one another as the army of trees fluttered to the stirring of a light breeze. If heaven has a fragrance, that orchard, on that day, was it. The scent tickled my nose; intoxicating and sweet. In fact, it was so potent I could taste it and that made me smile.

"How many trees are in here," I asked.

"I've never counted them," Barbara answered, "maybe sixty. The rows go clear down to the pasture."

We continued walking until I paused in what seemed the middle of the orchard.

"What's that scent?" I wondered aloud.

"It smells like incense," Barbara answered. "I think it's coming from that plum tree over there." She was pointing to a squat tree with deep purple blooms.

Barbara walked to a fallen apple tree and sat down on its trunk. It occurred to me that she was a perfect subject for the backdrop of white and purple blossoms that seemed everywhere around us. Her thick black hair was cut neck length and full. It framed a naturally pretty face with no need of artificial decoration. In contrast, my beauty routine consisted of creams and hair curlers before bed, and at least twenty minutes to prepare my face for the public in the morning, Barbara's amounted to a dab of lipstick and a quick brush of her hair. It seemed unfair.

I joined her on the prone tree trunk and asked, "Do you think you'll be happy here?"

"I think so," Barbara answered. "It should be a great place to raise the kids."

"Will this be your last baby?" I asked. I knew the answer, but wanted to see if anything had changed.

"We'll see," she said.

"Does Dale want more?" I pressed.

"We don't really talk about a number," she said, "and now that I've rejoined the church, it's up to God, isn't it?"

I could have argued that point, but what good would it do? If she was happy, I would be happy for her. I still doubted Dale was really on board. I say that, knowing I had little evidence either way and aware that my skepticism came from the knowledge of our shared history. Maybe he was just giving Barbara what she wanted because he loved her. That's what I hoped.

"Are you actually going to farm this place?" I asked.

"Dale says we are," she answered. "He's going to plant wheat in those twenty acres north of the house, oats in the next field over and maybe milo in the section behind the orchard."

"Are you going to raise any animals?"

"He's going to buy some sheep," Barbara said.

"Does he know anything about raising sheep?"

"Not that I'm aware of," she admitted. "But it can't be tougher than raising six or seven kids and we get that done." She rose up and offered me a hand, "Now, let's get back to work. We still have boxes to unload."

Sheep, I thought, *why sheep?* This was cattle and farming country. It made no sense. It was only later I learned that Dale had studied the issue. He knew that wool prices reached an all-time high in 1950 before fading late in the year. It was predicted that the trend would reverse itself and prices would turn up again. He intended to take advantage of it.

Dale was better informed than I thought. He was planning. The farm would make money through crops and wool production. But he would have to wait until Mike was old enough to help Barbara, and that was a couple of years off.

We strolled toward the house, in no hurry to leave the orchard.

∼

Barbara and I each picked up a box and walked to the mud porch. The much-delayed new addition was attached to the back of the house in a lean-to fashion that spanned the width of the original building. Though architecturally uninspired, it served its purpose. Two thirds of the space was the mud porch—the rest a combination laundry and bathroom. We carried our boxes through a screen door opening, over a plum-colored concrete floor, through the original back door and into a cramped dining area. Barbara's Formica kitchen table, white with stainless steel legs, was already in place. She had positioned two, six-foot long wooden benches lengthwise on either side. That's where the kids would sit. At each end of the table were wooden chairs with arm rests. The ruler's chair, Dale's in this case, sat on the far end of the long table beneath an exhaust fan. He would be isolated from the work that would eventually bring that table to life.

Boxes were placed in whatever room-name was written on the outside. The kitchen was my responsibility, I suppose because I was tall enough to reach the top shelves of her few cabinets. I surveyed the room's layout along the walls: A refrigerator, shallow work surface with cabinets above and below, door to the new bathroom, kitchen-sink built into a metal cabinet, a hot water tank, small stove, opening to Barbara's bedroom, a narrow stairway entrance leading to the second floor and a floor-to-ceiling cabinet. And that was it. All of it crowded into a ten by twelve-foot room.

I took in a deep breath and began my work, all the while wondering how nine people were going to fit into that small house. They bought the farm before even Hal was conceived, and now an additional baby was on the way. Where would she put all those kids? How would she prepare meals for so many people out of such a small kitchen?

∼

We underestimated Barbara once again. The move complete, she organized her limited space with quiet authority. The original parlor became her and Dale's bedroom. It had an entrance to the kitchen and another to the living room through a set of double doors. Hal's baby bed was placed along the wall adjoining the kitchen. A second baby bed occupied the wall opposite the living room. It would be put into service as soon as the new baby graduated from the rocker cradle that Barbara kept close to her bed for the first few months.

The only stairway was just wide enough for one adult to climb to the second floor. Wooden steps travelled up the dark passage and ended in a room not much bigger than a clothes closet. From wall to wall, there was barely enough space for the bunkbeds Barbara bought for Kelly and Stan. Kelly took the top bunk and Stan the bottom. It stayed that way until the day they left the farm.

Between the top of the stairs and the bunkbeds, there was just enough space to turn left and take three steps to the half bath and closet, or right to the girl's room. Calling it a closet stretches the concept to its limits. The space was little more than a cubby hole on the right side of the bathroom. You had to duck your head to move inside it. Between the stairwell and bathroom wall was a space exactly the size of a double bed.

The wooden door to the girls' bedroom was always closed, never locked. Initially, Carol and Linda shared a double bed, a small closet and a chest of drawers. During our weekend visits, that's where Al and I slept.

A second door in the girls' room led to Mike's bedroom. Even when fifteen people lived in that house, he had a room to himself until leaving for college. Al and I always said Dale had two children, Mike and Carol, while Barbara had thirteen.

Farm life was the beginning of both want and plenty for the Wilson kids. Everything was new and all around them a playground of discovery opened up. They inspected big targets first; the old chicken house, the two-car garage with a giant overhead hay loft, rail cars sitting on concrete slabs, a milk barn with curious contraptions made of wood and leather straps, the tree-studded apple orchard brimming with white blossoms, tilled land, and greening hay meadows. The only adult commandment they were given: "Do not go past the hedge rows. That's where our land ends."

A reliable rhythm developed once the family settled. Dale left for work on Monday morning before 5:00 a.m. and returned home on either Friday evening or Saturday around noon. In his absence, great joy animated the house and freedom reigned as the kids gained confidence by doing. When he returned on weekends, the house grew quiet with unquestioned obedience.

Dale kept his end of the bargain and bought Barbara a washer and dryer. Her life became a fraction easier. Next, he bought a self-propelled lawn mower from Sears. He taught Mike how to use it on their patchwork quilt of a yard. I felt sorry for Mike. He looked so small guiding that gold colored beast from one section of yard to another. He had to mow in the front and back of the house, on the west side that was long and wide, the Park 'A', in front of the tall cedar trees to the north and between the chicken house and garage. It was a lot for a young kid.

In late summer of that year, Barbara was ready to deliver her seventh child.

MARY MADELINE – AUGUST 1953
Number Seven

Mike – 9   Carol – 8   Linda – 6   Kelly – 5   Stan – 3   Hal – 2

Mary was the first baby born during the farm years. As usual, Al brought me to Parsons to stay with Dale and the kids while Barbara was in the hospital. I planned to spend a few extra days after she came home. I told Al I would call him when I was ready. They named the baby Mary Madeline. I think the name was meant to encourage me.

I was happy for Barbara and jealous at the same time. Each birth was a poignant reminder that I would never have a child of my own, and here she was delivering number seven. No doubt, I loved being an aunt to her kids, but it's like being a bridesmaid. It's just not the same.

Barbara called that Sunday morning to tell me it was time. We rushed around and made it to Parsons by late afternoon. I needed to be there so Dale could go to work the following day. I knew the kids would be starting school within a week. That meant I would have to make sure they had their school supplies, clothes and whatever else was needed to get them ready. I guessed Barbara had thought of all those things and was one step ahead of me. She tended to be prepared in the most unassuming way—it was uncanny. I would be staying in Barbara and Dale's room after that first night, so I left my bag there. I noticed Barbara had packed Dale's suitcase for the work week. His ironed dress shirts were hung in the closet next to the suit he would take with him. *Jesus*, I thought, *she must have done that as she was leaving to deliver.*

I told Mike, Carol and Linda to keep track of Kelly, Stan and Hal, shooed them out the back door and locked it behind them. It was time to walk through the house and make mental notes of what had to be done.

I started in the breakfast/dining room: *Clean after every meal. Wash and wax the linoleum floor at least once.*

Living room: *Deep vacuum. The room's long and narrow so that won't take long. Jesus, I can't believe the only phone they have is that wooden box on the wall. Look at that hand crank. Who still cranks their phone to get the operator? Oh, well.* I continued moving straight ahead and stopped in front of the free-standing gas stove. *I can't believe this one stove heats the whole house. That's not looking for some kid to get burnt this winter, is it?*

Maybe I should check on the kids? It can wait.

I noted that all the windows in the living room, including the six-paneled French doors going to Barbara's bedroom, would have to be washed. *That'll be a job*, I thought. Otherwise, their bedroom would be easy to clean.

On to the kitchen. I walked in hesitantly and thought: *Well, this is going to be constant cleaning. Three meals a day, maybe a snack in the afternoon…maybe not.* I sighed and went into the new bath and laundry room…more mental notes: *Toilet to the right…clean every day. Narrow closet, floor to ceiling; linens on top, everybody's dirty laundry in the cabinet below. Oh, my Lord! It's full—this will never end. Bathtub—everybody takes a bath Saturday after chores and dishes are done—water comes from a cistern so have to conserve it—clean on Monday. Straight ahead, a single sink—clean daily. Washer and Dryer—both full. Wall to the left, a door to the mud porch with the new baby's green bassinet in front of it—clean before Barbara gets home. I'm exhausted just thinking about it. I'm not even going upstairs.*

I went to the back door and hollered at the kids. Carol came out of the chicken house and called back.

"Do you know where all the kids are?" I yelled. She shook her head yes and pointed into the building behind her. That was good enough for me. Carol was imaginative and would keep them occupied with some new game or project. I went back into the house and began getting supper ready. Standing at the sink peeling potatoes, I thought about Barbara's life.

I can't imagine how she does it. After I'm gone and the kids are back in school, even though she just had a baby, every morning she'll have to get everyone up and dressed for school and then make breakfast and while they eat, she'll assemble sack lunches, back the old Packard out the garage, pray all four tires are intact, load up three school age kids, three young ones and a newborn baby and drive them three miles to St. Pat's, she'll get home and clean up the breakfast dishes, do laundry and get ready to make lunch after nursing the baby and changing her, Lord knows how many times, and after laying the baby down for a nap there's the never-ending job of washing cloth diapers that have to be pampered like a new baby to prevent diaper rash, followed by making lunch, putting the kids down for a nap, cleaning up the kitchen, cleaning a room or two between nursing and cuddling the baby, doing more laundry, ironing Dale's underwear, shirts, hankies and whatever else she's done to spoil him, and then she'll wake the napping kids, load them into the car for a trip back to St. Pat's to pick up the school children, drive home, fix the kids a snack, begin to prepare dinner—always a big meal of meat, potatoes and a vegetable, milk and Manor bread—clean up the kitchen, nurse and cuddle the baby, do some laundry, help the kids with homework, and do another load of laundry. She'll get the kitchen cleaned up, do some laundry and help the kids with homework. Lucky for her everyone does as they're told. Soon, she'll have more help and she's going to need it. Maybe this will be the last one.

Wonder where the kids are?

∼

Barbara came home after a week in the hospital. It must have felt like forever to the kids. I know it did to me. The house vibrated with excitement. Barbara worked her way into the living room with twelve little feet tracking her every step. She carried Mary over her left shoulder wrapped in a pink blanket. After sitting down in her rocker, she placed Mary lengthwise between her locked legs. The kids lined up in age order and stepped forward one by one to inspect the new baby. Some just looked; others touched her cheek or tried to rub her head.

"You have to be careful when you touch there," Barbara cautioned. "There's a soft spot right here in the middle of her head that still needs time to close up."

That's all it took to arouse even more curiosity, and it was exactly what Barbara intended. The kids lined up a second time and, in their turn, touched the soft spot ever so gently. Some of them jerked their hand away as if encountering hot coals. Others just smiled at Barbara while exploring the mysterious spot.

"What does she do?" three-year-old Stan asked.

Barbara chuckled and said, "Nothing yet, but she'll be playing with the rest of you in no time."

That fact set the other kids free. They all peeled away and headed outside, except for Linda. She lingered close to Barbara and the baby.

I stayed in Parsons long enough to get the kids started in school. It was September 8, 1953 and Mike, Carol and Linda were beginning their first year at St. Patrick's Catholic school. I packed their sack lunches, checked to see that they had their school supplies and told them to get to the car.

After one last check on Barbara and making sure there was a full pot of fresh coffee, I started for the back door. Mike met me there with the bad news; "The car has a flat tire," he said. "What do you want me to do?"

I pushed him outside to keep Barbara from hearing us. "What do you normally do?" I asked. "This can't be the first time you've had a flat tire."

"Mom calls the filling station," Mike answered. "They send a guy out."

"Stay here," I said, and walked to the wooden box of a phone hanging on the living room wall. I plucked the receiver from its cradle on the left, gave a couple of turns to the crank on the right and waited until I heard, "Operator."

"Would you connect me to the nearest filling station on the south side of Parsons off of 59 highway?" I asked.

She did and I told them my situation. They said someone would be right out. I left to be with the school kids in the garage.

The flat was on the back-right tire. All I could do was shake my head. *Why am I surprised?* I thought. *Why is Barbara driving this beat up '48 Packard? Those tires look as smooth as a baby's butt.*

Well, the young man from the filling station finally arrived. He wore jeans and a white t-shirt—a pack of cigarettes rolled up in his sleeve. His wavy hair was parted on the left side and he looked more like a teen idol than tire changer. Nonetheless, he patched the inner tube and remounted the tire. He charged $1.50 for his trouble.

After driving the kids to school, I escorted Mike, Carol and Linda to the principal's office and explained their tardiness.

With that, I had had it. I called Al and told him to come get me as soon as he could. All I could think was, *poor Barbara. How does she do it? Seven kids—it's just too many.*

26

LUCKY

Told by Carol

		Dale	Barbara			
Mike	Carol	Linda	Kelly	Stan	Hal	Mary

She came to us on a Saturday evening in early spring, 1954. Most of us were outside playing. Little did we know that an ordinary day was about to become *the* day.

I remember standing near the propane tank when I heard our driveway's familiar crunch. I looked toward the front gate. A pickup truck, pulling a two-horse trailer, eased through the entrance and stopped on the right side of the turnaround. His red trailer with white trim grazed the Spirea bushes as he moved forward. Dad appeared out of nowhere. That was odd since he typically avoided visitors. He directed the driver to a spot between the tip of the turnaround and the garage. Mike, Kelly and Stan joined me near the trailer. Linda led three-year-old Hal from the house to stand next to us. And then, strangely, Mom came out carrying the baby. The moment felt ripe with intrigue.

Dad engaged the driver. They shook hands and began speaking. The visitor looked to be in his thirties—thin and hard muscled, with a ruggedly handsome face. I imagined he was a real cowboy. His wide-brimmed hat was curved up on the edges and was surely as familiar to him as his name. I also noticed his cowboy boots were stained with horse sweat on the inner sides. They were wrinkled from the instep to the toe box; worn ragged by a rancher's life.

He opened a hatch at the front of the trailer and pulled out a new leather bridle. It had small silver medallions on either side of the brow band. He turned our way, smiled and raised his arms out wide, herding us to one side of the trailer. With the bridle draped over his shoulder and a short rope in his hand, he opened both back doors and disappeared through the right side. We heard heavy pounding against wooden floor planks. The trailer shuddered slightly. I held my breath. And then, in what seemed like slow motion, the most beautiful white pony on earth was backed out of that trailer and into our lives. It was magical.

The cowboy latched his lead rope onto her halter and began walking her around in wide circles.

"She needs to get her legs under her," he allowed. And then, after a few turns, he walked her in our direction and stopped just a few feet in front of Mike. "You look like the oldest here," he said. "Step up and pet her. She won't bite."

Mike did as he was told, his eyes as wide as saucers. I was next. I touched her pinkish nose. It was the softest thing I had ever felt; like a baby's skin with fine whiskers. She snorted and I jumped back. Everyone giggled. After spending time stroking her neck, I stepped away so the other kids could take their turns.

"What's her name?" I asked.

"Well," said the cowboy, "before we get to that, let me tell you a little about this old girl. This here is what's called a Welch pony. She's a riding type. She's around 13 hands tall but they can be taller. They're known for their athletic ability, and she'll take you as far as you want to go. On top of that, she's older than 4, so she's considered a mare."

"What's her name," I asked again.

"We call her Lucky," he answered, "but you can name her anything you like."

"Lucky," I said, "that's a good name. Can we call her that, Dad?"

"Sure," he said, "that'll do."

"Well, that's settled," the cowboy said, "now I'm going to teach you how to put a bridle on her and then we'll get to the saddle." He spent a few minutes showing us the art of sliding the bit into Lucky's mouth, pulling the headpiece over her ears, adjusting the chin strap and then buckling the throat lash. It was more for Dad's sake than the kids, but we felt important over it.

With that, he handed Dad the lead rope, walked to the bed of his pickup and pulled out a beautiful leather saddle. He held it down in front of us and named some of the parts. "This is the horn," he explained, "and here's the seat, these are the stirrups, this is the front cinch and here is the flank cinch." In his other hand, he held what looked like an oversized towel. "Now here's the saddle blanket," he went on. "You place it on her back first. Be sure to get it over her withers. Ok, now watch me saddle her up."

It all seemed pretty straight forward until he got to the front cinch. It was made of woven mohair, gathered in strands and attached to leather straps on both sides of the saddle. He positioned it right behind her front legs and began to pull it tight through a D ring with a clamp stop. "Come here and put your fingers between the cinch and Lucky's chest." Mike moved forward and did what he was told. "Does that seem tight enough to you," the cowboy asked.

"Yeah," Mike answered. "I can't get my fingers in there."

And then he asked Dad to test it out. Dad inserted a couple of fingers and nodded his head yes.

"Ok, now notice this," our instructor said. "Do you see her chest moving at all? No! it's not. She's a smart old girl. She'll wait until you cinch her up, then let her air out and it won't be so tight. You have to wait till she's breathing…then tighten it up again."

When finished, he asked who was going to ride her first. Dad pointed to Mike. He got on and the cowboy led Lucky around in wide circles. After a couple more kids took their turns, the young man said, "Ok, I think you've got the hang of it. I need to be movin' on." He gathered up his things, spoke with Dad for a minute or two, climbed into the pickup and was off again. And there we stood, in amazement and in love with our first horse.

Considering that cautious beginning, I doubt anyone could have imagined we would turn out to be exceptional riders. In fact, riding horses became second nature to us, and we were so good at it that a saddle was just a prop in our world. We rode bareback most of the time. We were even known to mount horses and guide them using only baling twine.

Lucky was an unimagined dream. She represented permanence, a connection to the farm that made it our own. Most of all, she was a message, living proof of how Dad really felt. What he failed to say in words, her presence shouted out with clarity—I love you.

27

YOU'RE GETTING BUMPED

Told by Linda

		Dale		Barbara		
Mike	Carol	Linda	Kelly	Stan	Hal	Mary

Average Prices in 1954

Average cost of a new house:	$10,250.00
Average Income:	$ 3,960.00
Average cost of a new car:	$ 1,700.00
Milk:	$ .92 gal
Gas:	$ .21 gal
Bread:	$ .17 loaf
Postage Stamp:	$ .03
T-Bone Steak:	$ .95 lb.
Kenmore Washer:	$154.95
24" Television Set:	$250.00
Dow Jones:	381.17

Bob and Evelyn Lett were Mom and Dad's best friends. On a summer day in 1954, two of the Lett kids and five of us Wilsons spent the afternoon spraying each other with the water hose in their back yard. After drying off and playing tag for a few minutes, Peggy, their oldest, said she wanted to show us something. We followed her through the back door, into the kitchen and on to the living room. She stopped in front of a mahogany cabinet. The line of kids bunched up behind her. The cabinet stood four feet tall and was maybe two feet wide. There was a ten-by-ten-inch glass surface in the upper right corner, about the size of a picture frame

Peggy pointed to it, "It's a TV," she said.

"What's a TV?" one of the kids asked.

"I'll show you," she said, as she reached for one of four knobs on the front panel. "Watch the screen."

Something behind the glass crackled to life.

Heads tilted one way and then another as we considered their new-fangled contraption.

You could barely make out human figures moving around behind the snow-covered picture. Their voices hissed and sputtered at us. "What are they doing?" I asked.

"I don't know," Peggy answered. "You have to watch from the beginning. And this channel isn't clear."

"What's a channel," someone asked.

Peggy took hold of a knob and looked back at us as she turned it. "You see these numbers? Each one of them is a different place where you can watch something. See, if I turn the knob to number 6, it's something else."

"It's more snow," I said.

"Well, nothing is on here right now," Peggy allowed. "And some channels are clearer than others."

We had to admit it was pretty amazing—strangers doing things in some other place while we watched and listened to them. And it was happening right there in Bob and Evelyn's living room. The group huddled in front of the TV for a few minutes longer. Each of us jockeyed for the front row and then fell back as another pushed forward. The whole thing would have held our attention longer if the picture and sound had been clearer. As it was, in those few minutes, part of our future had been foretold—we just didn't know it. Our interest lasted a few minutes longer before we concluded it was just a radio with a static filled picture.

In 1945 there were roughly 10,000 TVs in the entire country. By 1950, the figure had soared to around 3.8 million sets. Though still considered a luxury in 1954, over 26 million units had been purchased. No other home technology, not the telephone or indoor plumbing, had ever spread so rapidly.

Our first television was delivered in the fall of 1954.

According to Mom, Dad had a habit of laboring over expensive purchases. He spent time researching his options and typically brooded about it for weeks, sometimes months, before finally making a decision. In the case of our television, after weeks of deliberation, he chose a 24" Sylvania Halolight. The name referred to a lighted boarder around the screen.

The manufacturer's claims were questionable and compelling at the same time. They were designed to speak to the public's basic distrust of anything new, and television was surely that. The Halolight supposedly made viewing more enjoyable and protected children from going blind by watching too much television. There was no proof that either thing was true. Regardless, every Sylvania salesman had heard of the unfortunate Wisconsin family whose children had gone completely blind from watching TV.

The first program I remember watching was a ballet performance from New York city. Mom had taken us roller skating earlier that day—either to keep us out of the house while the TV was delivered, or because they wanted to surprise us when we returned home. I'm guessing it was just to keep us from getting in the way. Regardless, the prancing people fascinated and disappointed in equal measure.

Television eased into our lives gently, as nearly every new technology does. Whatever suspicion it caused lasted only a few weeks. Soon, no one could remember what sat in place of the glass screened, brown box in our living room. We tuned in to its offerings willingly, our capacity to resist dulled by the power of curiosity. What started out as intriguing turned into fixation.

27 YOU'RE GETTING BUMPED

In the beginning, Mom rationed TV for all of us. I think she instinctively knew there was a downside. She complained about our "wasting" time watching TV, and regularly chased us outside to "do something".

"But we can't find anything to do," we'd whine.

"*Can't* never got anything done," she'd counter, and that was the end of it.

I doubt she worried about any long-term consequences. She was concerned with *now*. Why would it occur to her that the Anderson family of "Father Knows Best", might become the impossible standard by which all families were measured? How could she know that television programming might shape our thoughts, and that the advertising that came with it would turn desires into needs? How could she know that television was just a vast experiment? It happened because it *could* happen, and there was money to be made.

There were four networks at the time, ABC, CBS, NBC and DMN; the forgotten network. In the beginning, DuMont Television Network rivaled NBC and CBS for the top spot in commercial broadcasting. DMN gave us Jackie Gleason and Father Fulton J. Sheen.

MIKE # 1

Up on the Roof
(And I don't mean the Drifter's song)

We generally watched just two stations. Tuning in to the third or fourth meant someone had to go up on the roof and adjust the antenna. That duty fell to me. It always revolved around a program Dad wanted to watch. Since it took a little forward planning, and of course the alteration had to be reversed, he kept antenna fine-tuning to a minimum. Each time, without fail, he lectured us about how dangerous it was to climb up on the roof. And with the same regularity, he gave strict orders that we were not to attempt it unless he were there. That seemed illogical to me, as if I could only fall from the roof in his absence.

The procedure was always the same, Dad stationed Linda at the living room door and Carol in the front yard with a clear view of me on the roof. He delivered orders to Linda; she passed them to Carol, who forwarded them to me. It was nerve wracking trying to keep my balance, knowing Dad was so easy to frustrate. Linda made sure to express his orders precisely the way he gave them. If he barked, "Tell him to stop moving it unless I say so," Linda barked it at Carol and she barked it at me. And on it went until I heard Carol scream, "Stop! Don't do anything else."

After six months of that insanity, Dad bought a remote system that turned the antenna automatically from a control box he kept near his chair. And that was the end of my roof climbing, antenna adjusting, Carol screaming "Stop!" days.

Dad may have had many reasons to buy the television. No one knows for sure why he bought it at that particular time. He traveled all week and must have stayed in motels that had television. He might have become accustomed to watching certain shows and wanted to see them from home also. For myself, I believe it was all about *The Gillette Cavalcade of Sports*. He never, and I do mean *never*, missed the Friday night fights when he was home. Some of the greatest fighters of his day – including the likes of Rocky Marciano, Sugar Ray Robinson, Archie Moore and Rocky Graziano appeared on the broadcast.

In addition, Gillette owned the sponsorship rights to the World Series, the All-Star Game, the Cotton Bowl Classic and the Orange Bowl, not to mention major horse races like the Kentucky Derby. There may have been other reasons he bought the TV, but if I had to bet, I'd put my money on baseball and the fights.

∽

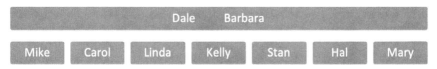

Speaking of Boxing
(And I don't mean on television)

It's impossible to guess what Dad was thinking, or trying to accomplish, when he came home one weekend with two pairs of boxing gloves. It eventually became clear what he expected, and Kelly and I were his experiment.

A weekend ritual began that day. Dad picked one of us to manage and Mike took the other. The middle of the living room, lined with furniture, became the boxing ring. Mom's rocking chair sat diagonally across the room from Dad's recliner so each became our respective corners. They slipped the gloves over our hands and tied the lacings around our arms.

Dad said we would have two-minute rounds with thirty second breaks. In the beginning, it was unclear how a winner would be decided. In the end, a bloody nose, or any blood at all, determined the outcome. I remember being ambivalent about the whole thing. Was I supposed to actually try to hurt my brother? Did he want to hurt me? Feelings require experience, they demand some point of reference, so what was I supposed to feel about *this* moment?

We began in our own corners with Dad or Mike whispering instructions into our ears we would never use. They made us touch gloves, just like real boxers, and the fight began in earnest. We circled one another, threw a punch here and there, mixed it up in flurries, but generally withheld any real aggression. The round ended after two minutes and we went back to stand next to our respective managers. I wish I could remember even a single thing either Mike or Dad said to me during those breaks. If they tried to give me a strategy, they failed miserably. All I knew was that I would rather be someplace else.

I'm sure Kelly was going through the same thing. We were being forced to do something neither of us wanted to do. Absent any personal ambition, our motivation, the only goal that made sense in our predicament, was a desire to please Dad. I remember he seemed happy during those battles. And while that may seem like a small thing, making Dad smile, causing him even a second of joy, was rare. I'll bet every one of my brothers or sisters can remember the first time they made him smile or laugh. And I'll bet more than once would be stretching it.

What I know for sure is that he enjoyed the bouts and whoever he managed won. It was always his fighter who initiated a shower of punches and Mike's who defended. Eventually, the kid who threw and landed the most blows, was likely to have his glove raised up in victory.

The Saturday afternoon fights stopped when the boxing gloves suddenly disappeared. Dad took it better than I expected. Maybe he knew it was nearly impossible to misplace something like that. They had to be missing on purpose. On some level, I think he was relieved about it. I found out later that Kelly had burned the gloves with some ordinary trash. I know it was true because a month later, I saw remnants of them while cleaning out the incinerator.

I wish I could say I put those boxing lessons to good use. I wish I could say they helped me in another part of my life. A story like that should have some profound impact. To be fair, maybe they taught me something I've simply failed to recognize. But in my heart, I believe they were just live shows leading nowhere.

Back to Linda

A pestering problem developed around the television each evening. Our living room was very small and the only seating was Mom's rocker, Dad's recliner (not an option) or the couch. With so few possibilities, some of the kids were forced to watch TV from the floor. To avoid that discomfort, arguments broke out when kids tried to protect their spaces on the couch. If they had to go to the bathroom, they placed someone younger in their spot until they returned. "Don't let anyone take my place," was the typical order.

Of course, little kids are useless to defend against older, bigger siblings and physical removal was common. The original owner would return, demand the seat back, and the battle was on. Invariably, the interloper would protest, "Mom, they can't save places." And the aggrieved party would counter, "Mom, it was my seat first. I had (name a kid) save it for me." "Mom, he's hurting my arm." "Mom, you need to stop him."

It's funny how life changes in an instant—how it can pivot on the utterance of just a few words. And that's what happened to us on an evening while watching TV. One of the seating arguments broke out and the kids were imploring Mom to get involved. She came in from the kitchen and stood at one end of the living room. This petite, thirty-three-year-old, dark-haired mother of seven kids with an eighth on the way, was about to issue a proclamation Solomon might have envied.

"Pay attention," she said. "From now on, if you are older than someone sitting in a seat you want, you give them the thumb and say, 'You're getting bumped'. And that's the end of it. The younger one moves and there will be no arguments."

"But that's unfair," someone said. "Why do they get to boss us around just because they're older?"

Mom took her time with the explanation. "It's not just because they're older," she said. "First, you should respect someone older than yourself. Plus, the older kids do all the work for the rest of you. The boys do chores morning and night. The girls help prepare meals, do the dishes and clean the house. They all help to look after the younger ones, and you'll do the same thing when it's your turn."

"What if the next baby is the last one?" I asked. "That one won't get to boss anyone around."

She patted her swollen belly and said, "I don't think that's going to be a problem."

From that day forward, there were only a few fights over seating. It typically started with, "Mom, do I have to?" or, "Mom, I was here first." But she stuck to the plan and merely said, "He/she is older. Get up." That's all it took and soon the rule was universally accepted and the fights ended. There were a few exceptions, like when an older kid would give the thumb and say, "You're getting bumped." The younger kid dutifully moved over, only to have the older one follow along and bump them again. That lasted exactly one evening. All Mom had to say was, "Do that one more time and you lose your privilege." Case closed.

Then, there was the time Pat was on the toilet and Ginger walked into the bathroom and said, "Up, Pat. You're getting bumped." Pat hollered, "Mom, she can't do that, can she?" Mom clarified the rule and from that time forward, the "bump system" as we all called it, was an unalterable fixture in our lives. The fights stopped.

In an odd twist, when the little kids visited friends, they just assumed everyone practiced the "bump" system. While attempting to use their seniority over younger kids in other families, they were met with disbelief and fierce resistance. The rest of the world failed to get the word.

Madeline – Barbara's Sister

I was called back into service just after Christmas when Barbara went to the hospital to deliver baby number eight. I was exhausted from the holidays, but it would have been rich to complain considering the circumstances. Thankfully, I had become a passable substitute after seven previous week-long visits.

VIRGINIA ANN (Ginger) - 1955
Number Eight

Mike – 12   Carol – 9   Linda – 8   Kelly – 6   Stan – 5
Hal – 3   Mary – 2

The first couple of days were always the same—the kids shadowed me and were on their best behavior. If the weather allowed, I chased them outside and set about deep-cleaning Barbara's house. I put Mike and Carol in charge, though I knew they lost track of some of the kids almost immediately. Had I imagined the kind of trouble they were capable of getting into, I would have locked all of them in the bathroom. As it was, Ginger was born in January and the weather was brutally cold, which meant the kids stayed indoors. I used it to my advantage and put each of the older ones to work. My popularity plummeted after that.

If I heard it once, it must have been asked 1,000 times, "When is Mom coming home?" The kids were homesick to see Barbara. I understood, but you had to be a certain age to enter the maternity ward. In desperation, I contacted the nun in charge at St. Mary's and asked if there were some way for them to see their mother.

She suggested we take the kids to the lawn in back of the hospital. Once assembled, the staff would bring Barbara to a window to wave hello. All went as planned. I lined them up, oldest to youngest, with Mike and Carol holding Hal and Mary. Within a few seconds, Barbara appeared in a window on the third floor.

"Wave," I said. "There's your mother."

We could see the nuns standing behind Barbara, smiling and waving along with her. The kids hesitated until they were convinced it was really her. They waved tentatively at first, and then the little ones began to cry. Soon, the tears started falling in earnest. Even some of the older ones became teary eyed.

The good nuns caught on to the drama and moved Barbara away from the window.

"Who wants ice cream?" I offered.

The older kids encouraged the younger ones to get on board and we were off to the car.

Well, that was a mistake, I thought. *At least I won't have to worry about it again. Surely this will be Barbara's last baby.*

28

THE TRUTH WAS FUNNY

Told by - One of Dale's Managers

Dale and Barbara Wilson. Dale and Barb. They were a curious pair. He was stern, understated and guarded, while she was one of the most approachable, accepting and generous individuals I ever met. They surely seemed a mismatch on the outside, but I wonder if one rounded the square corners of the other. Maybe what was soft in her tempered his hardness, while his certainty gave her courage. Maybe her goodness made up for his harsh punishments as his intensity countered her calm. Maybe fate demanded they find each other and create something greater than themselves. Or, maybe their relationship was just a harmony of coincidences.

Why it happened is a note. *That* it happened is a song.

I managed one of Dale's territories for Manor Baking Company. In that capacity, I saw him often. One of the routes I supervised included his family farm just north of Parsons, Kansas. As a result, I also got to know Barbara when I filled in for her route driver if he was sick or on vacation. I really enjoyed that stop. I liked talking with Barb—liked watching how she mothered those children. I always wondered how, in a house hungry for chaos, she contained it all with such patient dignity.

It seemed Barbara was pregnant every time I saw her. 'Seemed' hell, she was! That probably owed to my infrequent visits, but it became funny over time. In fact, some of the guys and I enjoyed inside jokes about Dale, "the boss", and his apparent sexual prowess. Of course, we were careful to keep it to ourselves. Dale was no one to trifle with, and all of us knew to avoid any risqué jokes. Now, that statement might make Dale sound somber and stiff, but he was far from either. In fact, he was one of the cleverest men I ever met, he just kept it to himself most of the time.

One morning around 6:00 a.m., just as the route drivers were beginning to disperse, one of them told me that Barb had gone to the hospital in the middle of the night to deliver her eighth baby. Parsons, Kansas had just one hospital, so I drove to Mercy, bounded up the steps, I think it was to the third floor, rushed to the nurse's desk and asked for Barbara Wilson's room. A white clad, all business type nurse directed me down the hall to the left. She told me to look for the fourth door on the right. I reached the room all out of breath from the stair climb. It caused the moment to feel ripe with urgency.

Barb was propped up on one elbow talking with Dale, who was sitting in a straight-backed chair next to the bed. I was struck by how typical she looked. Her nearly black hair was brushed out, full and curled like she always wore it. She rarely used much makeup so her oval face looked as natural as ever. And then she smiled—a kind, loving smile that felt like it was fashioned only for me.

In quick succession, I was thinking, *She has just had a baby* and in that same moment, Dale jumped to his feet.

"What's wrong?" he asked with alarm.

"Nothing's wrong," I answered in a halting cadence. "I just wanted to see Barb *once* when she wasn't pregnant."

Suddenly, I was unsure of what to expect. Had I misjudged the moment? Dale may have used his dry wit sparingly, but it was wielded with the precision of a sniper, and much to my relief, he chose to use it then.

With a wry smile he said, "You're too late".

29

LAND, KIDS, SHEEP, COWS AND HORSES

Told by Mike #1

Dad believed the farm could make money, if only he made the right decisions. Whether by dumb luck or solid reasoning, he was on target when it came to raising cash crops. The land was profitable every year. Living things were another matter.

He started with sheep, because at the time he bought them, wool prices were at an all-time high, which was great, but irrelevant. The wool from our herd (and I'm using the word liberally) of ten ewes and one ram barely covered the feed bill that first and only year. Negative earnings were bad enough, but their real crime was that the sheep considered our fences mere suggestions. I cringed every time the good nuns at St. Pat's announced, "Wilsons, you have to go home, the sheep are out." In spite of the fact that there is nothing cuter than a newborn lamb, there is nothing more damnable than its fence-busting mother. The sheep experiment ended almost as quickly as it began.

Next, Dad turned to cattle. After months of study, he settled on registered Herefords. They were the heart of his memories and fantasies. He remembered watching them graze on rolling hills of grass as he travelled by bus to see his mother. They were the stuff of cattle drives and cowboys. He was convinced buying Herefords was the right decision. They would make the farm profitable, while satisfying his childhood dreams.

One Saturday afternoon, Dad told me that on his way home from work, he had bought a few heifers from a local rancher. They would be delivered the following Wednesday. I missed school that afternoon and waited for the new arrivals. Mom told me to shut the gate to the orchard and put them in the barnyard. All was ready when two men in an oversized pickup, pulling a stock trailer, pulled into the driveway a little past noon. I had them back up to the wide, white gate that led to the barnyard.

The rancher was an easy going fellow. I liked him. He brought one of his sons to help unload the cows. He too was calm and purposeful. While the son prodded the cattle from the brown trailer, I listened to the rancher's take on Dad's visit.

THE RANCHER REMEMBERS

In the mid-1950s, our 400-acre ranch spread out just East of Parsons, Kansas. The land had been in our family for over 100 years and was primarily made up of cattle pastures. We also farmed a couple of hay fields and about 60 acres of tilled land used to grow feed stock for the winter. Our core business was buying and selling registered Herefords—'white face' is what some people called them. I never had to advertise my cattle because all the locals knew I'd put a price tag on pretty much anything that walked. The one exception were my kids, and I even considered selling a couple of them when they acted up. So, it was no surprise when one Saturday morning in spring, Mr. Wilson drove up the long, graveled driveway to my place and parked in the shade next to the propane tank.

I remember him for a couple of reasons—first, he didn't pretend to know anything about raising cattle, and second, even in his ignorance, he had a good idea of what a registered Hereford was worth. It was obvious he had done his research and I was sure he would walk away if the price was anything but dead center. He was a few inches shorter than me, 5'8", maybe 5'9" I'd guess, and strode out like he knew where he wanted to be. I noticed his suit fit perfectly—more a fixture on his thin frame than something just worn. He struck me as all business, though he was easy to like almost as soon as we shook hands.

He introduced himself as Dale Wilson, explained that he was on his way home from work, and said he was interested in buying a few young heifers. I told him I had a small group nearby and led him down a single path to a cross-fenced pasture where I kept the yearlings. He said little, while still coming across as completely engaged. I could tell he was immune to small talk, a guy who was used to quickly sifting through the BS to get to what mattered.

As he stood with a foot resting on the bottom rung of a pipe fence, a fickle breeze challenged his wavy hair.

"Do you have a family?" I asked.

"I have a wife and eight kids," Dale answered, while never diverting his eyes from the stares of curious heifers.

"Damn!" I said, "How many more are you planning on?"

"We named the last one caboose," he said. A restrained grin tugged at the corners of his mouth. He had a nice smile. I don't know why, but I guessed he used it sparingly. Maybe the pressure of raising eight kids would do that to a man.

I found out later he added five more cabooses to that train: Hard to imagine.

Back to Mike

I'm pretty sure the rancher thought I'd like the compliments he was passing out. And he was right. Kids rarely think of their parents that way—like other people. In an odd twist of remembering, parents are human only after *we* have lived long enough to become one of them.

It was near that same time Dad decided I was old enough to milk a cow. He bought a black and brown Guernsey the kids named Sally. She had an udder the size of a basketball. Her former owner taught me, Dad and Mom how to milk her, though we all knew pigs would fly before Dad would do any milking.

Speaking of pigs; he bought two of those also. The kids named them Bob and Evelyn after Mom and Dad's best friends. They lasted maybe six months before Bob became aggressive and within days, they were the stars of Sunday morning breakfasts and weekend dinners.

Now that we had cattle, Dad reasoned he needed a horse to move them around the property. Lucky wouldn't do—she was a kid's pony. He wanted something big and sturdy. It took a few weeks for him to make up his mind.

He settled on a full-bodied, grey gelding named Silver. A quarter horse breed, his hazy blue eyes made him appear blind and a little scary. After buying him a proper saddle and bridle, he took Silver on a few test rides. He was too docile for Dad's taste, but his gentle nature was just the peace of mind Dad needed to pass him down to Mike.

His next horse was exactly what he wanted. Thunder was a chestnut thoroughbred with an aristocratic bearing, intelligent eyes and spirited nature. He was fast and agile and Dad sat high in the saddle on his back. He rode him nearly every weekend, taking Mike on Silver, and Carol on Lucky, along for company.

The farm was taking shape—and then, a wrinkle.

The breeding Hereford bull Dad bought sported a set of impressive horns. The following year, the heifers began producing steer calves with nubs that would eventually develop into horns also. Dad began worrying over a kid being gored by one of them. The Herefords had to go. Dad was sometimes a walking contradiction, and no more so than when it came to the kid's safety. Remember, grownups had to hold my hand going up and down stairs until I was five. And now, at thirteen, I was milking cows, plowing, discing and harrowing sizeable fields, and caring for cows, horses, chickens and kids. Carol was in the mix and Kelly and Stan would be joining me soon. Considering all of that, in the name of caution, Dad was willing to sell off all the Herefords and begin buying Registered Black Angus. He was going to have cattle and Angus didn't grow horns.

Our pastures became dotted by black cows instead of red ones and we were back on course.

30

THANKSGIVING DAY

Told by Velva – Dale's Sister

Harold and I saw less of Barb and Dale once the family moved to Parsons, and I regretted it. They were a fun family to visit. The kids were clever and inquisitive and had begun to express their own ideas—at least in Dale's absence. By failing to listen to them, I thought he missed an important part of being a dad. I eventually realized Dale was interested in what a person had to say only after they reached a certain age or level of experience. Children were to be disciplined, taught their place in the world and never, ever allowed to question his authority. At the same time, he would kill to protect any one of his kids. I knew he worried about them, probably too much. He lived a contradiction he inherited from our dad, who learned it from his dad. Dale was just continuing the tradition.

The family's saving grace appeared to be Barb. She maintained order in a house designed to resist it. She did it with calm, kindness and compassion. She taught through example, while consistently helping each child express his/her unique character. She was the opposite of Dale in nearly every aspect of parenting. So, which one of them made all those kids so successful? It probably doesn't matter. When it comes time to cross a bridge, do you ask who built it?

Barb delivered babies like Dale delivered bread—dependably, and often. The time between learning of a new baby's arrival, and the announcement that the next one was on the way, began to feel like months rather than a year or two. While the rate appeared to quicken, in fact, Barb was fairly consistent. The gap between her babies averaged about nineteen months.

Our best opportunity to keep up with the family happened every year on Thanksgiving Day. I'm unsure how it happened, but our side of the family went to the Wilson's at Thanksgiving and Barb's relatives were there during Christmas. We were more than content with that arrangement as it saved us buying and hauling a car-load of presents to Parsons. We also knew Madeline and Al were closer to Barb's family, after all, sisters share a special bond. Beyond that, they were childless and treated the Wilsons as their own. I told Dale I was on to him. He raised so many kids because he never had to go anywhere—we all came to him. Even though I was kidding, I think I saw him grin.

Harold and I looked forward to Thanksgiving like no other holiday. It was the one opportunity for Nathan, Dale and I to be together. Nathan typically brought his second son, Doug. I brought pies and we always had candy for the kids. We were there for just one day, as Dale and Barb's farm house was much too small for overnight guests. Of course, that was just an excuse. We knew Madeline and Al spent many a weekend there.

The routine was always the same. Barb bought the biggest turkey she could find from a local farmer—typically, between 25 and 30 pounds. On Thanksgiving morning, she got up between 4:00 and 4:30 a.m. to stuff the bird and put it in the oven in time for its 2:00 p.m. unveiling. She prepared an assortment of vegetables, made her own cranberry sauce, baked homemade rolls, mashed a ten-pound sack of potatoes, cooked a delicious giblet gravy and served it all hot and on time. I was amazed she could prepare such a meal from that kitchen. The size of a small bedroom, it had maybe five feet of counter top.

Barbara was as busy as Dale was uninvolved. Little changed from year-to-year. He sat at the kitchen table, smoked his cigarettes and drank his coffee and chased the kids outdoors with a scowl and a toss of his head.

When it was too cold to be outside, the youngest were moved upstairs while the older ones sat in the living room and watched the Rose Bowl Parade. As soon as the women began setting the table, he moved to his recliner and watched part of a bowl game.

Back in the kitchen, Thanksgiving trappings were everywhere. The fragrance of a steaming turkey, bread crumb stuffing, hot yeast rolls and spice scented pumpkin pies drifted throughout the house on a wave of heated air. The entire day felt like the definition of family, and there was no other like Barb and Dale's. Once we gathered around the table, Barb always asked Nathan or Harold to say grace. I'm sure the kids noticed. They were used to the Catholic blessing before a meal—the sign of the cross and a standard prayer, followed by another sign of the cross. This day was different. Barb let Dale's family do it their way, and I loved her for it.

31

THE ASSEMBLY LINE CONTINUES

Told by Madeline

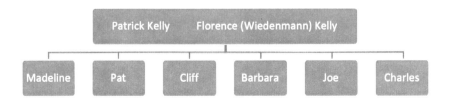

I swear, it seemed like no more than a heartbeat between Ginger's birth and Barb's announcement she was pregnant again. My conviction that Ginger would surely be her last baby turned out to be pure fantasy. I decided I might as well just keep a bag packed for the next inevitable trip to Parsons to fill in for Barbara.

PATRICK DELANEY (PAT) – 1956
Number Nine

Mike – 13   Carol – 11   Linda – 9   Kelly – 8   Stan – 6
Hal – 4   Mary – 3   Ginger – 1

Pat was born into a world still transitioning from WWII. Just two years before, England finally stopped rationing critical goods. In America, the middle class established a foothold and the economy was humming. Innovation, sparked by technological advancements, created new products at a dizzying rate. Americans were working and they wanted modern conveniences. Money in the hands of the masses was the key to prosperity.

We began trusting that the future would turn out like the present we were living. We could relax a little and there were clues Americans were letting their hair down. When Elvis Presley made his first appearance on The Ed Sullivan Show, Barbara told me Dale was at odds with himself over whether to let the kids watch. He finally decided it was okay, though he grumbled about the gyrating hips and hair tossing during the performance. Few of us realized the sea change that performance suggested was on the horizon.

Mike was milking Sally and doing all the farm chores himself. Early that summer, Kelly began helping with some of the lighter chores in the morning and evening. Stan followed close behind. Mike continued doing the heavy work on his own.

Sally had to be laid off for freshening at least once per year. Freshening is when a cow is allowed to dry up prior to calving. They bred Sally to a Hereford or Angus bull and the mixed breed calf was eventually used for butchering. During Sally's layoff, Barbara bought farmer's milk so she could continue using the cream on top for Dale's favorite hand churned butter. As soon as Kelly was able to milk, Dale bought a golden colored Jersey they named Tiny. Her addition allowed Sally and Tiny to trade off during freshening, and we always had a supply of milk.

Dale continued traveling from early Monday morning until late Friday night or mid-day on Saturday. That left Barbara to raise nine kids, including a new baby, pretty much on her own. She also had to pay all their bills with a meager allowance and manage a farm just for good measure. I honestly don't know how she did it. That said, what really amazed me is that she never complained.

I heard about cows getting out, pigs rooting under their fences and heading to the pond for a nice roll in the mud, clever hens hiding their nesting places from the kids and eventually strutting through the barnyard followed by a clutch of chicks, extracting a long-dead sheep–one limb at a time—that had wedged himself between hay bales, likely when a horse chased him into the barn, horses with colic, cows calving, "pulling" a colt stuck in his mother during birth, attending school events and of course, the inevitable cuts and scrapes that befall most young children. She told it all with good humor, and not once did I detect a hint of self-pity or implied regret. She lived her life joyfully, and it inspired me. Truth be told, all of that makes her sound much saintlier than she was, as the following story illustrates.

Told by Stan - #5

My First Day of School

I was excited about going to school until that first day. The older kids worked overtime trying to prepare me. They focused my attention on the new clothes Mom bought and how lucky I was to have my own Chief tablet. Linda laid out a box of Crayola crayons and my two yellow pencils. While helping me get dressed, they talked of what to expect from the nun teaching first grade. I listened skeptically. All I could think about was my upset stomach.

Mom was still driving us to school and picking us up at the end of the day. She treated me just like the other school kids. Our sack lunches were lined up on the kitchen counter like a column of soldiers. I was the last to grab mine. Mom pulled the old black Packard out of the garage and waited for the kids to load up. My walk in her direction felt like a trip to the firing squad.

Until that day, I doubt I had been away from Mom for more than a few hours—at least, not that I could remember. Even then, I was with my brothers and sisters so her absence felt unremarkable. Now, driving away from home on our way to school, I was being asked to leave the only security I knew and enter a world I could only imagine. And I was imagining the worst. I had heard stories about the nuns, and they were rarely flattering. My only exposure to them was at Sunday morning mass—eying them suspiciously as they sat side-by-side in the first two rows of pews.

Ours were the sisters of Saint Joseph who wore full length black and white habits. The kids willing to toy with eternal damnation, whispered that they looked like penguins. Topped by a veil over the bandeau, their faces were exposed from just above their eyebrows to below their chins. The guimpe, a stiff, white cardboard looking shield draped their shoulders and chest. Below it, a wooden cross hung from a chain around their necks. Their pleated, black tunics were tied at the waist by a woolen belt from which a rosary dangled over their hips.

I also remember that, other than the small window to their faces, only their hands enjoyed the light of day. It was traumatizing to see any other part of their bodies. Once, when my second-grade teacher raised her arm to write on the chalkboard, her sleeve collapsed and we could see a bare arm clear up to her shoulder. The room shivered. We never wanted to see it again.

Anyway, what with the dread of leaving Mom, the whole penguin heavy images racing through my head, the nun inspired fright that had me on edge, I decided to take a stand. There, in the Packard on the way to school for my first day, I announced, "I'm not going."

The other kids looked at me curiously, but I had the sense they had heard that line before. Just the same, most of them encouraged me as best they could. Mike called me a "big baby" and Mom drove on as if she hadn't heard a thing. As I think about it now, it must have been difficult for her to go through that same ordeal thirteen times. She had talked about how heartbreaking it was to force the first few kids away. She never said so, but I'm guessing when the middle group came along it felt more like a dreaded duty. And by the time she reached the last two, she probably wanted to drop kick them out of the house. I was number five— somewhere between heartbreak and duty.

There was a line of parking spaces in front of our blonde brick school building. Mom swung the car into an open slot and watched the kids clamor out. Linda took my hand and helped me arrange my sack lunch, Chief tablet, crayons and yellow pencils. Only steps away, I began crying, dropped my supplies, ran back to the car, opened the door and took a seat. I looked to Mom for guidance. She draped her arm over the seat back, looked me square in the eyes and told me I had to go. I crossed my arms and said, "I'm not going." She checked on three-month-old Pat lying on the front seat next to her.

In a flash, she disappeared from behind the wheel and in what felt like a second, I felt her grab my arm and pull me out of the car. Linda had picked up my supplies and lunch and was standing half way between us and the school building. I think the plan was to hand me off to Linda, but before Mom could make the exchange, the baby began crying and diverted her attention. In the confusion, I shook away and ran back to the car. This time, I grabbed hold of the curved, silver bumper. It, and I, were going nowhere.

Mom did the best she could to yank me away from my anchor. She tugged and I held tighter. She tried to pry my fingers away which caused me to gain greater control by wrapping my arms completely around the bumper. Pat was still crying and Mom, trapped between a lesson and her heart, gave up.

"Either you go to school or I'm going to spank you like never before when we get home," she warned.

"I'll take the spanking," I said.

She put me in the car, drove home and the second she parked, said, "Ok, let's go."

My plan suddenly felt flawed. I chewed over my feelings and decided, *well, at least it isn't Dad.* I enjoyed a split second of courage by convincing myself Mom's spankings were always pretty tame. As that miscalculation breezed through my head, I was turned over her knee and walloped by a barrage of hand swats. Now, if anyone thinks that kind of spanking is relatively harmless, they haven't been spanked by Mom on a mission. I would be going to school the next day and she was leaving no doubt.

The second day was like a script from the first. Each of the kids picked up a sack lunch and loaded up for the trip to St. Pat's. I was paid little attention, though I could feel the dread building up as we got closer to the school. This time, much to my surprise, a nun was standing on the sidewalk in front of an open parking space. Mom pulled in, told the other kids to get to class, hurried to my side of the car and plucked me from my seat. After a hesitation so slight a hummingbird would fail to notice, Sister, whatever her name was, took me by the back of the neck and marched me into the building. I can still feel that steely grip guiding me forward. And that was my first *real* day of school.

Back to Madeline

Dale continued to buy Black Angus cattle and eventually ended up with between ten and twelve cows, four heifers and a bull. Calves soon followed. To his surprise, though less slippery than the sheep, the cows also treated the Wilson fences as hints rather than barriers. Now, instead of opening the classroom door and announcing, "Wilsons, your mom's here, the sheep are out," the good nuns inserted "cows" and no one missed a beat.

The cattle roamed farther from home than the sheep. Though larger and easier to spot, they also covered more ground and did it faster. On one trip, they took a three-mile stroll into Parsons before Barbara knew they were out. After hours rounding them up on foot, Mike, Carol and the boys surveyed the fence line, found where they had escaped and spent the remaining daylight repairing it.

Both the interior and perimeter fences on that farm looked like a patchwork quilt of fixes.

Dad Was So Proud

Told by Carol - #2

Cows are interesting creatures. Even when their own pastures are lush with green grass, the other side of a fence is apparently more inviting. Given our experience, I began to think it was either the thrill of the escape that motivated them, or they just enjoyed driving us crazy. Either way, we went through a period when our cattle prompted so many calls from one particular neighbor, it lit up the switchboard down at Southwestern Bell. In the beginning, he was nice about it. Over time however, his patience wore thin and his calls became terse and unneighborly—who could blame him?

In this case, the cows were going through one of our interior pasture fences and into the wheat field. They would then cross the gravel road in front of our property and trample another fence to get to a neighbor's wheat field.

Why they considered his spring wheat growth better than ours is beyond me, but they did. It began to feel like they were just doing it to prove they could.

Dad protected his solitude like a lion guards its pride. He was fine with all the kids around, but the outside world was unwelcome. One of the ways he controlled his privacy was refusing to answer the phone. He ignored the most insistent ringing and waited for someone else to answer it. Unless it was work related, we knew to say he was gone. Then, one Friday evening while Mom was visiting a sick neighbor, the phone rang. Caught between his sense of duty, (what if it was about work?), and his obsessive reluctance to answer an unknown call, he caved in and picked up the receiver.

"Your cows are in my wheat field," the frustrated caller said.

"I'll take care of it," Dad promised.

The next day, after they did chores and finished breakfast, Dad rounded up Mike, Kelly and Stan to help him fix the fence. I volunteered to go with the boys, suggesting they needed all the hands they could get. To be fair, it was really because I preferred being outside over helping Mom and Linda clean house. Dad liked that I wanted to be with him and rarely worked me like he did the others. While ordering them to do whatever he needed next, he allowed me to pitch in as I saw fit.

Dad and Mike did most of the post hole digging. They used railroad ties for the corner posts, sunk them into the ground at least two feet and just for good measure, planted a second one a few paces from the first. The same pattern was used for both ends of the fifty-yard fence run we were creating. Between those braced anchors, they strung field fencing to t-posts spaced six feet apart. Over that, they attached two strands of barbed wire. To insure everything was taut, Dad mounted a cross-bar onto the three-point-hitch and stretched the wire with the tractor. It took all day and at the end of it, we were exhausted.

Dad had his first "coke" around 5:00 pm—his second, thirty minutes later. By 6:30, he had edged into his "happy" stage and that was exactly where we wanted him. It was in those moments he actually smiled and said a few nice things to us. We welcomed his drinking because it made him more engaging. After ordering us to load the tools into a wheelbarrow, he stood back and admired his work. The fence looked invincible.

"They won't be getting through there," Dad predicted. He tipped his coke toward the fence for emphasis. After a few more minutes of regarding our efforts, we headed to the house. Mom had cooked Dad's favorite meal of chicken and homemade noodles. We finished supper and then watched Bonanza. Most of us went to bed early, content to believe we had finally gotten the best of those pesky cows.

Dad typically slept in on Sunday mornings, while the rest of us went to 6:00 a.m. mass at St. Pat's. Instead, the next morning he was up at dawn and headed outside to check on the cows. Only a few feet beyond the back door, with a clear view across the road, he stopped dead in his tracks. There, in the neighbor's wheat field, were all of our cattle, including the milk cows, lying on a deep, green bed of wheat grass, chewing their cuds and looking altogether content.

We missed mass that Sunday.

Back to Madeline

Shortly after Pat was born, Dale bought a second farm. It was 120 acres roughly three miles West of the home property. Its christening took place at a breakfast one Sunday morning. While discussing what had to done with the new property, Linda asked, "Where's the other farm?" From that moment forward, Dad's addition had a name. Sixty percent of the other farm was tillable. Dale placed it on the Soil Bank, a program where the Federal Government pays a farmer a flat rate not to plant cash crops for five years. He had a neighboring farmer plant sweet clover, a perennial crop that adds nitrogen to the soil every year. The remaining forty percent of the property was pasture and a fine pond.

One thing was certain, Dale tended to get what he wanted. The farm was his idea—that's where they were living. He wanted sheep—they bought sheep. He wanted Herefords and then Black Angus—they bought both. He had always dreamed of having horses—they now owned three of them. He wanted the other farm—they bought that too. Around that same time, he also bought into three oil wells promoted by a friend of Velva and Harold's.

Al and I, along with my brother Joe and his wife Mary Lou, also became partners in the venture. We liked the idea of owning a small stake in J. Paul Getty's world, regardless of how brittle that notion might be. It was fun hearing the names of those wells: The Steiner, The Becher, and The Claussen. Shortly after signing the paperwork, we all travelled to western Kansas to inspect our investment.

It was a cloudy, damp day. Winter had claimed the landscape and everything around us was in some stage of decline. We drove down a gravel road, pulled into a turn-around and parked the cars in front of two silver holding tanks. A flat, handrailed bridge spanned the width of both tanks about two thirds up their height. We climbed metal stairs leading to the walkway. Off in the distance, steel horse heads nodded up and down in rhythmic cadence, each stroke depositing a bottom-hole-pump quantity of oil into the tanks in front of us.

There was a hatch built into the top of each tank. Dale leaned over, tripped the latch on one of the lids, tipped his head toward the opening and listened to the sound of fluid cascading into a body of liquid. Dale looked up and asked, "Do you know what that sound is?" He smiled his wry, devious smile and said, "It's the sound of money." We all laughed.

The Steiner, Becher, and Claussen were short lived. They were stripper wells and soon oil prices and our production had a race to ruin. Operating expenses began to exceed income and the General Partner decided it was time to give up. Our oil days were over as quickly as they began.

I was struck by the irony that Barbara constantly worried about finances while Dale invested in land, cattle, horses and oil wells. I asked her about it one day and this is what she said, "All of these kids are my dream, Madeline. He lets me live it every day. I won't take his away from him."

32

COUSIN MERLE

Told by Kelly #4

Dale	Barbara

| Mike | Carol | Linda | Kelly | Stan | Hal | Mary | Ginger | Pat |

The extended Wilson family history was as shrouded as the Kelly's was transparent. Dad's immediate relatives—his mom, sister and brother were fixtures in our lives. They and their families were synonymous with Thanksgiving Day. Mom mentioned he also had a few aunts, uncles and cousins who lived out in Colorado, but they were like ghosts to us—alleged, but unproven.

The veil lifted slightly one Saturday in June of 1959 when a gold-colored Cadillac coasted through our front entrance. Summer came early that year so the afternoon heat was building. Carol, Stan and I were in the back yard waiting to see what Dad wanted to do next. Unfamiliar cars were rare, so we stopped to watch it ease into the driveway. It came to a stop close to where we were standing. The motor went silent. A smiling woman, sitting shoulder to shoulder with the driver, offered a tiny wave. The middle-aged man to her left nodded his head at us, and then opened his door and scooted from under the steering wheel.

He bore an uncanny resemblance to Dad. At roughly 5'8" tall, he had a similar tanned complexion with a high forehead and lively, deep-set eyes.

"This is Dale Wilson's place, isn't it?" he called out.

Our heads bobbed up and down. Within seconds, Dad came from the house and walked right up to the man and shook his hand. After a short conversation, they both encouraged the woman to get out of the car. She did. Out in the open, she looked closer to a girl than a woman. She wore a white, sleeveless halter top tied at the neck. Her legs were bare to just above mid-thigh. The amount of visible skin was both interesting and a little unnerving. Her bleached blond hair was cut short, unlike the curls and waves most women preferred in those days.

Dad led the new arrivals toward the house. As they passed by, the woman stopped and said, "And who do we have here?"

Dad gave her our names.

"Well, I'm Adele and this is your Daddy's cousin Merle. We're heading to Colorado."

We were conditioned to silence around Dad, so no one spoke, which probably seemed odd to the young woman. Dad continued on toward the house. He told Stan and I to stay outside—no surprise there. Carol followed close behind the group as they disappeared through the back door.

They were gone for only minutes when Merle reappeared and made his way back to the car.

"How bout a little tour of the place," he suggested to no one in particular.

Stan and I followed him to the Cadillac's trunk. He popped the lid and then leaned down to pull aside what appeared to be a bed sheet. There, occupying the very center of his belongings, were two full cases of Coke—24 bottles each. We had only seen that kind of wooden container in the grocery store and had no idea people might actually buy so many at one time.

"I'd offer you one," Merle said, "but I put medicine in these."

Sure enough, each cap in the case bore a slight wrinkle across its top edge, indicating it had been opened. Most of them were empty. Merle snatched up one of the few full bottles, popped its top and took a long swig.

"Now, show me the place," he said.

We took him to the chicken house first, then to the barnyard where we explained how each building was used. Next, we guided him through the orchard and out to the pond and pasture. He looked around a lot, seeming to enjoy the tour. I noticed him keeping a close eye on the coke. I guessed he needed to know how much he had left. It was medicine after all.

Merle was content with silence, another trait similar to Dad. I might have left him to his quiet, except he was a relative none of us kids even knew existed until that day. I was determined to learn something about him.

"So, you're Dad's cousin," I confirmed as we walked along.

"Yes, I am," he answered.

I kicked up a little dust in front of me and said, "Well, we didn't know he even *had* cousins".

"He never said anything about his own family?" Merle asked.

"Not that I remember," I admitted.

"But you knew he had aunts and uncles, didn't you?"

"Guess we just never thought much about it," I answered.

"Well, it's not important," Merle said. He sounded almost disappointed, maybe a little hurt. I quickly changed the subject.

"Is that your wife," I asked, "the woman you drove in with?"

Merle looked at me and smiled, "Not yet," he said. "But she will be if I have anything to say about it."

"Why don't you just ask her," I suggested.

Merle chuckled. "It's not that easy, son," he said. "You can't make somebody want something just cause you do." We walked on a few paces more before he added: "Sometimes you're the kicker, and sometimes you're the can."

I kinda knew what he meant. And then I asked, "When will you know?"

"You ask a lot of questions, don't you," Merle said.

"I guess," I answered.

"But how else ya gonna know anything?" he said. And that was that. We took just a few minutes to check out the pond before Merle noticed his medicine was almost gone. He immediately turned and headed back to the house.

Once we got to the car, Merle opened his trunk again. He pulled the sheet aside, deposited his empty bottle back in its place and told us to go get Dad.

As soon as Dad got to the car, Merle showed him something hidden under a blanket. Dad chuckled and ran us off. That might work with city kids, but we were resourceful and were bound and determined to see what they were doing. Stan and I simply walked to the chicken house, found a pair of hard used binoculars, a good vantage point and watched from there.

First, one-by-one, Dad handed Merle unopened bottles. He carefully popped the cap and poured out about a fourth of the Coke. Next, he pulled a larger bottle from the trunk and unscrewed the lid.

"That must be the medicine," I whispered to Stan.

Merle then refilled the Coke bottle and capped it using some kind of tool to crimp the edges. This went on, bottle after bottle, until the job was done.

"Wonder what that medicine is?" I asked, while giving Stan a turn with the binoculars.

"I don't know," Stan said. "But he just gave Dad one of the bottles and he's drinking it. Do you think he's sick too?"

What seemed interesting in the beginning, had become strange.

"I want to see what kind of medicine that is," I said. "Give me those." And just then Merle set the bottle on top of the car.

"What does it say on the bottle?" Stan asked.

I focused the spy glasses and started snickering. "Jack Daniels," I answered.

33

THE CHICKENS CAME HOME TO ROOST

Told by Carol #2

	Dale	Barbara			
Mike	Carol	Linda	Kelly	Stan	Hal	Mary	Ginger	Pat

I remember how excited I was the day Mom took me to the feed store to buy some new chicks. She planned to sell eggs to make extra money and this clutch would be the beginning of her empire.

"You can't make any money selling eggs," Dad told her.

"*Can't* never got anything done," she said. It was her mantra; her guidance. And she repeated that statement many times during our lives.

We brought home around forty chicks. Not long after we moved to the farm, Dad let me convert the chicken house to a skating rink since it had a concrete floor. Now, with Mom's new chicken business hatching, it would serve its original purpose. Mike helped Mom build nesting boxes and scaffolding so the chickens could climb to their chosen spaces. He also reframed a couple of openings for them to move in and out of the hen house. Next, we added feed and water troughs and fashioned nests of hay in their boxes. Mom was ready.

All went according to plan. The chicks passed through an ugly molting stage and were within a month of laying their first eggs. I could tell Mom was getting excited. She made arrangements to sell the eggs and had begun collecting cartons to deliver them. Her talk of an egg business excited the kids. We would have to feed the chickens and collect their offerings every day. Next, the eggs would be washed and dried, placed in cartons and sold. No one gave a second thought to how sick we might become of all those duties. Plans are free of struggle.

Everything seemed in order when Dad unexpectedly decided we were going to take our first trip to Texas to see his mother, Virgie, and Mr. Snead. The timing was fine with Mom—we would be back before the egg harvest began. She arranged for neighbors to feed and do chores. They also had to take care of our three dogs, Monte Dick, a black and brown collie, Midge, a toy terrier, and a brown and white mutt who showed up a few weeks earlier. We were still debating on a name for him.

The trip was made possible because Dad had recently purchased a decent family car. The old black Packard was sold off—replaced by a used, 1947 Ford Woodie Station Wagon. It was green with gold wood panels. The kids were amazed by its three seats. The middle one was three quarters in length to allow for a step up to access the third level. It was a welcome improvement over the Packard and we loved it.

None of us had ever traveled far from home, so the prospect of a long trip to Texas sounded exciting. We left the farm around 7:00 p.m. one Saturday evening and drove all night. Dad figured it would be less stressful for everyone if the kids were asleep during most of the trip. As it turned out, sleep was our only option as Dad laid down the law early. No one was to make noise.

Mom was happy. She enjoyed whatever travel came her way. It was a break from the hectic pace of her daily life. Pat was in her arms with Mary and Ginger sitting between her and Dad. The rest of us were spread out between the shorter middle and full back seat. Oncoming headlights proved the rest of the world was moving along, while only whispers testified that anyone was in the car. Soon, even the whispers melted away.

The next morning, the kids and dawn awakened about the same time. The car wheels hummed over a long, steel girder bridge as Dad announced we were leaving Oklahoma and entering Texas. I could tell it spoke to him—a connection to a past only he could recall.

"Look," he said, "that's the Red River."

I thought it looked more orange than red.

We were somewhere near Wichita Falls, Texas when Mom reminded Dad she needed to go to mass with the older kids. He stopped at a diner and asked for directions to the local Catholic church. Mom told Mike, Linda and I to get ready for mass, while she changed Ginger and Pat's diapers. Dad stayed to watch Kelly, Stan, Hal and Mary. It was the first time I had known him to look after any of us on his own. The whole thing seemed strange.

The church goers returned and we were off again. Reserved for most of the trip, Dad became animated as we topped a hill leading to a sandy plane stretching out as far as we could see. The treeless, empty scene lay in deep contrast to the green, busy landscape we recently passed through. Sagebrush danced over its sunbaked surface in rolling skids and wind-driven hops. That's when Dad pointed to a small building at the bottom of the hill.

"Look," he said. "That's where they tie up their horses when they go into the store for supplies." He was excited to see it, though I had trouble imagining why. It was just a little building with a hitching post out front. Mom told me later why it mattered. "That's where the bus from Joplin stopped each summer," she said. "That's where Virgie and Sid waited to pick him up." I suppose the little building and the hitching rail signaled he had arrived home—a home he always wanted, but could never have.

Dad slowed the car as we passed his memories. He studied it and took in its special meaning while we idled on. Just past the store, we drove onto a landscape none of us had ever seen. *Where was its grass*, we wondered. *Where did the green things go*? We travelled a mile or two before Dad turned off on a sandy trail marked only by a couple of wooden entrance posts. Up ahead, a tiny box of a house, looking forlorn in its isolation, sat Virgie and Sid's home. As soon as we rolled to a stop, Virgie came out of the house with Sid trailing close behind.

The kid's pressed close to the Woody's windows as they considered the barren landscape and wondered what they would do on a canvas of sand? The answer came soon enough. Within hours, they were chasing skittering sagebrush, tracking down bright green lizards and doing their best to outrun the wind-swept sand.

But that would come later. For now, we climbed out of the car and clustered together to say hello to Virgie and Sid. Most of us had never seen our own grandmother. That first encounter felt foreign. Her steel gray hair was curled and stiff, a shield against the morning wind. She looked small, yet sturdy beneath her plain cotton dress and full pinafore apron. A high forehead caused her features to appear to crowd the lower part of her face. Nonetheless, I imagined she was very cute in her time. The cute had faded away, and now she just looked like a grandmother.

Sid, while making every effort to stand up straight, still slumped. If he were ever handsome, it was hidden beneath the folds and wrinkles of skin long tested by the Texas sun and wind. He removed a beaten-up straw hat to say hello. There, shielded by the hat's brim, were the last vestiges of his youth—a forehead of smooth, creamy white skin.

Mom stepped forward, holding Pat on her left shoulder. She gave Virgie her warmest hug, long and firm enough to prove she meant it. Virgie's response looked awkward. When it was Sid's turn, his effort was mechanical, though well meant. Dad followed close behind. He hugged Virgie and asked, "How are you, Mrs. Sneed?"

Mrs. Sneed? Had I heard that right? Why hadn't he called her "mother?" Was it just a mistake? The question hounded me until I realized he *never* called her mother. She was always, Mrs. Sneed. Taking Dad's lead, Virgie and Sid became Grandma and Grandpa Sneed to all of us.

As the adults exchanged small talk about the trip and how the kids had done, I trained my attention on the weathered, wood building in front of us. It had a lean-to porch across the front. Patches of white paint mingled unevenly over bare wood. The house looked out of place, like someone had set it there by mistake. The bobbing iron horse heads all around us were the only testament to why it existed in the first place. Someone had to keep those wells pumping.

Inside, the house was even smaller than the exterior forecast. Past the porch and through the front door, we stepped into a small room with a dining table and chairs at its center. The living room was to the right, the kitchen straight ahead, with a small bedroom to its right. And that was it. *Where's the bathroom?* I wondered, and as if on cue, Virgie guided us to the back door and pointed to the outhouse. If it had ever been painted, there was no sign of it. I wondered why they had carved a quarter moon silhouette into its door. *Aaahhh,* I thought, *ventilation.*

We planned to stay for three days and two nights. Everyone slept on the floor, including Mom and Dad. The little kids found that funny. But they did it, and no one was any worse for the wear, except Mike. He opted to sleep under the lean-to where it was cooler. The next morning, his entire back was covered in tiny balloon-like welts.

"Blister Beatles," Virgie said. "I have some cream for that. The bumps will go away in no time." And they did.

As hard as it was to imagine, considering no bathroom, no running water and a hundred other ways their life seemed primitive, I believe Virgie and Sid were happy there. I think they were proud the world had passed them by. In fact, I believe they wore their difficult life like a badge of honor. *They* felt sorry for *us*. At least Virgie did.

Virgie served us big breakfasts of eggs, bacon, ham, biscuits and red eye gravy. She made the kids peanut butter sandwiches for lunch and we had ham and beans for dinner the first day and fried chicken the next. Mom and the girls helped Virgie prepare the meals and clean up afterward. Meanwhile, Dad and the boys joined Sid, who continued to follow his daily maintenance routine. They tracked behind him as he shuffled to a coal black, one ton truck. The bed had been modified for oilfield maintenance—just a flat platform where things were easy to get at.

"You've had this truck since I was a little kid," Dad said. "How old is it?"

"Oh… I'm not really sure off hand," Sid answered. He moved some tools around and added grease to a grease gun. "I've had her as long as we've lived here. Still runs fine. Doesn't get used all that much." He paused. His voice changed tone and he said, "Reckon she won't be needed much longer. Electric is coming. Those engines don't need lookin' after like these do.

The kids just shrugged off the comment, but Dad knew what it meant. Sid would soon be out of a job.

"It's about time you retire anyway, isn't it?" Dad asked.

"I suppose it is," Sid allowed. He surveyed the deep horizon. "I suppose it is."

The boys helped Sid with his chores and afterward they all fished together until lunchtime. We had sandwiches and milk before the little ones were put down for their naps. While they slept, the women prepared dinner. Clearly, Mom and Virgie had little in common. Their conversations centered around cooking and how the kids were doing in school. I was struck by how carefully Mom avoided ever mentioning the name, St. Patrick's. Virgie was still knotted over the suggestion that Dad might join the Catholic church. She was invested in a hellfire and damnation kind of gospel. In her world, nearly anything could cause a trip to hell. One thing was sure however, Virgie knew Catholics would be on the welcoming committee.

After dinner, we gathered in the tiny living room. Most of the kids spilled out into the adjoining dining area. Sid turned on the television.

"Do you folks like to watch wrestling?" he asked. "It's what we like best."

Dad just nodded his head and waited for Sid to adjust the antenna.

"What's that thing?" Linda asked, pointing to a thin, multi-colored transparent sheet over the TV screen. The top fourth was a light shade of orange, and beneath it successive quarters of red, green and blue. Behind the shaded sheet, the wrestlers were an odd assortment of those colors.

"That's so you can watch it in color," Virgie announced. "We bought it from a young man who showed up at the door one day."

No one said a word, though even the young kids looked skeptical.

Just before sunset on the second evening, Dad decided we needed to go home a day early. Virgie and Sid offered only a slight objection. Dad packed the car and the kids in record time. He offered Virgie a weak hug, shook Sid's hand and we were off again. I leaned my head against the window and thought about how nice it would be to have a bathroom again.

33 THE CHICKENS CAME HOME TO ROOST

I'm sure Mom was thinking about her egg business while Dad drove all night and half of the next day. I noticed she sat up straighter as we neared our driveway. And then I heard her gasp and ask, "Oh, Daddy, what happened?"

Everyone in the back raised up high enough to see over the kid in front of them. The carnage was shocking.

"How could this have happened," Mom wondered out loud. She seemed disoriented.

The answer bolted in front of us in the form of a chicken being chased down by that brown and white stray dog we never named. He had systematically killed every chicken he could catch. As far as we could tell, the entire flock would be wiped out as soon as he finished off his final victim.

"This is what happens once they get a taste of blood," Dad said. "There will never be another chicken on the place as long as that dog's alive." We bounded out of the car. "Get the wheelbarrow," Dad ordered. "Pick up every one of them and throw them into the old well. Pour some lime powder on them."

Mom held the baby close as she headed for the house. She turned and took one last look at her dreams spread out on the ground like fallen leaves.

"I'll just have to come up with something else," she said.

While we kids tossed shattered carcasses into the wheelbarrow, Dad grabbed the offending dog, tossed him into the car and took off. He drove deeper into the country. A half hour or so later, he returned. No one ever saw the brown and white dog again.

I'm sure glad we never named him.

34

THEY KNEW HOW TO GET THINGS DONE

Told by a Farm Neighbor

I'll tell you what I thought of Dale and Barbara Wilson—I thought they raised a great group of kids. Maybe I should say, I admired the results. Their children were always respectful and hard working. They did their chores as most farm kids do. The older ones milked cows every morning and night. Twice a day in winter, they wrestled bales of hay from various storage sheds around the barnyard. Each bale weighed more than any of the younger ones. Before they were big enough to pick one up, they rolled them from one flat side to another until they reached metal or wooden hay stands. There, they broke the bales apart and heaved individual flakes into the racks. If they had been teenagers, my telling of the story would seem completely unremarkable, but these were little kids who went about their work with grown-up determination.

In winter, wielding a double-bladed ax, they broke ice whenever the pond froze over, and in those days, it could be from six to 10 inches thick. Each time the cows got out, (as a neighbor I can tell you—it was often) the kids had to find them first and then repair the fence they had trampled over to freedom. They collected eggs and fed the chickens. They had to feed and water all of the pinned-up animals, consisting of colts or calves being weaned from their mothers, or the current year's butcher bound steer.

Those kids were no doubt resourceful and creative. They worked hard, but they also knew how to have fun. More than once, I watched them corner a group of horses in the deepest part of the pasture. The boys would spread their arms wide, then bob and weave to cut off any escape routes. Convinced they were trapped, the horses settled and the boys walked calmly to their chosen ride, wrapped both arms around their necks and then mounted them without benefit of a saddle or bridle. The rest of the horses bolted for the barnyard—conditioned to receiving oats at the end of their flight. The brothers, riding comfortably astride free running mounts, caught up to the herd and were suddenly surrounded by their four-legged clan. Racing through the apple orchard, the horses galloped under low hanging branches, trying to scrape the riders from their backs. The boys countered by spreading out flat against the animal's withers and neck. It was a standoff the boys generally won.

Those kids were engaging, curious and sociable too. It's unlikely those traits came through their dad. He never pretended to be like us country folk, though deep down I think part of him wanted to be. He was known as a gentleman farmer. That's what we called a guy whose real business was somewhere other than the farm. I was told Dale was a sales manager for a bread company. That struck me as an unlikely job for someone like him. He was passably friendly for the first few minutes you met him, and then he became the mystery his reputation suggested. That said, I liked Dale, not near as much as I liked Barb, but he was a solid guy.

I've got to give Dale credit for one thing though, farmer or not, he had the good sense to buy the hottest selling tractor in U.S. history—an 8N Ford model. It was small, but durable and mechanically simple to keep running. He bought it because of the wide front-end wheel base, "…less chance of it tipping over," he said. The only real farming they did with that little tractor was preparing the fields for planting. Every year, just after the wheat harvest, those young boys and sometimes even one of the girls, used it to pull a two-bottom plow over a twenty-acre field of dirt and wheat straw. I should mention, more than once, Dale burned the wheat straw and part of the neighborhood, but that's another story.

It's likely Dale gave the kids a lesson or two on how to plow a field, but I doubt the instructions amounted to much. Regardless, for all their inexperience, those little guys and that gal knew how to get the job done. They always began from the south end of the field. To assure a straight line, they aimed their tractor for a specific tree in the hedge row bordering the property's north end. Their target sighted, first gear engaged, they eased off the clutch to set the tractor in motion. Momentum in their favor, they then dropped the three-point hitch to a preset position and the plow shares cut into the earth. They looked back only after reaching their target at the opposite end of the field. It must have been disheartening for a young kid to travel so far, finally turn around, and see just two narrow rows of upturned dirt, knowing there were twenty acres to go. And that was just in one field.

After plowing, the field was disced and harrowed before a nearby farmer named George Dhooghe planted the winter wheat. It was called "winter wheat" because it was sown in the fall and needed winter weather to mature. In early summer, George returned to the Wilson farm on his combine. Dale never missed a wheat harvest. I know, because I liked to stop by when George showed up—my way of cheering them on. Dale's excitement was obvious and I could tell it rubbed off on the kids. I doubt they really knew what animated their father at that moment. Whatever it was appeared to make him happy and that was enough for them to value the day.

Personally, I think he got some kind of powerful pleasure from watching the wheat kernels blow from the combine into the bed of a hauling truck. Once full, he'd drive to the grain elevator, where they weighed the vehicle full, then empty, and measured the wheat's moisture content. The outcome defined what their hard work was worth that year, expressed in bushels per acre and dollars per bushel.

My wife and I were used to the comings and goings in the Wilson's wheat field. Only a bar ditch and a weary barbed wire fence separated it from the gravel road we travelled each day. To the east were additional fields where the kids plowed, disced and harrowed out of sight—their presence revealed only by clouds of wind-swept dust chasing the little Ford tractor from one end of the field to the other. That's where they planted cash crops of soybeans, or winter feed reserves like oats or milo.

I doubt the kids drew any pleasure from working that land. To them it was just another chore. It was different for Dale. I think it satisfied something deep within him; put him in touch with his roots. In an unguarded moment, he once told me there was nothing more beautiful than a field ready for planting or primed for harvest. He said it wistfully, as if speaking from some distant version of himself.

35

MOM MADE IT WORK

Told by Mike #1

Dale	Barbara

| Mike | Carol | Linda | Kelly | Stan | Hal | Mary | Ginger | Pat |

After five years on the farm, life had become three parts monotonous and one part unpredictable. Each morning, Mom called up the stairwell at 5:30, "It's time to get up, kids. Kids, it's time to get up." Kelly and Stan were helping me with daily chores, so, in bed at the top of the staircase, they were the first to hear Mom's call and zombie down the narrow steps to the kitchen. On cold mornings, they hurried to stand in front of the large space heater in the living room—the only heat in the entire house.

After warming our gloves on top of the stove, we headed for the barnyard. The boys milked Sally and Tiny while I took care of haying the cows and horses and making sure they had water. We finished around 6:15 and returned to the house to change into our school clothes and eat breakfast. It was always the same—oatmeal, cinnamon toast and milk. Occasionally, on days the Manor Man delivered, Mom bought sweet rolls as a treat.

While the boys finished their breakfast, Mom and the older girls prepared sack lunches of peanut butter and jelly sandwiches, a small bag of chips, a piece of fruit and some type of dessert, often, a Moon Pie. It was around then I received a learner's permit. On days Mom could do without the Woody, I began to drive the kids to and from school. Year-after-year, as soon as I parked, more and more kids spilled out of the Woody's doors. It looked like a clown car at the circus.

St. Pat's was a traditional Catholic school. Most classes were taught by the sisters of St. Joseph who were strict, but well intentioned. Most of them, wrinkled with time and seasoned by battle, were proof that the Order had grown old. Those nuns, Sister Hilarian, Sister Justin, Sister Ester, Sister Martin and many others, were some of the last of their type. Their habits, both worn and practiced, were soon to be tossed away in the name of progress. Some person, or some committee decided that those traditions stood in the way of attracting more women to the "calling".

We were generally home by 4:00, and Kelly, Stan and I were back in the barnyard doing evening chores around 5:00 pm, often in the dark during winter months. It was pretty much the same routine as the morning. By the time we got back to the house, Mom had super on the table and we all sat down together to eat.

Our farm life was a bailing twine existence. Why, we could fix anything with that blonde colored cord. Something breaks—tie it back together with bailing twine. The gate post wire snaps—refasten it with twine. You need an instant bridle to ride a horse—make one out of twine. Your belt breaks, bailing twine will keep your pants up.

That's how our lives worked—patches instead of permanent fixes. In the process, we learned to manage circumstances, instead of being managed by them. We learned to improvise because there was no way to buy our way out of a dilemma.

I was never meant for farm life. I remember feeling jealous of the town kids and only learned later that they were jealous of us. I suppose hearing about riding horses and going on cattle drives would spark the imagination of any little kid. But the reality was different, the farm world, for all its fun and novelty, meant work and separation from the more common experiences of our town friends.

I think Mom understood that clash of cultures and did everything she could to bridge the gap. While I failed to appreciate it at the time, she consistently encouraged us to join in activities that brought us closer to other kids.

It is impossible to remember a single interest she refused to nourish. The girls were in Brownies and Girl Scouts, some of the boys in Boy Scouts. When I decided to try out for the high school football team, she bought me everything I needed, while knowing I was too small to tackle a gnat. She supported Carol when she tried out for Cheerleader and made Kelly a homemade pair of shorts to complete his basketball uniform. Unfortunately, she missed the mark on the St. Pat's green and her effort to make him look like the other kids, further emphasized the differences. Small compromises like that one, were a clear indication of how carefully she had to watch her spending.

STAN - # 5

I liked the farm and the freedom it brought. Even as little kids, once outside, it seemed we could do whatever we wanted. I actually thought Mom was unaware of where we were or what we were up to. I thought that right up to the moment my backside paid the price for finding out otherwise.

The proof came one Saturday morning when the milk cows, Tiny and Sally, disappeared. We found a gap in the fence where they likely pushed through, so we had a good idea of where they went. Mom sent Kelly and I to track them down. We headed to the neighbor's farm house and asked Mr. Siefert about the missing cows.

"Haven't seen 'em boys," Mr. Siefert said. "Maybe they headed down to the pasture beyond the creek bed."

Creek bed, I thought, *I didn't know they had a creek over here.*

That surprise won our attention. We were used to the creek across the road from our house. It was like a honey pot to a bear in our world. We fished there and built teepees and played hide-and-seek and pretended we were

Tarzan in an African forest. It was a place ready-made for a little kid's imagination. And here we were, finding out there was another creek unknown to us within walking distance of our house.

We fully intended to find the cows in the pasture Mr. Siefert pointed us to. We walked in that direction and probably would have made it, if not for the creek. It was clearly marked by a stand of tall trees on either side of the ravine and stretching in both directions as far as we could see. As we stepped into the shade, we saw that the creek bed had dried up. That was contrary to everything we knew about a creek, but it had a magic all its own.

There were boulders strewn about, many of them worn smooth by whatever water typically rushed down its gorge. Trees laid toppled over, either due to old age or the creek bank giving way in places. We began running through the creek bed where water was supposed to be, the contradiction adding to our excitement. On it went—running, climbing rocks, jumping tree trunks, shinnying up the banks and sliding back down them. It was unlikely Sally and Tiny decided to spend their day in a dry creek bed, but we pretended it was possible. We worked our way to a spot where the bed crossed under a narrow, concrete bridge.

Just then, Mom, in the green and brown Woody, sped past us.

"I wonder if she's looking for us?" I asked.

"We'd better head home," Kelly said.

We ran back through the dry bed to where we had started, clambered up the creek bank and worked our way through the trees and back into the open field. It was then we saw our undoing. Riding toward us like three of the Four Horsemen of the Apocalypse were Dad, Mike and Carol. They were led by Dad on a red horse, the Conqueror come to exact a toll. He was flanked on one side by Mike on a pale horse and on the other by Carol on a white one. It was epic.

As they galloped toward us, we held out some hope that their only reason for being there was to help us find the cows. That delusion faded quickly as Dad pulled Thunder to a full stop. After swinging his leg over the saddle, he hit the ground with a thud. Our fate was laid bare when he reached for his belt buckle and whipped the leather strap through its loops.

The spanking progressed as it typically did—Dad holding our right arm (he was left-handed) as he popped the half-folded belt against our backsides. We cried, more to stop his punishment than because it hurt. His penalty exacted, Dad climbed back onto Thunder and galloped away, Mike and Carol close behind.

So, Mom *did* know where we were. And apparently, she worried about us. I made a note of that.

Pat Kelly – Barbara's brother and war hero

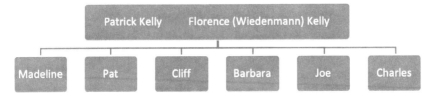

Barbara made things work on more levels than I could count. Number one was how she raised those kids and held her marriage together. By the late 1950s, we had given up complaining about Dale—as much. It was difficult to criticize him when he was making a good living for Barb and the kids. He worked long hours, had spirit draining responsibilities and traveled ninety percent of the time. On top of their own expenses, every month they sent money to Florence and Virgie because he insisted on it. Plus, they were willing to help any one of us, and we all knew it.

All of those things were true, but none of it made living with Dale any easier. That said, I think both of them knew he was spoiled and had figured out how to laugh about it—sometimes, even during extreme events. In fact, Madeline told me a story that illustrates the point perfectly:

Barbara was preparing to deliver her tenth kid—I think it was Terry. She had lots of experience, her timing honed to a fine edge, so her hospital bag was packed and waiting. Then, on a Sunday morning, the baby decided to arrive. It was the one day Dale could sleep late, so Barbara quietly moved the suitcase from their bedroom into the kitchen. She counted the minutes between contractions. Finally, when "wait" edged toward "hurry", she woke Dale and told him they needed to leave.

While he got up and dressed, Barb went to the bathroom where the washer and dryer were located. She unloaded clothes from the dryer, folded them and placed them on a bassinet. She then moved wet clothes from the washer to the dryer and started it again. After timing her contractions once more, she sat down in front of the laundry closet and separated whites from colors to reload the washer.

Dale came to the laundry room, leaned his shoulder against the door frame and asked, "Do you have time to make breakfast?" They both laughed as he helped her up and they headed to the hospital. Actually, I'm surprised breakfast wasn't already on the table.

Back to Mike #1

I often wondered why Mom had so many kids. If asked, she typically allowed that the Catholic church approved only of the "rhythm method" to limit babies. That's a birth control formula instructing couples to engage in sex only when the woman isn't ovulating. *Abstain from sex? Not on your life.* Dad was only home on weekends and I'm sure he wasn't about to honor any "safe days" routine. Besides, it seemed Mom could get pregnant simply by looking his way.

TERENCE EDWARD (TERRY) 1957
Number Ten

Mike-15   Carol-12   Linda-11   Kelly-9   Stan-8
Hal-6   Mary-5   Ginger-2   Pat-1

One afternoon while Mom was nursing Terry, she asked me to retrieve something from her dresser drawer. I had to move a couple of items and beneath one of them was a small, paperback book titled, "The Rhythm Way to a Happy Marriage". I found what she wanted and delivered it to her. I also handed her the instruction booklet.

"Isn't it a little late for this?" I asked with a grin.

"Put that back," she said.

It is possible Mom took Genesis 1:28 a little too seriously when it directed "…go forth and multiply." I think it had more to do with how much she loved babies and being a mother. She lived in a time when more women were beginning to cultivate professional careers in areas like law and medicine. Mom wouldn't have given a nickel for that life. She liked raising kids, and to our great good fortune, she was wonderful at it. The farm just made it more practical. It allowed her to leave us to our own devices, maybe on purpose—maybe because she had so few options. What made it all work was that she needed only a general idea of what we were doing.

If she knew how many frightful, truly dangerous things we were up to, I'm guessing she would have locked us in the house. In our defense, it's not as if we courted danger. Risk was just a by-product of farm life and creative play. A perfect example: One of us would drive the tractor while pulling a disc, which is a series of sharp discs lined up with their sides facing out in two rows, coupled by a steel frame. The implement is designed to break up larger clumps of recently plowed earth. Too often, a couple of kids rode on top of the disc, the spinning circles of steel grinding the ground into submission just below their feet. It was a bumpy ride, which made it all the more exciting. Granted, we could have fallen through the steel frame and into the path of the rotating discs, but our focus was fun and unsafe equipment was our playground.

Personal risk was everywhere and nowhere, depending on how you considered it. Hooking up an implement to the three-point hitch on our 9N Ford tractor was about as dangerous as anything a little kid could do. Yet, Kelly and Stan were connecting plows, discs, harrows and sickle hay mowers to the tractor when they were 12 and 11. Carol and I did the same thing in our time. We were given the responsibility to perform, the right to make mistakes and the confidence to believe we could do whatever was needed. We were as competent as we imagined ourselves to be.

Even real play involved hazards. We fished from the pylons of a steel girder bridge, about a quarter mile from our house. The ideal spot to catch fish was on the apron of a concrete support pillar right in the middle of the creek. It was maybe a foot and a half wide and we had to dangle from the edge of the bridge floor to get to it. Once situated, we were fishing from a narrow ledge, water rushing by, the creek sometimes swollen by spring rains—a misstep away from disaster.

I doubt she knew how many times Carol, Kelly, Stan, Hal and I maneuvered around in the middle of a herd of cows or horses, comfortable in that unpredictable animal community. To be head butted, kicked or trampled was an ever-present threat, one we countered with confidence.

Any one of us could drive the farm's three-quarter ton pickup long before we earned a learner's permit. The truck was in constant use. Its olive black body, steel hardened by design, housed a thundering motor that roared with authority. Dad added red painted stock panels to the bed for hauling livestock. We used it to move the cattle to the "other farm" in spring, and back to the home farm in fall.

There was one spot where a ground level concrete pad spanned a typically dry creek bed. Kelly and Stan were on their own this particular trip with a truck load of cows. They stopped in front of the creek. Stan questioned driving over the uneven surface. Unable to convince Kelly to turn back, he decided to ride standing on the side-board outside of the truck.

As the wheels rolled over the pad's lopsided edges, the truck rocked left and then right. The cattle shifted from one side to the other and the truck felt like it might tip over at any second. Stan jumped, more out of fear than good judgement. Kelly stopped just long enough to steady the load before moving forward again. Stan remounted the truck and they finished the job as if nothing had happened.

I wonder if Mom ever imagined something like that?

Maybe we *did* court danger.

36

THE SHETLAND PONY BUSINESS

Told by Carol #2

I know Dad had dreams. Why else would he invest in land, sheep, cattle, oil and stocks? His first problem was jumping into an investment just as the rest of the world was easing out of it. Second, his money-making ideas required a large-scale operation and ours was barely on the edge of existence.

His last attempt to make the farm pay for itself involved Shetland ponies. In the mid-1950s they were all the rage, commanding ever increasing prices for quality breeding stock. Dad had studied the trends. He knew the market was growing. And it did, right up to the time he waded in.

One Saturday afternoon in the early summer of 1958, Dad took Kelly, Stan and I to visit a local Shetland pony breeder. The ranch was located along a busy highway just outside of Parsons. Dad pulled onto a long driveway flanked by white board fences. He parked in front of a green and cream-colored barn and told us to stay in the car. We watched him walk to the building and disappear through a double wide entrance. A few minutes later, an older man with a sizeable belly led a grey mare into the open. Dad was close behind. He motioned for us to come join them. While turning the mare in one direction and then another, the wide-bodied man commented about her breeding, age and what fine colts she raised. He took the grey mare back into the barn and returned with a palomino. After a few turns and highlights of her resume', he exchanged that one for a sorrel, and finally paraded a black and white pinto in front of us.

Dad directed us back to the car and then trailed the man and pinto into the barn. We milled around and waited. Shortly, the two men appeared in the doorway again. They shook hands and Dad turned and walked toward us as we piled into the car. As we eased back toward the road, Dad said, "Well, we're in the Shetland pony business." No three kids could have been happier.

Over the next few weeks, he bought a couple more mares and a showy stud named Dodo (as in the Dodo bird). His dappled grey color was mixed with white patches and he could pull a surrey which Dad bought along with the last group of mares.

The original four mares were delivered the following day. As I watched them back out of the trailer, their heads held high and their eyes dancing with interest, I wondered who would get which horse. The thought seems silly now. We would go by ages as we always did. The oldest would get first pick and then right on down the line. It was the "bump system" all over again. No one questioned it. Any grievances concerning the primacy of "age" had been resolved years earlier during the chair wars.

I was out of the running as I had claimed Lucky during the early days when Dad bought Thunder for himself and Silver for Mike. I continued to ride her until she was bred to a thoroughbred and foaled a solid black filly. We named her Flicka and she was mine from then on. Kelly chose Miriah, the grey mare from the Shetland purchases. Stan picked Nelly Belle, the palomino, and Hal was left with Dolly, the sorrel. Two weeks later, Miriah became ill and died. By default, the Pinto, SusieQ, became Kelly's. She turned out to be the fastest Shetland on the place.

~

Dad was never more content than when he was riding Thunder and leading us on road trips. On a horse's back he could be the cowboy figure he admired in Western movies. He seemed happy. A confident rider, he sat high in the saddle and reined his mount with authority. In those rare moments, he dropped his guard and we saw a man at ease with himself—a sight so curious we doubted our own eyes. It was a chance for happiness to claim him.

The Shetland years were the most exciting of our farm life. In summer, we rode nearly every day during the week and joined Dad on weekends. A ride with him typically began with, "Have Mother fix me a Coke. Tell her to put it in the flask." That was the signal to round up the horses. On most days it was a simple trail ride, but once in a while, a real adventure took shape—like the spring day Dad decided to drive the cattle from one farm to the other.

In the past, we had always hauled them a truckload at a time—a sometimes dangerous, always eventful and stress-filled day. Driving them over on horseback sounded like a lot more fun. What seemed a simple thing to do, became an exercise in futility until we figured out how to keep the cattle heading in the right direction. The twenty head or so herd, intent on making things difficult, turned down the first driveway we expected to pass. They then spread out in the surrounding pasture and resisted every effort to reorganize them. Once they had been assembled again, Dad stationed one of us back on the gravel road to the left of the entrance, making sure they headed in the direction we wanted. From then on, one of us rode ahead to each driveway entrance, unfenced creek bed or fork in the road to stop them from turning in the wrong direction. It went on like that for the entire three miles.

After four hours and countless tense moments, we finally reached the other farm. Since most of us rode bareback, our jeans, heavy with the sweat from our ponies, began to stiffen the moment we dismounted. The last leg of the drive involved herding the cattle down a fenced lane stretched out between two fields of clover. After latching the gate between the lane and pasture, it was finally over. We enjoyed a sense of relief and accomplishment. Dad in particular seemed satisfied, which lifted all of our spirits. We would repeat the exercise at the beginning of spring and end of summer every year from that point forward.

∽

Where sheep and cattle were a passing phase, horses were a staple in the lives of the older kids. Later in life, Stan and Hal became accomplished jockeys until they were no longer able to make weight. Hal married Holly Tackett, whose father Bill was a renowned auctioneer and race horse owner/breeder. He had recently acquired a well-bred stud by the name of Here We Come. Bill suggested that Stan buy himself a mare and he could breed her to his stud for free. Stan, after serious research, went to an Arkansas Thoroughbred sale and bought a mare named No No Danielle for the bargain price of $6,700.

The offspring of No No Danielle and Here We Come ran out over $1.3 million.

Around that same time, Kelly began betting horses as a serious business. In his second season of full-time wagering, he hit a Pick Six for $250,000. Three months later, he hit another for over $103,000.

Dad may have failed to make money on horses, but his investment paid dividends through his sons for many years.

37

BABY DUTY

Told by Velva

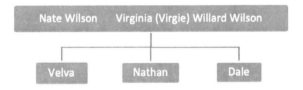

What Things Cost in 1959

Car:	$3,200 Average
Gasoline:	$0.25 cents/gal
House:	$14,329 Average
Rent:	$97.00 Month Average
Bread:	$0.20 cents/loaf
Milk:	$1.01 gal
Postage Stamp:	$0.04 cents/stamp
Average Annual Salary:	$5,016
Minimum Wage:	$1.00 per hour

TIMOTHY WADE 1959
Number Eleven

Mike-16   Carol-12   Linda-13   Kelly-11   Stan-10
Hal-8   Mary-7   Ginger-3   Pat-2   Terry-1

In April of 1959 I was called to help when Barb went to the hospital to deliver baby number eleven. I'll have to admit I was nervous. To start with, my being there was unusual. Barb's sister, Madeline, had always taken care of the kids during hospital week. This time, she claimed a heart attack. I personally think it was a panic attack in anticipation of another week alone at Barb's.

I'm kidding, of course. At least I'll pretend I am. The fact is, it was a tough week for anyone. I feared the responsibilities that would come at me in waves—the cooking, cleaning, getting everyone ready for school, making sure chores were done, straining milk morning and night and after a short stay in the refrigerator, skimming off the cream to churn butter later. Then there were the endless mounds of dirty clothes. Oh, the assembly line of laundry! Those were just a few of the *planned* activities. I shuddered at the thought of how the *unplanned* might spice my day.

Mike had begun driving the kids to and from school, and that was a blessing. I was left with the three little ones, Ginger, Pat and the baby, Terry. The first day felt overwhelming. I believed I had to be in charge and in control, that everything was up to me. By the second day I realized no one needed to be in control of much because Barb's kids knew what to do. They were self-reliant and more than willing to help one another. Dale may have been the reason they toed the line, but Barb molded them into valuable human beings.

As I moved through the bustle of Barb's days, it was difficult to imagine anyone wanting the kind of life she had carved out. It was even tougher to imagine making a success of it. I learned quickly that she needed stamina and multiple skills to deal with the complexities of her life. She managed two farms, ran the household on a meager budget and organized sales strategies that included milk, eggs, apples and animals. She could milk cows, fix fences, kill and dress out a chicken for dinner, supervise a small army of kids doing daily and weekly chores, wean calves and colts, attend school activities for seven children and regularly fit in afternoons at the city park or pool in summer. She helped with homework and attended nearly as many parent/teacher conferences as the teachers themselves. The very thought of it wore me out.

To my great good fortune, I had Carol and Linda to help me with whatever they were old enough to do. Carol was a teenager by then and Linda was a few months short of it. Barb told me that Carol was a natural organizer and could keep track of the older kids, while Linda's mothering instincts suited her to caring for the toddlers. We made an effective team.

The older boys, Mike, Kelly and Stan took care of outside chores in the morning and in the evening after school. I made a point of avoiding asking even a single question about what they were supposed to do. I just trusted they knew and would get it done.

There was a mystery to how it all worked. I sometimes stood silent and watched the tornado of activity swirl around me. Ten kids, in varying degrees of motion, crowded the mornings, and then there was a short break for school, followed by late afternoon and evenings thick with living. I have to admit, I rarely knew where most of them were from one moment to the next. Maybe that's why Barb's faith was so essential. Her entire existence depended on it.

Barb always said, "We raised the first five kids and they are raising the rest." It was during that week I finally understood what she meant. She was too busy keeping the train on schedule to worry about how it was maintained. Hers was a top-down organization, and during that week I learned her secret. All you needed to know about her philosophy was to understand the "bump system". She delegated authority through a lesson everyone understood. If the oldest was gone, the next oldest was in charge. Like getting bumped, there were no questions asked.

One morning I was feeling a little overwhelmed. The farmhouse felt small, even when seven of the kids were away in school. I opened the doors and windows to let in the cool April air. There was something about inviting in the outside that took me back to my childhood on our truck farm. I liked being in touch with that part of myself. It was a simpler time, a time when I found pleasure in taking care of Dale while Virgie and Nate worked the fields. It's funny how we fool ourselves. We cling to memories of a less complicated past, forgetting the struggles that made simple things feel special.

KELLY # 4

A Mess of Greens

I liked having Aunt Velva stay with us for that whole week. In the past, we had been with her only on Thanksgiving Day, and that amounted to little more than a few hours.

Velva sparkled. Though a product of hardship, her dirt-poor upbringing simply informed, it did not define who she was. She raised herself up to middle class respectability along with her husband Harold, in spite of just a fourth-grade education. It was during that time Virgie was forced to sacrifice Velva's childhood to Dale's care. Later on, after her divorce from Mark, she took bookkeeping classes, which led to a successful business career. Velva was life's equal, absolutely comfortable in her own skin.

Tim was born on a Saturday. Dad stayed home for a couple of days before Velva arrived the following Monday. He was uneasy being in charge, anxious, like a caged bird with clipped wings, wanting to fly but unable to take off. Dad knew nothing about changing diapers, doing laundry or cooking. Carol and Linda did their best to fill in for Mom, but it was like a bantam weight fighter taking on a heavyweight. To his credit, Dad was understanding when their bacon burned, biscuits tasted like cardboard and the sunny side up eggs were frisbee flat—nothing sunny about them.

As happy as Dad was when Velva arrived on Monday, he barely accepted a kiss on the cheek and immediately left for work. She took his and Mom's bedroom. There was little time to think about what had to be done and she wasted none of it. After listening to a quick summary of where things stood, she folded a load of laundry from the dryer, deposited the washer's load into the dryer and reloaded the washer with dirty clothes.

I gave her a little time to settle in before beginning to ask questions. A new person in the house was like catnip to me, and Velva was a great opportunity. She humored me. She even commented early on: "You sure ask a lot of questions, don't you? Is it just because I'm new, or are you always so curious?"

"I never thought about it much," I said. "I just want to know things."

"Well, don't change that," Velva said. "I'd rather know too much than too little."

I trusted she meant that and through unmerciful questioning, found out more about Dad's life in a week than anyone else had in a lifetime. Now, she was telling me things I never imagined, and confirming many of Aunt Madeline's and Mom's stories.

⁓

On Friday evening, the day before Velva went home, she asked me to get a bushel basket and follow her to the yard.

"What are you going to do with this," I asked, with the basket dangling from my right hand.

"I'm going to cook you kids a mess of greens," she said. "You're going to see how we used to eat when I was a kid."

Hmmm, I thought, as I followed her out the back door, *what's she going to find in the yard that anybody could eat?*

"Stay close," she said.

Her beige, cotton dress swayed in the breeze as she walked around the yard and focused on the ground at her feet. Occasionally, she bent over to pluck green leaves, flowers or stems from plants we had always considered weeds. I was familiar with dandelions, as we had plenty of them, but many of the others were a total mystery.

"You're going to cook those?" I asked.

"I sure am," Velva answered.

"But, they're weeds," I said.

At that point, she ignored me and continued to add more greens to the basket. I used the opportunity to ask questions about her family. What was Dad like as a kid? Was he a good student? Why did his mother leave him? And on it went—she picked weeds and put them in the basket while I peppered her for information. She seemed to enjoy it.

We moved to the fence line that separated our yard from the Siefert's corn field. There, Aunt Velva found many more options. When the basket was about ¼ full, she led me back to the house where she washed her greens and immersed them into a large stock-pot half full with water. She added some bacon grease and potatoes and began simmering her concoction. Carol, Linda and I watched in horror. Weeds!

She tasted and salted, tasted and peppered, then added a little more bacon grease before calling out, "Time to eat, kids."

That wasn't going to happen. Aunt Velva spooned some greens into a bowl and handed it to me. "You get to try it first because you helped me," she said. It was an honor I could have done without. I sat unmoved as the other kids got their helpings. We all paused, waiting for someone else to start. Finally, Aunt Velva sat down and showed us how it was done. I followed suit and nearly gagged. The other kids pushed their bowls away as if they contained poison.

"You all have to take one bite," Aunt Velva said.

I had already walked the plank so I watched as the others nibbled on their own weeds. After one bite each, the experiment ended. We had learned something about Dad's early life. It was awful and Velva's lesson was more information than we ever needed.

To our surprise, Velva, smiling and unperturbed said, "Mike, go to town and buy some ice cream. I bet they'll eat that."

Back to Velva

I began the week entertaining thoughts of reconnecting with Dale. I thought we might find some time together without other adults around. Maybe he would talk with me like when I picked him up at the bus stop in Oklahoma and drove him back to Joplin. It would have been nice, but he laid those illusions to rest right away, barely speaking ten words after I arrived on Monday. I understood, he wanted to see Barb and the baby and planned to leave for work soon after that. Even so, it was easy to find his attitude ungrateful. I thought exactly that, and then filed it away with all the other excuses I used to dismiss Dale's faults.

∼

After my eventful week with the kids, Dale arrived back home on Friday evening just as it was getting dark.

"How's Barb and the baby?" I asked.

"Good," he answered. "It smells like greens in here."

He took his place in the throne chair at the end of the table nearest the wall. The kids milled around, studying him out of the corners of their eyes. I think they wanted to see if he would eat what I cooked. I set a piping hot bowl of greens in front of him. He looked at it for a few seconds. It must have brought back long forgotten memories. I thought I saw him sigh. Whatever stirred his thoughts caused only a pause and he took a small bite. "Do we have any vinegar?" he asked.

Carol found a bottle and brought it to the table. Dale drizzled it over his meal and took two more bites to impress the kids. I think he felt obligated to pay homage to his past, to show how to live "poor". The kids continued to consider him, not completely sure that a couple of bites proved anything. He had had enough and ordered, "Go play." The kids scattered like a covey of quail.

After the room cleared, we sat alone chewing on small talk and sipping coffee. When I tried to dig deeper, he grunted or just ignored the question. To make his attitude clearer, he lit a cigarette and began hiding behind a newspaper he brought home from work. He would dip the paper down long enough to nod his head or give me a word or two.

So, this is what Barb's life is like, I thought. *This is what she puts up with, constantly interpreting Dale's actions, testing the wind to see if he's in a good* mood, living on hope for a positive word. Thank God she has enough love for the both of them and for all these kids.

I stirred some sugar into my coffee and thought about the man behind the newspaper. *I wonder why he shuns these kids so much. I know he loves them. Why can't he show it? He sure has made the rest of his life exactly like he wants it. Maybe the kids are Barb's prize for putting up with him. Lord knows she deserves something for all she does. How did they ever get together? It's like Dale was looking for a mother and Barb needed a daddy. Well, they got what they wanted if that was the case. I wonder what he's thinking? He smiles about as often as you'd see a bat in daylight. Is he just unhappy? He probably still blames me for Virgie giving him up. Maybe I deserve it. Maybe I should have done more. It had to be terrible for him, living with someone like Marie. She was a child herself. Nate never should have married her. I always told Virgie she got her revenge by Dad marrying his own hell. Life works that way sometimes. He traded for a newer model and ended up with a lemon. That's what I think anyway.*

Out of the blue, "How's Harold?" he asked. "How's the hearing aid business?" He tilted the newspaper down, but it was still close to covering his face.

I answered with the same enthusiasm he offered me, "He's fine," I said. "The business is good." I picked up my cup and his full bowl of greens and headed to the kitchen. I took one last pass at explaining him.

He's a shadow, I thought—*neither completely hidden nor clearly revealed.*

The girls had filled a crock with the leftover greens—which was most of them. After a long look at what was left in the soup pot, I mixed it all together and told one of the kids to pour it out in the garden. I began thinking about the week and how I learned to see Barb in a whole new light. She was superhuman as far as I was concerned. It was impossible to appreciate how much she did, and how beautifully she did it, unless you had to do it yourself. She inspired and encouraged and accepted the march of time and all the changes that came with it. I was in awe of her.

While considering Barb's many qualities, I had to come up with at least a couple for Dale. *Well,* I thought, *he provides for this whole bunch. I have to give him credit for that. Oh, and at least he hides his liquor when I'm here. He knows how I feel about it. I guess that says something about caring. I know he loves Barb. I know he loves the kids. He works long hours. If I had time, I could think of more.*

For now, I need to get home and rest.

38

THE GROCERY STORE MANAGER & THE LA-Z-BOY

The Grocery Store Manager

I kept an eye on the woman in the white maternity dress in case she needed my help. She shopped at my grocery store once a week for more years than I can remember. People mill around in my mind as they do in the store, disconnected from time or events. I do know Mrs. Wilson had five kids when she first started shopping there. I remember, because at that time she was filling only one basket and now, with eleven kids, she was filling three.

Mrs. Wilson was special. I knew it, and so did everyone in the store. Her dark brown, almost black hair was thick and varied in length over the years. She was average size, maybe 5'4" inches tall and weighed around 120 pounds—more when she was pregnant, which was a lot of the time. What I remember most is that she always smiled at me as if I was somebody special. She wanted me to know I mattered. At least that's how I saw it.

We knew the Wilsons lived on a farm about three miles outside of town and just beyond the stockyards. We found out they butchered a calf each year, which is why we rarely saw Mrs. Wilson buy beef. She was a once-per-week grocery shopper. I figured that was as much time as she had to spare with so many kids. Watching her fill one basket after another was almost entertaining. Then I considered how much work those groceries would lead to and my amusement turned to admiration.

I found something curious about that family. In all the years I saw Mrs. Wilson and the children in the store, I never saw her husband. It was as if she produced those kids all by herself. I don't mean to make a case out of it, but you'd think we would have seen him at least once, but it never happened. And I'm sure of it because I made a point to ask the checkers if any of them had ever seen him. No one had. He was like a ghost to us.

Actually, his presence was known to everyone in the store—we just didn't know we knew it. It came to us through the kids. They were always dressed neat, but humble. The hand-me-downs were pretty obvious. Their outfits only half fit some of the little ones, while the older kids consistently wore very basic clothes; drab and unremarkable. But what the clothes couldn't hide was a striking curiosity in each of them. I loved how they looked with wonder at the neatly stocked shelves and bins filled with food. I remember thinking how lucky they were to gain so much pleasure from such a simple thing.

They did this - the looking with wonder - while behaving with absolute calm. Children typically didn't act that way, especially little ones who can meander away from their mothers for no reason at all. Not these kids, they stayed close to Mrs. Wilson as if they were tethered to her by some imaginary rope.

One day, I asked Mrs. Wilson how she maintained so much control over all of them.

"It's easy," she said. "All I have to say is, 'I'll tell your dad.'"

That was obviously a potent threat, and it was how we knew he was a force in their lives. We may have never seen him, but he was there.

THE LA-Z-BOY

Told by Terry #8

As a kid, when I thought of Dad, he was typically leaned back in his La-Z-Boy recliner. If a man's home is his castle, that chair was Dad's throne. Most often, unless he was laid back all the way and getting a little shut eye, he sat with it half way up, and it was from there he ruled his world and gave orders like:

"Coffee." He would hold out his empty cup and within seconds, someone, anyone, rushed to the kitchen, scooped up the coffee pot and returned to refill his chalice.

"Turn the channel." This one caused the kid closest to the TV to hop up and begin twisting the knob from one station to another—pausing at each new channel until finding one that satisfied Dad.

"Go out to the car and get me a pack of cigarettes."

When we lived on the farm, Dad kept a carton of cigarettes under the driver's seat. The car was parked in the garage under the hayloft and Dad always seemed to want a fresh pack after dark. No matter how black the night, the garage was blacker. It was scary. If the order came to Kelly, he latched on to one of the younger kids (too dumb to know better, which sometimes included me) and encouraged them to go into the garage in front of him. I suppose he figured if they got snatched up, he'd have time to run.

"Time for bed." On that command, the kids lined up next to his chair. Dad would offer his cheek, and one by one we gave him a kiss goodnight. It was a ritual—like brushing our teeth. What I remember most about the routine was how prickly his whiskers felt. They made my face itch.

There was another reason the chair was special. That's where he revealed a soft side we rarely saw when, out of the blue, he would say, "I love you, Mother."

"I love you too, Daddy," she echoed back.

The La-Z-Boy enjoyed a mystical quality. It was the personification of Dad when he was away. None of the little kids dared sit in it. If fact, he gave strict orders to stay out of his chair from Monday until Saturday when he returned. The older kids were immune to the threats, knowing there was no one to back them up. They bumped their way into the guilty pleasure of mounting the throne while watching TV.

One day, when I was five and half years old, I found myself alone with the chair. Against everything taught and holy, I decided to taste the forbidden fruit. I approached it cautiously at first, checking to see that the house was empty but for me and the chair. Its frame was covered in red leather, the seat and seat back, in black and white upholstery. I placed both hands on the cushion, pausing just long enough to be sure my sin caused no immediate punishment. I hiked one knee onto the seat, hesitated again, and then brought up the other. I turned and eased my back into the curve of the seatback and sat silent, a sense of power washing over me. It felt right and wrong at the same time. I pretended to give orders like Dad did, mouthing words with no sound. I crossed my legs and rocked my foot up and down. Just as I was becoming comfortable, a rustling sound from the kitchen threw me into a state of panic. I flew out of the chair, bolted through the screened doorway and raced away from the house until I felt safe again.

That chair was something.

39

A PINHOLE IN THE DIKE

Told by Madeline — Barbara's Sister

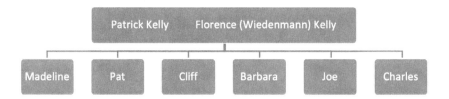

The 1950s unfolded like an airplane in a holding pattern. The Great Depression, two world wars and the Korean conflict conditioned us to expect an unstable future and likely more of the same. When it didn't come, we welcomed the stability that came with sameness. We wanted an orderly life and believed those wars were fought to create it. People felt lucky to have jobs, and conservative traditions became our norms. Consumerism was in full swing and 'keeping up with the Joneses" motivated people to wear, live-in and drive their priorities.

Just below the surface of that "accumulation" culture was a small band of dissenters called Beatniks. They advocated for personal reliance, purification and illumination through sensory awareness. Many professed allegiances to the principles of Buddhism and made literature and poetry their primary tools of enlightenment. Like the hippie generation they eventually spawned, their collective inspirations were sex, drugs and music. Lacking a broad common cause, something to advocate *for* or *against*, reduced them to the fringe of society. Waiting in the wings, the hippie generation would soon show them how it was done.

By common measure, Dale and Barbara were doing well, though Dale, still hounded by nightmares of the depression, continued to keep Barbara on a pauper's budget.

"Why do you put up with it?" I asked one day.

"Put up with what?" Barbara said. "I'd like the kids to have more, but they're happy and I can make do with what he's giving me."

"Barbara," I said, "I know you're stressed every month. He could afford to give you more."

"He's putting money back," Barbara countered. "He's trying to plan for our future. It isn't easy, Madeline, keeping up with a family this size."

I had to admit Barbara was half right. It must have been a mental and emotional strain on Dale to keep up with so much responsibility. Plus, he was just being the kind of father he was taught to be. But Barbara was also part of the problem. She was a product, and a victim of her upbringing. Most of us believe the rest of the world is living roughly the same kind of life we are. As far as she knew, all women catered to their husbands, and there was ample evidence to support that notion. In those days, the man earned everything the family had. He lived an emperor's life, if only at home. Money gave him power—tradition enshrined it.

My own life was much the same—I just refused to give in to it. Al controlled *our* purse strings too, except for the money I slipped into my purse from his billfold on paydays. Over the years I accumulated thousands, squirreled away in curtain hems, envelopes taped to the back of headboards or stuffed in the upright vacuum cleaner bag. When a hiding place reached $2,000, I found a new one. If things ever turned against me, I was prepared.

I wish Barbara had had that luxury. Unfortunately, Dale was more aware of his money than Al, and Barbara's ethics curbed any bent toward larceny.

She changed the subject by announcing, "I'm pregnant again." It was obvious the idea made her happy.

It would be short lived.

The pregnancy ended in her second miscarriage. Barbara faltered, but only for a couple of days. Nothing seemed to break her.

John F. Kennedy's announcement on January 2, 1960 spurred Barbara to a new awareness. A Catholic was running for President of the United States—a Catholic who had a chance to win. He represented possibilities.

Just after Nixon and Kennedy squared off, Barbara announced she was pregnant with number twelve. She was as happy as I had ever seen her. I think losing the last baby made this pregnancy more important than ever. By November, she was slightly over six months along. About that same time, I detected an air of independence she had never shown before.

The proof surfaced a couple of weeks before the election. It was only a hint—a few raindrops just before the downpour—but it was there for all to see.

We were sitting at the dining room table. Barbara placed a freshly churned bowl of butter in front of Dale. Al reached across the table, scooped up a spoonful of it and said, "We're voting for Kennedy."

"Not us," Dale allowed, "we're voting for Nixon."

Barbara heard the exchange from the kitchen and returned to the dining room.

"I'm voting for Kennedy too," she announced.

"I'd better not find out you did," Dale warned.

"You'll never know how I voted," Barbara said.

And that was it. That was the moment we knew something had changed.

Kennedy and Barbara won.

1960 was the end of an era for our family. Florence was unable to take care of herself as Parkinson's claimed more and more of her independence. The brothers and sisters traded taking care of her for the final five years of her life. Even Dale and Barbara took their turn. In that small house, with 13 people already living there, they made a makeshift bedroom out of the front half of the living room for Dale and Barbara and gave Florence their room. Eventually, Mom was unable to speak and swallowing became impossible. As much as we hated it, Florence had to be placed in a full care facility. She was moved to a specialty hospital near Joplin, Missouri. She died there in 1960.

∼

TERESA LOUISE – FEBRUARY 1961
Number Twelve

Mike – 19   Carol – 16   Linda – 15   Kelly – 13   Stan – 11
Hal – 9   Mary – 8   Ginger – 6   Pat – 5   Terry – 3   Tim – 2

I took care of the kids while Barbara was in the hospital delivering Teresa. Everyone was excited. After three boys in a row, we were ready for a girl. The week progressed as it typically did, except this time I was more relaxed and willing to leave well enough alone. Oh, I cleaned and cooked and did laundry, but it was winter and the kids were housebound most of the time. Keeping house was secondary to keeping my mind.

∼

One week after Christmas in 1962, Barbara announced she was pregnant again. It had almost become seasonal. We quit hoping *this* would be the last one, though many thought there was an elegance to stopping at a baker's dozen.

During that '62 summer, Monsignor Gunning, pastor at St. Patrick's, announced that the parish needed additional financial help from the congregation. They would begin charging tuition for high school students, grades nine through twelve. Dale decided the cost was too high. Carol, Linda and Kelly were in high school that fall and Mike would be leaving for St. Benedict's College in Atchison, Kansas at the same time. A private college was expensive and except for scholarships, the entire cost fell to Dale and Barbara. Al and I felt the other three kids were sacrificed for the benefit of one.

To be fair, making sure Mike graduated from college turned out to be an important decision. Whether a stroke of genius or just dumb luck, a precedent had been set. The kids who followed assumed going to college was a natural and expected next step after high school. In the end, nine of the thirteen kids would graduate from college. The eight after Mike did it all on their own. It also turned out that a college education was not for everyone and was a poor predictor of success. The four who bypassed college turned out just as well-off as the kids who graduated with university degrees.

∼

ALPHONSE JOSEPH (AL) – JULY 1962
Number Thirteen

Mike – 20   Carol – 17   Linda – 16   Kelly – 14   Stan – 12   Hal – 10   Mary – 9   Ginger – 7   Pat – 6   Terry – 4   Tim – 3   Teresa – 1

The kids were out of school when Al was born. Barbara told me Carol and Linda would be taking care of things while she was in the hospital. Al and I called the morning the baby was born, but decided to wait for the weekend before driving to Parsons. We were in no hurry to revisit the disappointment felt at the arrival of the last three boys. In each case, we had lobbied to have Pat, Terry or Tim, named Alphonse Joseph. Al's name had been passed down through his family for generations. With no children of our own, the name would die with him. The thought caused Al real pain. We knew Barbara was fine with it, but Dale had the final say and he refused to consider the name. He was afraid bullies would have an easy target.

As fate would have it, the baby was the biggest Barbara had ever delivered; 9 pounds, 14 ounces. Though he came on a Wednesday, Dale decided to stay home until after the weekend.

Dale and Barbara typically named their babies on the first day. This time was different. Barbara explained what happened:

> No one mentioned what to call the baby that first day. I wanted to name him after Al, so I purposefully avoided throwing out

options. Shortly after Dale arrived the next morning, I told him how I felt. He said, "No."

I dropped the subject, but offered no alternatives.

Dale spent the day on the farm, working on whatever projects he dreamed up to keep the boys busy. Around 5:00 p.m., he had his typical highball and celebrated the new baby with a couple of extras. By the time he made it back to the hospital, he was feeling pretty good.

"Maybe we should name him after Al," he said. "This is the biggest kid we've had. I think he'll be able to defend himself."

And that was it. The name lived on.

∼

One weekend in late 1962, Barbara and I were preparing dinner when she told me there was a rumor that Manor Baking Company might be sold. She added that Dale doubted route sales would continue.

I stopped peeling potatoes and asked, "What are you going to do?"

Barbara spoke, while continuing to flour the round steak she planned to fry for supper. "Dale's talking about starting an insurance agency for Farmers Insurance Group." She paused. "But it would have to be in Coffeyville, Kansas."

"Where's Coffeyville?" I asked.

"About 40 miles southwest of here," she said.

"What about the farms?"

Barbara wiped her hands and said, "We'll have to sell both of them. But I don't care."

I was taken back, "You don't care?"

"Not really," she said. "I'll enjoy having neighbors."

"How about the kids," I asked. "How will they feel about it?"

"They'll be fine," she said. "Some of them may not like it, but they'll adjust."

That was Barbara's way–don't worry about what hasn't happened.

We continued on, peeling and flouring. "Have you looked for a house?" I asked.

Barbara stopped what she was doing and rested her hip against the counter top. "We have," she said. "We've found exactly what I want. It has seven bedrooms."

"Seven!" I repeated. "It must be huge."

"No," Barbara admitted, "and it only has one full bathroom with a half bath upstairs. But we've been dealing with less. The rest of the house is perfect."

40

THE FARM AUCTION

Told by Kelly #4

The Wilson family called no grand meetings where decisions were discussed or announced. Dad typically decided what was going to happen and Mom took care of the details. And so it was with our move to Coffeyville and a planned auction of everything on the farm. The news simply filtered down through the ranks. Mom answered our questions, and like bees in a hive we organized to prepare for the upcoming sale and move.

We had lived on the farm for over twelve years. It was all some of us knew. This next phase was more than just a move—it was a completely different life. Each of us processed the news in our own way. I was excited about it. The farm was a lot of work and I had had my fill of country living. I knew the five oldest would get jobs. Even on the farm, four of us worked in town anyway.

As excited as I was about the idea of moving to town, it was an abstraction until the day we saw the fliers announcing the auction. *Farm Equipment, Registered Angus cattle, Horses…* Wait! What? Horses? "We can't sell Lucky. She's been here since the beginning. She's family. And what about Flicka? She's Carol's. What would happen to her?" In the end, it was decided they would find a place near Coffeyville to stable Flicka, but that was it.

Mom knew many of us were upset about the idea of selling Lucky. All she had to offer was, "We'll figure something out."

As luck would have it (ironic, isn't it?), Lucky died of natural causes about a week before the sale. We found her lifeless body lying behind the pond dam. I was sad…and relieved. As much as I hated seeing her go, I could never imagine not knowing where she was or who was taking care of her. Crisis averted.

∼

The auction took place on a Saturday in August.

Our farm life was sold to the highest bidder that day; the auctioneer's clipped cadence moving the memories of one family to dreams of another.

We parked the tractor and all its implements in a line along the row of evergreens north of the circular drive. In front of the two-story garage, saddles straddled wooden racks, while bridles rested on folding tables next to boxes filled with assorted pieces of our history. People began showing up early in the day. Potential buyers headed to the auctioneer's table to sign up for a numbered bidding placard. Their registry secured, they began weaving their way around and between the equipment, studying each item while fanning themselves with their numbered cards. From a distance, it looked like a sea of butterflies.

Mom had us move a stock tank near the house and fill it with pop, then cover it with ice and water. She placed a cloth covered table next to the tank and laid out sandwiches and chips. We sold the pop for ten cents each and the sandwiches and chips for a combined price of twenty-five cents. Customers gathered in groups to eat and chat. The day felt festive.

I stood in front of the garage, while horses and cattle were sold in the corral behind it. Nearby, Dad rifled through boxes sitting on the folding table tops. He had been watching the sale just minutes before. Shetland mares that he bought for $250 each were selling for $50 and less. I had the impression he wanted to be anywhere but there.

A minute later, one of the auctioneer's bid spotters walked up to Dad and said, "Your daughter picked up a thrown away bidding card and bought that gold and white filly she calls Candy. She doesn't have any money. What do you want us to do about it?"

My first reaction was fear for Carol. And then I regained my senses. She was one of Dad's favorites. He had two in particular at that time; Mike and Carol. The only question now was whether he would let her keep Candy.

Dad pulled Carol aside and had a short talk with her. She walked away crying. He then spoke with the auctioneer and Candy was returned to the sale a second time. I felt sorry for Carol, but then I remembered she was the only kid who was allowed to move a horse to Coffeyville. My sympathy turned to indifference.

The sale ended in late afternoon. The crowd dwindled to a few stragglers loading horses and equipment onto trailers or flatbed trucks. I heard the last pickup tires crunch over the gravel road in front of the house. As the sound faded, a strange quiet settled over the farm. Where mooing cattle and whinnying horses had once dotted the barnyard and orchard—where tractor growls had rumbled over tilled fields—where the voices of spirited children had pierced a million moments, a dull silence now reigned.

We helped Mom gather a few items from the house and loaded them into the Woody. She and Linda then drove the youngest kids to Coffeyville for their first look at our new home.

Dad, Mike, Carol, Stan and I stayed the night. We loaded what was left of the furniture into the bed of the paneled ¾ ton truck. Dad took us out for hamburgers and later to a double feature, (Westerns of course) something unimaginable to all of us. After a night of sleeping on the floor, we packed the last few items from the house and tied it down with cotton ropes.

Just before leaving, Dad walked away, alone. His stride appeared heavy and uncertain. He eased past the walk-through gate and stopped near the center of the barnyard. His head pivoted left and right as he scanned the outbuildings and the dirt worn spaces in between. They marked the comings and goings of every living thing on that farm for the last twelve years. He then walked to stand under the huge oak trees guarding the entrance to the orchard. Their massive limbs slumped together in the still summer air. He pulled back his shoulders and stared into the distance, past the apple trees, beyond the pond and into his version of the past. I wondered what he felt. Was our time there an ocean, or just a wave?

PART V

THE TOWN YEARS

*Small towns are the foundation upon which
This country was built.
They are proof of our origins,
Evidence of our humanity.*

41

THE NEW HOUSE

Told by Linda #3

Dale	Barbara

| Mike | Carol | Linda | Kelly | Stan | Hal | Mary | Ginger | Pat | Terry | Tim | Teresa | Al |

Mom stopped in front of our new house in Coffeyville and said, "This is it."

"It sure looks small," I said.

Mom smiled and told us she had thought the same thing. "In fact, when the realtor first brought me here, I didn't even get out of the car. I told her our family would never fit into a house that size. But wait until you see the inside," she said.

I found out later that our house was the original Etchen Bungalow of the Etchen Bungalow addition. It was built by Mr. Etchen himself and was designed with a narrow profile in front to resemble a bungalow, while extending back more than seventy feet. "You'll see," Mom said.

Seven of the kids scampered out of the car and stood on the sidewalk waiting for Mom and I. She carried baby Al, while I gathered up Teresa. Mom led the way up two sidewalk steps and further to three steps leading to the porch. There was a screened in area to the left and an open porch with a pergola overhead to the right. My doubts swelled.

Mom unlocked a thick oak entry door, stepped into a small foyer and then opened another wooden door leading to the living room. The kids pushed by us and into the house. They spread out in all directions, gaping with wonder at the many rooms and tall ceilings.

"Does the fireplace work?" I asked.

"No," Mom answered. "It was converted to gas years ago."

"What are those?" I wondered, pointing to two contraptions on either end of the living room. They turned out to be steam radiators, found in nearly every room, which were heated by a gas-fired furnace in the basement that provided heat for the whole house.

Mom and Dad had purchased a new couch and a couple of cushioned comfort chairs. They added a coffee table and two side tables with lamps. Dad's recliner sat at the far end of the newly carpeted room. I didn't like the carpeting. Mom said it was called, "candy cane." Its multi-colored straight lines made me dizzy.

The living area we entered was separated from an adjoining room by double hung French doors. The dark oak baseboard and doorway trim made the house feel rich and substantial. We continued through the second room, a dining area, and pushed open a swinging wooden door with a glass window on top. It led to a spacious kitchen, at least by our standards. At the back of the room on the left, was another door leading to a mud porch and the refrigerator. To the right was a breakfast cove. It was perfect for the picnic table Mom bought and where the youngest would eat.

I then noticed another wooden door to the right. "Go on," Mom said. "Go through there."

I stepped into a hallway. "It's like another whole house," I said. Wooden door after wooden door, spaced out down the length of a very long hallway, led to three large bedrooms, the bathroom, steps to the basement and a hall closet. Further down the hall were doorways to the living and dining room. To the right, a wooden staircase climbed to the second floor.

The little kids scrambled up the stairs and when they reached the landing one yelled, "There are more doors up here!" Upstairs, there were four more bedrooms, a half bath and a recreation room roughly fifteen by thirty feet. On either side were storage spaces that ran nearly the length of the room. To the left and right were more doors leading to two of the upstairs bedrooms.

I had to admit, it was amazing. It was difficult to imagine having all that space considering the small house we just left. I could tell Mom was proud and happy. Even she had a look of wonder on her face. I was thrilled for her.

The house was located near the middle of Coffeyville. It sat across the street from Holy Name Catholic church and grade school. A one-half block size playground spread out behind the church and directly in front of our house. It was perfect for a bunch of kids fresh off the farm.

I have to say, I felt sorry for the new neighbors. Think about it, Pete and Jean Stover, along with their one daughter, Peggy and Jean's father, Bud had lived next door to maybe two to three people for years. The same was true for the Pazeys and every other neighbor with adjoining property. It had to be frightening–earth shattering–unimaginable that fifteen people, thirteen of them children of the corn, would now be living in a house right next to them.

Mom changed their minds quickly. She took to town living with the same grace she did most other things. She baked bread for the neighbors and spent time with them whenever possible. They seemed to like her–admire might be a better word. I think most of them were in awe of how she managed to raise thirteen kids. She had to appear soft to them, because she was soft, but not in the way most people imagined it. You see, that softness gave her great power. Her loving spirit inspired us to protect her, especially against our own shortcomings.

I doubt Dad met any of the neighbors, except for the Stovers. He liked them and I think he felt real compassion for how they must be feeling. He had been selling insurance in Coffeyville for a few months, so he knew some of the locals. He was particularly friendly with Paul and Betty Zimmer and their daughter, Paula. They became the family's first friends in Coffeyville.

There was little time, and even less interest, for the kids to worry about how we were being accepted. The beginning of school was only days away and we had to get organized. Carol would attend Coffeyville Junior College. Kelly and I were enrolled at the high school, while Stan, Hal, Mary, Ginger and Pat simply walked across the street to Holy Name. Terry, Tim, Teresa and Al stayed with Mom.

Dad was home throughout the week now, and it took some serious adjusting for everyone involved. Twelve years of Dad-free weekday living had spoiled us. Mom began to defer to him over decisions she had made for years. That led to uncertain outcomes, which called for a little extra planning. We learned that the best strategy was to avoid asking him.

Most of what we wanted to do began in front of the house. The playground was across the street. Friends would pick us up on Fifth Street between the house and the playground. No one wanted to go through the front door where Dad had a clear view of our comings and goings. Our solution was simple. Dad's living room chair sat next to a window with a view of the house next door. A narrow space of roughly eight feet separated the two houses, with stone pavers creating a walkway down its middle. If we wanted to leave the house, the best strategy was to exit the back door, take the walkway to the front of the house with a strategic "duck" as we passed under Dad's window.

He knew it was going on all along. I'm sure he understood it was the *threat* of his punishment that really mattered. As long as we ducked, he could count on us doing the right thing.

42

COFFEYVILLE

Told by Mike #1

Dale	Barbara

| Mike | Carol | Linda | Kelly | Stan | Hal | Mary | Ginger | Pat | Terry | Tim | Teresa | Al |

We moved to Coffeyville, Kansas in the late summer of 1963, just weeks before I returned to college.

I settled into one of the many bedrooms in the new home. Everyone knew it was only temporary. Soon, the entire house would be animated by my move back to Saint Benedict's. A chain reaction of bedroom upgrades was about to follow me out the door. I could feel the anticipation building all around me as the future heirs circled nearby. I understood. Ours was a hierarchy of age and my leaving was seen as an opportunity. What really mattered to me was knowing I would never again have to plow a field, milk a cow or stitch together broken-down fences.

That fateful year, benign to a fault until it wasn't, marked a turning point in America. In a matter of months, a president was assassinated, the Beetles popularity eclipsed Elvis, the Supremes introduced America to Motown and news of the Vietnam War, simmering since 1955, blanketed the front pages of every newspaper on the planet. A picture of our future would soon resemble a disordered Picasso rather than the Norman Rockwell world we were living. The pace of change was accelerating and a revolution gathered on our doorsteps.

All of that would happen soon enough, in the meantime, on a lazy Saturday afternoon, I prepared for college. After packing my bags, reviewing my class requirements and making a checklist of books I needed to order, I looked for something to do. It was a little unsettling. I was used to a life littered with Dad inspired projects. No more. I decided to walk to town.

Coffeyville, with a population of a little over 17,000 people, was the poster child for life in middle America. Downtown was vibrant, especially on weekends. Shoppers mingled easily as they wove their way between shoe stores, dress shops, department stores like Read's or the local Western Auto. Teenagers were respectful and most little kids tagged along behind their mothers rather than being tethered to their hips.

It felt good to wonder down a sidewalk without a care. I watched my reflection tracking me through store front windows, while discreetly checking out a few girls walking past. Cars angle parked up and down both sides of the street—the city's steel-gray meters marking the comings and goings of their owners. A brand-new Mercury Monterey with its reverse angled rear window, was parked next to a Ford Thunderbird and I experienced by first attack of car envy. Older models, like a blue Ford Falcon and a red Chevy Impala, dotted the line with color. The only pickups I saw belonged to farm families shopping for weekly supplies.

It was magical in a way—the beating heart of a community in rhythm with itself. There was an air of stability about this place that dated back to its beginnings. As with so many other small towns like it, that luxury was about to fade. Few of us knew that Sam Walton had opened his first Walmart in Rogers, Arkansas in 1962. His power to transform the face of America had just begun. No one imagined that "downtowns" like Coffeyville's, would soon become like dinosaurs—known only by the bones that once surrounded their thriving businesses.

During that first walk, I started at Bynum's, traveled up Ninth street for two blocks and then cut over to Eighth Street, the main drag through Coffeyville. It was there I discovered the Dalton Museum, located just past the business district and near the railroad tracks. The unassuming, one-story building would have inspired sympathy if not for the mural painted on its west side. Instead, a color faded scene out of Coffeyville's horse and buggy days suggested something interesting inside. The museum was a historical account of the day the Dalton Gang attempted to rob the town's two banks at the same time. They were the villains. The heroes were townspeople who stepped into the breach and gave their lives to protect Coffeyville.

The gun battles that day lasted 12 minutes. When it was over, four citizens had been killed, along with the entire Dalton Gang, except for Emmet. Emmet suffered twenty-three gunshot wounds and survived, was given a life sentence, paroled after fourteen years and lived to age sixty-six in California.

After leaving the museum, I toured the bank buildings–walked into the alley where the Daltons had tied up their horses, and milled around in Isham's Hardware store where the townspeople had gathered to plan their defense. I'm sure it was just my imagination, but it felt like something epic had happened there. Maybe it was because one of the iconic bank buildings was in its identical location and Isham's was still open for business across the street. Or, maybe it was seeing people going about their day, much like on the morning the Dalton's lost their gambit. I realized how easily "typical" can explode into chaos without notice or regard.

∼

After returning home from my walk, I sat in the living room, sometimes reading, sometimes watching Mom go about her business in the new house. She was obviously happy. The differences between her farm life and how things would be in town were enormous.

The older kids had jobs within a matter of days. Carol became a checker at a grocery store. Linda and Kelly went to work at the local A&W, and Stan began to clean floors in the evening at Piggly Wiggly. I'm unsure how Mom and Dad influenced that kind of initiative, but no one had to tell them to get jobs–they just did it.

The five oldest worked for both noble and practical reasons. They did it for Mom because they knew how she struggled to make ends meet. And on a practical level, the only way to *have* money was to *make* it. Their initiative helped prove one of Mom's most familiar claims, "Dale and I raised the first five kids and they raised the rest." That was partially true. It would have been impossible to accomplish everything she did in a day without help from the five oldest. Town life didn't change that.

Regardless of where we lived, each day began with a breakfast of oatmeal and toast. Moments after turning off the heat from under the oatmeal, dropping four more slices of bread into the toaster and placing milk and sugar on the kitchen table, just like on the farm, Mom went to the staircase and hollered, "Time to get up, kids. Kids, get up!" Shortly, in no particular order, they began filing downstairs and out of bedrooms on the first floor. The younger ones, without direction or question, took their places at the picnic style table in the kitchen. The older kids joined Dad at the long formal table in the dining room, each taking a specific place on the bench seat against the wall, or one of the chairs on the opposite side. And so it would go at every meal.

I noticed a change in Mom in those early days in town. She began keeping track of everyone as best she could. It wasn't like that on the farm. There, she seemed relaxed about not knowing where everyone was minute by minute. In fact, we roamed freely and only rarely checked in, typically around lunchtime and always at supper—the big meal of the day. Nobody missed supper.

Town life was different. The farm had acres and acres of space to roam. Now, we could walk around our property in less than a minute. In Parsons, Mom knew all of our neighbors. In Coffeyville, she knew very few. Everything outside of our house was foreign and Mom was intent on keeping the kids from it; whatever "it" was. I knew that would change. The first five of us were formed by hard work and creative play. We had experienced freedom and any attempt to reign us in was hopeless. Even in those early weeks, I watched the younger kids begin exhibiting that same independence. They were learning.

Mom welcomed the move to town. Her sociable nature was tailor made for this new kind of life. She liked people and they liked her. Dad was another matter. It had been fourteen years since he lived at home full time. How would life change with him constantly present? I knew it would be challenging for the family–Dad was difficult by nature–maybe "complex" is more accurate. To make it work, he would have to become a different version of himself, a version I was unsure existed.

All of this moving from one place to another had me thinking about things I rarely considered before. What in the world brought Mom and Dad together in the first place? She was a river of love–he, a desert of affection. She poured herself into being a mother. He was a part time father. She taught by example. He demanded obedience. She was an active part of our lives. He experienced us from a distance. So, did she love us more than he did? Not on a bet.

I once asked him, "Why are you so strict?"

"Somebody has to be in charge," he answered. "Little kids will take over if you let them and they're not very good at it. I decided from the beginning that I would be running things." And he was right. Absent his steady hand, even when it targeted our butts, it's hard to imagine how we might have turned out.

Great things can happen when one parent loves you to success, and the other one expects it. I'm pretty sure that's why it worked.

43

CAMELOT LOST

Told by Carol #2

Our first few months in Coffeyville were great. We settled into a routine and everyone seemed content with their new lives. Mom's large lunches brought everyone together at noon. Dad appeared to have accepted his fate—a daily member of a family he once ruled from afar. The kids liked their schools, and even the neighbors appeared to be adjusting to the upheaval our family created.

Linda, Kelly and I made cold calls for Dad's insurance business. He paid us $5 for any referral leading to a sale. We all had jobs, so calls were made whenever we could work it in. No one knew how Dad's business was going, though we hoped we could help him succeed. His distant, sour moods–more frequent than rare–offered little insight into how he was feeling. We were just kids and kids rarely worry about their parents. They have their own worlds to negotiate.

In my case, I found John Kennedy's vision of the Peace Corp inspiring. I began speaking about joining the Corp in vague terms, knowing full well Dad would object. Each time it was mentioned he said, "You're not going to the Peace Corps." He knew I might end up in another country and that was too much for him to consider. He failed to realize the decision was already made. I had submitted my application and was waiting to see if they would accept me for training.

And then it happened. We had just finished lunch on November 23, 1963 when Bud, our next-door neighbor, knocked on our back door. One of the little kids let him in. I followed Mom from the dining room into the kitchen. Bud looked stricken.

"What's wrong, Bud?" Mom asked.

"President Kennedy has been shot," he answered. "In Dallas. They don't know how bad it is yet. I heard it on the radio."

He then turned, shaken and unsteady, and headed out the back door.

Dad was partial to Walter Cronkite so we turned the television to CBS. The soap opera "As the World Turns" was playing when, at 12:40 CST, Cronkite's voice-over announced the President had been shot. The station returned to regular programming. We learned later that as soon as students returned from lunch, the nuns at Holy Name school guided them to the church to pray for Kennedy. Mom also hurried to the church. I stayed with Terry, Tim, Teresa and Al. Dad slumped in his chair and stared at the television coverage.

Time staggered. I was in a fog of disbelief. No one spoke, hoping against hope he might survive. Soon, Dad was bent forward with his elbows on his knees, his gaze fixed on the television. Mom returned from the church at around 1:15 p.m., her face strained with worry. She sat in her recliner and talked about how all the kids were in church praying. "The nuns were leading them in saying the rosary," she said. If Dad heard her, there was no sign of it. We waited.

It was roughly 1:35 CST. We now had a camera view of Cronkite. He read from a sheet of paper in front of him: "President Kennedy died at 1 P.M. (CST)". Cronkite was visibly shaken. Dad leaned back in his chair. His eyes watered. Mom sobbed. Camelot was lost.

Kennedy's assassination turned out to be one of the most accurately remembered moments in most people's lives, "Where were you when you heard about John Kennedy's assassination?" I'm guessing most everyone could answer that question without hesitation.

～

From the beginning, Mom was quietly supportive of my Peace Corps goals. She encouraged me, helped crush any doubts, prodded me forward and shared my dreams as if they were her own. I'm confident she pleaded my case with Dad when they were alone. She knew how to negotiate his objections. Her strategy was never to gain his approval. She knew the best she could do was stop him from forbidding one thing or another. More often than not, when it really mattered to her, she won the day. In the end, Dad just quit commenting about it, though I know he hoped I would fail to follow through.

Against all odds, I was accepted into the Peace Corps and began classes in Montana in 1964. After completing my education there, my class was sent to Mexico for two weeks of immersion training. At the end of that process, we were given our assignments. I was posted to a village in Ecuador. We were allowed to return home for a few weeks before leaving for our permanent duties.

Dad had given up his open resistance, but it was apparent he continued to brood over the prospect of my leaving. They said it many times, as reported here, that Aunt Madeline and Uncle Al always said, "Dale had two kids; Mike and Carol. Barbara had thirteen." I objected to the characterization, though secretly I thought it was true. In fact, I thought it was true up to the moment I disobeyed him and joined the Peace Corps. He was at odds with himself about the whole affair. I know he believed there was value in what I was doing, while being incapable of imagining me away for two years.

The entire family joined me at the Joplin airport on the day I left for Ecuador. It was joyous and sad. Mom told me later:

> We stood on an outside observation deck and watched you walk across the tarmac toward the boarding stairs. We all waved as tears began showing up on one face and then another. I think some of the kids were crying because I was. I looked over at Dale.

He leaned against the pipe railing as if needing help to stand up. His stone-faced gaze began to fade and I knew he was fighting back his emotions. He turned and backed away from our group. Some of the older kids noticed too and began casting quick glances his way. The looks on their faces proved just how rare it was to see that kind of emotion from Dale. He was wiping his eyes and collecting himself as quickly as he could.

I took no joy in hearing Mom's account.

44

THE GREAT ADVENTURE

Told by Linda #3

1964 was full of surprises. Carol's Peace Corp work in Ecuador made her both happy and sad. In a matter of months, she was homesick and offered to pay Mom's travel expenses to come visit. It seemed an outlandish idea—surely Dad would put a stop to the notion. Then, to everyone's surprise, and without a real discussion, Mom told everyone she intended to go. She talked with Aunt Madeline about joining her. Madeline was enthusiastic. They arranged to leave that summer for a month-long trip.

The older kids were shocked. It was unlikely Mom had ever traveled to more than five states in her entire life and now she was going to South America. How was that even possible? Plus, we would be left with Dad in charge, and that was a frightening thought. I imagined none of us would be going anywhere for those thirty days. The opposite turned out to be true.

Soon after Mom and Aunt left, it became clear Dad had little interest in running anything. He came and went as always, content to know his *threat* value was undiminished. Mom left money for food with instructions for how to spend it. For the first week, things continued to run as they always had. Whatever apprehension I felt, melted away with the demands of taking care of the little kids. I was maternal before I could walk, so the new responsibilities seemed natural. There was no fear; no hesitation. Kelly, Stan and Hal went about their jobs and helped whenever I asked. Mary and Ginger supervised the kids and did their parts to prepare meals and clean up afterward. It was summer, so we took the younger ones to the pool nearly every day. Otherwise, they were fine with playing together upstairs in the rec room or across the street at the Holy Name playground.

Dad took care of himself for the most part. He came home for lunch and always had his highball after 5:00 each evening. His clothes were laundered as Mom would have done. If a person avoided tunneling down too deeply, things appeared pretty typical. Yet, I felt we were operating on a knife's edge. We may have been pulling it off for a few weeks, but Mom's absence was beginning to take a toll. We were an unanchored boat; afloat, but drifting aimlessly. She needed to get home. Dad's one or two highballs became three or four on some nights, and his disposition began to sour.

~

Meanwhile, Mom, Aunt Madeline and Carol were having an incredible time in South America. Carol filled us in:

> We stayed in Quito, Ecuador for a few days and then travelled by bus down the west coast. My Spanish, formal by local standards, was solid, so I easily negotiated our way through most situations. While in Lima, Peru we were trying to make arrangements for transportation further south. Standing near us was a very official looking gentleman who Aunt Madeline mistook for a policeman.
>
> "Maybe this joker could tell us what to do," she said in exasperation.
>
> The man turned in her direction and in perfect English asked, "How may I help you, Ma'am?"

Aunt Madeline, statuesque and uncommonly pretty, blushed and issued a strained chuckle. "I'm so sorry," she said, "I thought you were a policeman."

"Not a joker?" the military man replied. But then he laughed and asked where we were going.

It turned out he was a General in the Peruvian army. He invited us to travel in his car and said he would take us to his headquarters and arrange further transportation from there. "Load their bags into the trunk," he ordered.

The General, a graduate of Harvard, was good natured and charming. I filled time by giving him background information about Mom and Aunt Madeline.

"Thirteen children?" he commented. "You look too young for that. Did you leave them with a nanny?"

Mom, dressed conservatively in a light sun dress, her black hair brushing the folded collar, smiled and said, "I'm afraid we couldn't afford something like that."

"So, your husband is taking care of them?" the General asked.

"That'll be the day," Madeline said.

I jumped in to explain the bump system and how the little kids knew to mind the older ones, and that they were more than capable of taking care of things.

"The "bump system," the General repeated. He took a minute to consider the thought. He slapped his thigh and said, "You're running an army. You're just like me. You're the General," he said to Mom. "And when you leave, your second in command takes over and on down the line. I love it."

After a few more miles, he tipped his head toward us and said, "Three beautiful ladies. What good fortune."

> We reached the base and enjoyed a beer and a late lunch with our new friend. It was exciting to travel with the General. It should have ranked as the most memorable part of our road trip. But it paled in comparison to bus rides over one lane roads hugging the sides of towering mountains. If our bus met another, one of the drivers had to back up to a short passing lane cut just wide enough for the two vehicles to pass. Thankfully, there were few of those roads to travel."

Mom's favorite story was about a ride from Quito to Machala on Ecuador's western coast. She told it like this:

> We always tried to sit close to one another on the bus trips. Typically, Madeline and I sat together and Carol took the aisle seat across from us. That was the arrangement when we left Quito. Sitting next to Carol was a casually dressed young man, maybe in his mid-twenties. He minded his own business for the first forty miles or so, only occasionally glancing our way if we laughed about one thing or another.
>
> I leaned my head against the seat back and closed my eyes. The bus hit something that caused it to lurch up enough to wake me. At the same moment, I noticed the young man placing his hand on Carol's leg. She slapped it and pushed him away. She pointed to her canvass tote and spread her hands apart as if measuring something. The young man's body stiffened and he stared straight ahead. And that was that.
>
> When we reached our next stop and were alone, I asked Carol what she had said.
>
> "I told him I had a knife in my tote this long," she spread her hands as before, "and if you ever reach toward me again, I'll stab you in the leg."
>
> Madeline and I winked at one another."

~

Mom returned home after a full thirty days. I came to the conclusion she took that trip for two reasons. She obviously wanted to see Carol and experience the adventure. But I think there was another purpose. I'm convinced she wanted Dad to miss her, to see what life was like without her.

I wondered how that had turned out.

45

A TRIAL PERIOD

Told by Hal #6

There were two trials going on in the first three or four years in Coffeyville. Neither was planned and both were life altering.

The first determined whether Dad could make it in the insurance industry. That turned out to be impossible. It takes years to build a profitable book of business and with thirteen kids, one in college, there just wasn't enough time. The second trial was less obvious. It was lived every day and would prove whether Dad could be more than a weekend father.

He did the best he could. The adjustment from two days a week to full-time parenting had to be brutal. I'm guessing he felt guilty about missing our events, or avoiding simple things like Parent/Teacher conferences. Traveling throughout the week had guaranteed him a perfect alibi, and now that excuse was gone. His new life came at him in waves and he was constantly swimming upstream.

The trial outcomes looked ominous.

Dad gave up the insurance business in 1965. He began working with Aunt Velva and her husband Harold in their hearing instrument office in Columbia, Missouri. He spent the week there, training under Uncle Harold. On weekends, he sold hearing aids in Coffeyville. Kelly and Linda continued to make cold calls for Dad, except now they were offering free hearing tests as opposed to insurance quotes. Dad seemed relieved to have made the change.

By 1966, Mike had graduated from Saint Benedict's and was working on a law degree at Washburn Law School in Topeka. (Later in life, tongue in cheek, our brother Tim liked to tell the bluebloods back east that Washburn was the "Harvard of the West.) Carol was back from the Peace Corps and enrolled at Kansas State College in Pittsburg, Kansas. She was a Residence Hall director. Linda lived in Parsons, Kansas with her new husband and baby. Ten days after graduating from high school, Kelly joined the army. He knew the family was unable to help with college expenses and the military's Veteran benefits would pay for a significant portion of his education.

Just weeks before Dad was ready to strike out on his own, disaster struck. On Tuesday, September 20, 1966, Dad called to tell us Uncle Harold had died of a heart attack. He was only sixty years old. According to Velva, they were working in the office, Harold at his desk, she filing paperwork. Suddenly, Harold sat straight up, arched his back and said, "This is it, Velva." He was dead before his head hit the desk.

Dad was shaken. He and Harold shared a rich history dating back to when they frequented bars and partied together before Harold got religion. He was like a big brother and Dad looked up to him. His sense of loss was personal and profound. Adding to his grief, Velva was devastated and her pain became his. She looked defeated, lost, and I think everyone realized she would, from that day forward, lead a half-life without Harold.

Soon after Harold died, Dad announced he was going to start a hearing instrument business in Topeka, Kansas.

His plan totally surprised Mom. She had assumed he would be working in Coffeyville, but there was no point in objecting. She knew Dad had probably brooded over the move for months and that his decision was final. What she found out next was unexpected.

"I guess I should begin looking for a house up there," she said, dreading the thought of it and loath to leave Coffeyville.

"I'm going alone," Dad replied. "I'll be home on weekends."

Mom put up a halfhearted protest, arguing that he could start the business in Coffeyville.

"It's not big enough," Dad countered. "It would end up like the insurance business."

She knew he had made up his mind, and that issue was settled too.

If you took a survey of the older kids, as shocking as the news was at first, they welcomed it. We were accustomed to a weekend father. The younger ones would learn soon enough how much more enjoyable life could be with a two-day-a-week dad. Some worried his absence might lead to chaos. How would the kids behave with him away all week?

It turned out the amount of time he spent at home, within reason, was irrelevant. Everyone should have known little would change. While we might enjoy a greater sense of freedom, our behavior was rooted in a code written by Dad. Mom was the glue that held our family together, but Dad was the bottle it came in. Nearly any important decision we considered took into account what he would think or do.

Maybe two days a week was exactly right. During the week we were like horses running free. On the weekends, our bridles were restored and the reins tightened just enough to remind us who was in charge.

TERRY #10

Mom could function normally, even through her most troubled times. She typically kept the truth to herself, opting for privacy over drama. For instance, none of us knew how she felt about Dad moving to Topeka, but her actions proved it had shaken her.

I was in the second grade when it happened. I came home from school one day and said, "Mom, Sister and the other kids sang happy birthday to me today. Is today my birthday?"

Mom stood motionless for a split second. She then swept me up and hugged me. It caught me by surprise. I doubt she had held me like that since I was a toddler.

"I'm so sorry," she said. I watched tears well up in her eyes. "After lunch, I'll make you the best birthday cake you've ever had. Whatever you want. And you get to choose your birthday meal too?"

I chose a chocolate cake with chocolate icing. As for dinner, the older kids typically bribed the younger ones into asking for fried chicken, mashed potatoes, gravy and corn. Little did they know, we would have asked for that anyway, but there was no harm in bargaining for a reward. Mom's fried chicken was amazing.

As soon as lunch was over and the kids left for school, Mom took my hand and guided me to the kitchen. She lifted me onto the counter top and kissed my cheek. There, we talked about everything and nothing as she went about baking my cake.

"Don't I need to go back to school?" I asked.

"I'll call Sister," Mom answered. "She'll understand. This is *your* day and I want to be with you."

She whisked and stirred, stirred and whisked. As I think back on it now, maybe she was working out her guilt for overlooking my birthday. The thing is, she smiled a lot too, rubbed my back when things slowed down, patted my leg as she worked around me. She made me feel happy and special.

I got to lick the wooden spoon she used to mix the cake batter and stir the icing. Without my knowing, she arranged for one of the older kids to buy a few presents. They were given to me after everyone sang happy birthday and I blew out the candles on my cake.

It was one of the best days of my life.

Mary told me Mom swore it would never happen again. As far as I know, it never did. The biggest surprise is that it happened only once. Later, we learned there was a good reason for her scattered attentions.

46

ALTAR SOCIETY FRIENDS

Told by Mom's Friends

We were lucky to know Barbara through the Holy Name Altar Society. Our group was responsible for things like the hosts, wine, vessels, linens, vestments, candles and flowers used for daily services at the altar. We gathered for spiritual duties, and along the way we became great friends.

Barbara stood out in our group for many reasons, the most obvious was that she was raising thirteen children. Consistently kind and considerate, she lived her life with what we all called 'chaotic calmness'. We marveled at her serene response to a conveyor belt of problems that spilled into her life. She created order wherever possible. But in the end, thirteen clever, bright, productive and mischievous kids will win out over any effort to corral them. None of it seemed to unsettle her. She faced all of that unpredictability with humor and patience.

"How do you deal with so many kids?" was an early question.

Her answer was direct, "We've tried to raise them to do the right thing," she said. "I know they're not perfect, but I have faith they'll make good choices. It's really all a person has, isn't it?"

One cold winter day, after we served a funeral lunch, a few of us gathered around for a cup of coffee and our choice of leftover desserts. Someone asked Barbara about living on the farm and how the kids were adjusting to town life.

She told us a number of cute stories, including one about Pat.

"After the first day of school at Holy Name," she began, "Pat (a first grader) walked across the street to come home. Our neighbor's house looked a lot like ours. Jean Stover's dad, Bud, was sitting on their front porch. He watched Pat cross the street and head directly toward him. Pat climbed the porch steps, saw Bud and looked around in confusion. 'I think you have the wrong place, young man,' Bud said. 'You live over there,' pointing to our house. 'Oh. Okay,' Pat said. He took another look, just to be sure Bud knew what he was talking about, then reversed course and headed home."

Barbara wore very little makeup or jewelry. She felt life was complicated enough without keeping track of useless things. Her treasures tended to be simple items like a silver charm bracelet made up of eight boy and five girl silhouettes. On one side was the name of a child, on the other his or her birthdate. The multi colored birthstone ring on her right hand was another reminder of what mattered most. Her favorite necklace was a gold cross and chain given to her by one of the kids to help hide the faded scar from a thyroid operation. She wore a tiny diamond engagement ring on her left hand, though if a diamond were present, it was tough to distinguish from the setting.

Those were the only decorations Barbara needed. Don't get us wrong, she cared about how she looked. Neat and well groomed, Barbara had her hair cut and styled at the local beauty college every month or so. I heard she took her hairdresser a loaf of homemade bread on most appointments—lucky hairdresser.

We know Barbara sacrificed a lot to provide for Dale and all of those kids…and she sure had fun doing it. She laughed easily, loved generously, gambled with enthusiasm and was curious about nearly everything. Some said she gave up her own life for the family. They miss that the family *was* her life. In that regard, we never met a more satisfied human being.

Barbara was a prolific communicator and we were her loyal friends, eager to listen. She told her stories in vivid detail and absent the slightest effort to conceal the truth. Some were about boldness and courage, like when her daughter Carol joined the Peace Corps and left for Ecuador. Others were about dread, like when her son Stan enlisted in the Army and was sent to Viet Nam just as the war was ramping up. And we heard about notoriety like when her son Mike defended a high-profile pro football player in a widely published court case in Wichita. We learned about kids winning speech contests and debate tournaments, about others winning tennis matches, baseball games or swim meets. A number of the girls were chosen football or basketball Queen and one was an attendant for both.

We also heard of harrowing stories like when Pat, the little boy at the wrong house, now all grown up, owned a butcher shop in downtown Independence, KS. One morning, a gas leak developed in the underground piping beneath his building. It seeped out in all directions, filling spaces where only fumes could go. Along its path, now far-reaching and unimpeded, it found a spark. Pat's building exploded along with half a block of other businesses on that street.

"Thank God it happened on a Sunday when no one was at work," she said.

We were never surprised when she entered the room offering up the latest report of injuries. We heard about broken arms or legs, finger tips cut off with a meat slicer, minor car wrecks, Al walking into the street with a stocking cap pulled over his face and bumping into a moving car, or Terry nearly losing an eye in a sledding accident. She generously revealed the good and the bad of her life, though by her telling, it was difficult to know which way she saw it.

She advanced by miles and retreated by inches.

47

OFF TO THE RACES

Told by Stan #4

Mom and Dad created standards of behavior we all followed. The lessons were passed down from the oldest kids to the youngest. On a systematic level, it began with the "bump system," which was simple and effective. It established an order to our lives and insured continuity. There was no magical age when things became different. We were simply in a line of progression. You listened to anyone older than you, and you were responsible for anyone younger.

Some believed it was just good fortune we turned out the way we did. But I knew better. *I* knew early on that Mom gave each of us only the amount of responsibility we could handle. She knew our abilities and limitations because she had fixed fences with us, showed us how to milk cows, raise chickens, gather eggs, feed weaning calves, plant and weed a vegetable garden or any of a hundred additional things a farm kid needed to know. She made sure Dad prepared us for driving tractors and using farm equipment. She left it up to him to teach us how to ride horses and raise sheep, horses and cattle. Once we had mastered the basics, she trusted we would learn the rest by doing.

We knew what to do on the farm—knew its gifts and demands. The move to Coffeyville challenged all of that. I always believed the transition was toughest on Hal. He could claim to be a farm kid *and* a town kid. A few younger than him might remember being *on* the farm, but he *lived* it. I think he was six years old when Kelly and I first had him pushing bales of hay, one quarter turn at a time, from the storage loft over the garage to the hay rack in the middle of the barnyard. He weighed less than the bale of hay. Within a year, he was milking cows when needed, or cutting holes in the pond ice in winter.

This is how Hal told it:

> I thought living on the farm was great and I had mixed feelings about moving to town. Kelly told me I hadn't lived there long enough to resent having so much responsibility. That may have been true, but I remember being happy, even when I started doing chores. It was like joining a club when I began working beside my brothers. Along with work, came the pleasure of riding horses with them too – Kelly leading on SusieQ, Stan riding Nelly Belle, and me bringing up the rear on Dolly. I know they picked Dolly because I was the youngest and least experienced and she was gentle and kind.
>
> I once rode her into the orchard, reigned to a stop under a tree loaded with apples, reached up and plucked a piece of fruit from a branch, laid back with my head on Dolly's hips and ate the apple while thinking about how lucky I was.
>
> Mom encouraged the partnership, knowing I would be looked after. We did everything together, including swimming in the farm pond, which was full of some of the muddiest, brownest, most disgusting water on the planet. And we loved it. We went swimming at least a hundred times every summer. Twice a day was common. The highlight was when Mom joined us. She wore a one-piece, black swimsuit with thin straps over her shoulders. She generally had on a tight swimmer's cap that made her look smaller than she actually was. She could swim like a pro, her free style stroke long and graceful. She played games with us and stayed as long as we wanted.

Mom was great that way. She had an innate sense of how kids think and what mattered to us. Every year, no matter what other expenses might be weighing on her decisions, she bought a family season pass to the Parsons municipal pool and later to Coffeyville's. We used it often. One summer day, when I was about nine years old, uncle Charles, Mom's youngest brother, was in Parsons for a visit. He agreed to take Carol, Linda, Kelly, Stan, Mary, Ginger and I swimming at the public pool. While paying for himself, he began laughing as one kid after another filed past the desk staff and said, "Wilson," "Wilson," "Wilson,". Finally, the clerk said, "Ok, ok, I know. You're all Wilsons."

The move to town changed our environment, but the rhythm of our home lives remained the same. Just like on the farm, Dad continued to give us burr haircuts about once per month. We lined up in the hallway and sat with our backs against the wall like captured prisoners awaiting our fate. Then, one-by-one, we entered the bathroom where we sat on a chair Dad had carried from the kitchen. He then draped a towel over our shoulders and back. The clippers were always oiled first, though they still occasionally grabbed our hair instead of cutting it. When we were younger, he nearly turned us into versions of future skinheads. As we aged, he left our hair a little longer on top, but the results would never pass as "style." There was no greater incentive to get a job and pay for a real barber than avoiding Dad's haircuts. It's possible that was his plan all along.

～

Many of my friends wished they lived at my house. Mom had too many kids to try to keep track of them moment to moment. She just learned to trust that we would do the right thing, even when we were doing something questionable. Once, when I was around twelve years old, a couple of friends and I decided to spend a little time in the church bell tower. You had to pass through the choir loft and up some rarely used steps to get there. We failed to calculate that the choir might be practicing that evening. They were, and we were stuck.

As daylight faded, we began hearing parents calling out the names of my friends in the tower. "My Dad's gonna kill me," one of them worried. "Mine too," another said. From our lofty perch, we could see people coming out of their houses looking for us.

"Nobody's looking for you," one of them said to me. "Jesus, I wish I was a Wilson." And that's the way it was. Mom knew I would get home safely and a little darkness did nothing to dissuade her.

Back to Stan

We all knew Dad kept Mom on a tight budget. As much as she may have wanted, there was no way to help us financially. I think it bothered her, though she hid whatever she felt about it. Instead, she championed any cause that helped us earn our way through life. While we were still in grade school, she let us sell mistletoe or Christmas cards door-to-door during the holidays, or the non-slip clothes hangers we made by hand. She dropped us off in a neighborhood of her choosing, left to do her grocery shopping, then picked us up afterward. A young family friend once commented, "I knew Tim would be a success. While the rest of us were catching candy thrown by a fat guy on a sleigh during the Christmas parade, Tim was weaving his way through the crowd, pulling a little red wagon and selling mistletoe he had either climbed a tree to get at, or shot it out with a BB gun from the ground.

Mom sometimes helped the boys roll newspapers or slide them into a plastic sleeve to deliver during rain showers. She also drove them on their routes during snow storms. She filled in for the girls when they had to miss a babysitting job. She did our chores if one of us was sick. I can't think of a single instance when she failed to back us up.

We once decided to save returnable metal containers to sell at a recycling plant. We collected large plastic bags of the treasure, convinced we were going to make a killing. On the day our hard work was to pay off, we loaded all the bags into the Woody and Mom drove us to the recycling facility. They weighed the car with the bags in it, and then again after they were removed. The anticipation in the car was electric. How much would we make?

A thin man wearing a baseball cap, walked toward the car. Our heads pivoted to his movement. He gave Mom the weight slip and deposited some change into her open hand, then walked away.

"How much," someone asked?

With no judgement or apparent disappointment, Mom answered "Eighty-four cents."

That business plan was dropped along with the first collection.

There was a certain synergy to the younger brothers and sisters work patterns. Starting off as babysitters and paperboys, they progressed to clerks in fast food outlets, ice cream parlors, grocery stores and eventually to cashier jobs at a local bank. The positive reputation of one, fueled the rise of those who followed.

A perfect example: One of the first jobs the boys could get was taking a paper route for the Coffeyville Journal. I started an unbroken line of Wilsons who threw the paper up Fourth Street and down Fifth for over twelve years. As the baton was passed from one brother to next, some of our customers failed to realize a different Wilson had taken over.

Our life-clocks typically march in undetected ticks. But once in a while, events expose time and a person's life is changed with striking certainty. It happened to me when I decided to go out for the high school football team. Mom encouraged it, though she understood my size was no match for the desire that motivated me.

That first day, after changing into an ill-fitting uniform, the coaches tried in vain to find a helmet that wouldn't wobble on my head—no luck. I was assigned to a group of players on the offensive line. Everything was fine until the coach threw me into my first—and mercifully, last play. A defensive lineman twice my size, nicknamed Tuna, bulldozed over me like I wasn't there. I stood up, walked to the sideline, tossed my useless helmet to the ground and headed to the locker room. *"There has to be something better than this,"* I said to myself.

I drove to the fairgrounds where Flicka was stabled and asked around for a horse trainer by the name of Clyde Hulet. We heard he was a no-nonsense horseman who was respected by everyone in the race horse business. I found him in a dirt covered corral next to his stables.

"Can you ride a horse," Clyde asked after I told him I was looking for a job.

"Yes, Sir," I answered.

"Then show me," Clyde said. He led me into a wood-rail corral where an antsy three-year old colt was tied to a gate post. He was sporting a black training saddle. The wide-eyed bay came to attention as we drew near. Clyde legged me up and led the pair of us to one side of the corral. After letting lose his hold on the reins, he backed away to the center of the lot. Clyde nearly always carried a long bullwhip at his side when training younger horses, though it never touched one of them. The *"cracking"* sound was all he needed to keep their attention.

"Take off," he said, and he gave the whip a meaningful "pop."

Though I had never ridden a training saddle, the position of the stirrups, high up on the horse's shoulders, caused me to begin posting automatically. Posting is basically when you're standing in the stirrups, your upper body bent forward. I rode like I had been doing it all my life. In essence, I had.

After a few trips around the corral, Clyde held up one hand and motioned me over to where he was standing.

"Get here as soon as you can after school every day," was all he said.

Word spread quickly that there was a new rider at Clyde Hulet's place. After my first week of riding, trailers were lined up along Clyde's driveway each afternoon. Race horses were hauled in from all around for me to exercise. I was paid a flat fee for every horse I rode and even more for riding in races on the weekend. I was earning more money than any kid my age.

When I could no longer make weight, Hal, following me from the paper route to cleaning stalls and hot walking horses, replaced me at Clyde's and the money-making machine rolled on.

"What did your parent's think of that?" a friend asked.

Well, it's the darnedest thing—Mom was happy we were doing something we loved and could make money to boot. Dad, on the other hand, while avoiding an outright ban, warned us of the danger and never watched either of us ride a single race. Mom was the opposite. She loved going to the races. In time, she began doing more than just watching.

Pari-mutual betting was against the law in Kansas and Oklahoma while we were riding. However, that did little to stem the demand and availability of wagering on the races. Folks would stand around the saddling paddock and wait for odds makers to state their positions. The money changers milled through the crowds, inconspicuously making their opinions known and by what odds they were willing to back them.

"I'll take the eight horse and give the field," one would say, "even money." If there were ten horses contesting the race, he was saying you could have the other nine entrants and he would get only the number eight. Chances are, he knew something about that horse and if the truth were known, the bettor should have been getting better odds to play against him.

Another might say, "I'll take the even numbered horses against the odd numbers at two to one." If there were ten horses in the race, the odds maker is taking the 2, 4, 6, 8 and 10 and you get the 1, 3, 5, 7 and 9. He's giving two to one odds, so if you put up a dollar and one of the odd numbered horses win, he has to pay you $3, your dollar, plus two more.

Or, it might become weird like when a guy hollered out, "Even up, I'll bet the number seven is leading at the first light pole." If someone took the bet, a couple of young men were dispatched to the light pole to declare the leader.

Most of the betting was done as the horses were being saddled before the race. After she became knowledgeable about how it worked, Mom would venture into the middle of the wagering crowd to make a bet. With experience, she became crafty. If one of the bookies was giving odds on even numbers over odd, and Mom's horse was an odd number, she jumped on the bet knowing she was picking up some additional insurance. Money would change hands and she would return to the stands.

It was dangerous sitting next to Mom during a race if she had a stake in the outcome. When the announcer broadcast that the last horse was entering the gate, if they valued their body, the kids near Mom created some distance. She would screech, call out encouragement, bound to her feet and invariably beat on the person next to her as the horses approached the finish line. Her enthusiasm infected everyone around her, though few knew why the outcome was so important.

One afternoon, a man to her left took a particularly aggressive pounding on the arm and shoulder as the horses raced down the stretch. He happened to be the guy who covered Mom's bet. The winner was announced and he paid her. The bruised man said, "Excuse me, Ma'am, but I've watched you for a long time and I can never tell why you make the bets you do. Is it the trainer? Do you know the horse's owners? What's your angle?"

"I bet on the jockey," Mom admitted. "I have two sons who ride. If they're in the race, that's who I'm betting on."

"Well, I'll be damned," the bookie said. "Are either of them in the next race?"

"One of them is riding the 3 horse," Mom said.

The bookie moved up two rows.

That's the way Mom inspired work. She supported every one of us in whatever job we could find. Whether shopping at the supermarket where Carol worked, buying shoes at the store where Kelly was a janitor or rooting home a race horse Hal or I were riding—she was there.

48

MOM THE DISCIPLINARIAN

Told by Mary #7

Mom rarely used corporal punishment, but when she did, it made an impression. As youngsters— three years to six or seven—a hearty swat on the behind was about as severe as it got. However, when it concerned our safety, she spared little effort to make her point. I'm convinced, like Dad, she believed that if you want a child to remember a lesson, tie it to something dramatic— something extraordinary. Regardless, always in control, she measured her response against the degree of the offense.

Throughout our lives, Mom used the threat, "I'll tell your dad" to win the day. That was enough to strike fear into the hearts of even the boldest among us. We knew Dad was prone to immediate, unquestioned, decisive action, so the threat carried a sobering vision. Luckily, Mom rarely followed through, but the mere possibility turned steely nerves to quivering jello.

Somewhere along the line, Mom began using a new tactic to make her point. Given that nearly all of us were tall enough to see over her head when standing face to face, she equalized that disadvantage by using her reach. Mom became a slapper. Its power lay more in the shock of the moment than any hurt. It's akin to petting your purring cat who suddenly springs into action and scratches or bites you. "What the ….?"

Al, the youngest, has a good example of such a moment:

> I was nine or ten years old, playing with a friend who lived maybe a block and a half away from our house. She was my age. For the life of me, I don't remember what she did to set me off, but I know I called her a bitch and immediately headed home.
>
> I walked into the house. Mom was on the phone. I moved to her side and began hugging her. A few seconds later, she hung up the receiver, created a little distance between us, and *whack*, a solid face slap. My first thought was, *how did that girl's mom make the call so fast?* Speed dial was years away, but she had gotten the story from her daughter, dialed Mom and explained her beef, all before I had run one block. I was impressed.

Only a few of the brothers and sisters remember one of Mom's slaps, because it happened so rarely. In fact, I avoided it altogether, but I recall being a central character in one of those events.

Ginger and I were closet smokers. We hid our cigarettes in an old metal lunch box and squirreled it away in a deep corner of our closet. Periodically, we would collect a couple of cigarettes, exit the back of the house and walk a well-worn path through the back yard leading to an unfinished opening dad had sledge hammered into the garage. I'm still amazed we avoided being caught in the act. When a pack was empty, we just left it in the lunch box, afraid of being discovered with the evidence on us, or throwing it in a trash can where Mom might find it.

One day, while hanging clothes in our closet, Mom noticed the metal lunch box. She slid it from its hiding place and walked into the living room carrying it with the lid hanging down in defeat. Empty Marlboro packets peeked over the edge. When I saw the evidence, my heart stopped and I began sweating. "That Ginger," Mom said. I had a momentary urge to fess up, but instead, just looked surprised. I was sitting on the couch, Mom hovering over me. We could see through the front storm door and at that moment Ginger came walking up the sidewalk steps. Mom moved to the front entrance. She held the proof in her left hand and waited. I stopped breathing. Ginger stepped into the living room, took one look at the lunch box, half grinned and *whack*.

Maybe I should have admitted my guilt that day, but it's important to understand the whole story. Most of the kids considered me a "goody two shoes", because I was. I hovered, I protected, I tried to anticipate danger and steer us away from it. Grounded in Mom's sense of service, I believed in the value of trying to make others happy by my own efforts. I think my most grievous crime was adding too much ice cream to a cone for one of my friends when I worked at Peter Pan.

Ginger, on the other hand, was a known agitator—bolder than her small size justified. A good example: She created a space known as "Duke City" in the horseshoe formed by two garages across the street from the playground. If an argument arose between a couple of kids, she stirred the pot until they agreed to meet at Duke City after school and there, through varying degrees of physical exchange, the differences were resolved. She was Don King and Duke City was an MMA cage before either thing existed. Sometimes, she arranged matches just because she enjoyed it. She particularly liked watching our brother Pat duke it out. "He's scrappy," she liked to say.

Another: Ginger once became irritated by one of the nuns who taught music class. The cheerleaders wanted our youngest sister, Teresa, to act as mascot for Holy Name's sports teams. Sister said "no" and called Teresa a "picklepuss". In retaliation, Ginger—riled by the unwarranted name calling—persuaded the entire choir to remain silent when directed to sing. The next day, Sister entered the room, laid out sheet music on a lectern, considered it for a moment, raised her arms, waved them up and down like a flying seagull and directed the choir to begin the assigned song—silence. "Sing! Sing!" she encouraged—nothing. "Sing!" she demanded—zilch. "Now!" she cried – the hush overwhelmed her.

She left the room in defeat.

Justified or not, I took comfort in believing the cigarette-provoking slap was just one penance Ginger had coming.

On a redeeming note, Ginger was capable of valuable things too. Every Saturday morning, while Mom went to the grocery store, Ginger gathered the younger kids together in the living room. She named each room in the house and wrote them on a separate piece of paper. The kids were then forced to draw for which room they would clean that day. It was efficient and ruthless.

Those events are great examples of how Mom prioritized crime and her response to it. The recently found cigarette packs brought out the big guns. Whack! But when Mom found out about Duke City she simply ordered, "Stop that!" I think I saw her smile as she turned away.

And then there were the "in-between" crimes—the ones where a slap amounted to overkill, but a simple admonishment was inadequate. In those cases, Mom relied on her most potent weapon, "I'll tell your dad."

A case in point—Terry told me about this the day it happened:

Mom had great faith in the older kids looking after the younger ones. Experience proved she was generally right, but sometimes her confidence was shaken. During one summer break, Stan and Hal took up calf roping. After exercising horses at Clyde's, they practiced on real calves at the fairgrounds. Then, back home, they decided on a new routine that involved Pat, Tim and I.

The three of us were led to the alley. Stan and Hal each carried a rope, which made me worry about how things might go for us. They lined us up facing the street, about half a block away. Pat was first, next me, and then Tim. Stan fashioned the end of his long rope into a loop and circled it over his head a couple of times.

"When I say, 'go', you take off," he told Pat. "Now, GO!"

Pat was fast and he outran Stan's toss.

Stan stepped back to gather up his rope. Hal moved forward with his rope primed.

"Now, you, Terry," he said. "GO!"

I took off, but Hal had learned from Stan's mistake and threw his loop before I had time to build up a head of steam. Caught.

Then, it was Tim's turn. Before stepping up to the line, he asked, "Why do you need all three of us? There are only two of you."

"We need to keep our bulls fresh," Stan said. He and Hal laughed and one of them stomped a foot.

Stan gave the 'go' order and Tim got caught too.

On and on it went for the next half hour or so. Some of the throws caught us around our bodies or legs, others slapped against our heads or backs and the ropes slid off in crumpled defeat. We danced our way back to the line when they missed us.

No telling how long it would have gone on if not for one errant catch. Tim was the bull—Stan the calf roper. Tim took off. Stan threw his loop. Tim was running hard and fast and had learned to duck his head after the first few yards. Stan's aim was right on target. His rope glided over Tim's bowed head but came to rest under his chin, the noose riding on his bent back. When Stan pulled, the loop gathered around Tim's neck. His forward motion tightened the rope and caused him to flip backward.

Stan and Hal ran to see if Tim was okay. They stood him up, dusted him off and removed the rope from around his neck.

"Look at that rope burn," Stan said. "Mom's gonna be pissed."

"Go put on a dickie," Hal said. "That'll hide it."

"He can't wear a dickie till it heals," Stan said. "Just stay away from Mom," he told Tim.

Tim said he would and headed for the house. He honored their demands for a total of ten minutes. Stan and Hal's new practice scheme had to be stopped, and Tim knew how to do it.

The minute he was alone with Mom, he asked, "Do you think I need to change this shirt?"

When she looked his way, he held his head up high.

"What's that around your neck?" she asked.

The jig was up. Mom got the truth out of Stan and Hal. After a thorough berating, she ended with, "Do it again and I'll tell your dad."

The bulls were put out to pasture.

And then there were the times she could have taken action—probably *should* have in fact—but opted to remain quiet.

For example, Stan was home from the army and going to school at the junior college. Our dog, Sassy, was in the front yard minding her own business. Someone from animal control spotted her, saw that her collar was missing and gave Mom a ticket. Mom was generally strapped for cash, so the fine upset her. Stan was livid. Now, I can't say he did it, but the next day a headline in the Coffeyville Journal announced, "Dogs Released from Pound."

Mom read it, looked at Stan and asked, "Was that you?"

"I don't know what you're talking about," he answered with a sheepish grin.

Al #13

Mom always said the older kids raised the younger ones, and she was right. She knew her grasp far exceeded her reach. I was the youngest, so I essentially had thirteen 'mothers' watching my every move. Here are just a couple of examples: I was just a little kid when one day Terry and I were picking up a few things for Mom at the local grocery store. As soon as we stepped outside, I pulled a handful of Brach's candy from my pocket and showed it to Terry.

"Where'd you get that?" Terry asked.

"You know," I said, "in that display near the checkout."

He grabbed me by my shirt collar, marched me back into the store, found the manager and made me give it back and apologize.

At least it wasn't slap worthy.

Another time, we were mowing and cleaning up the church and school grounds for Father O'Hare. It was the end of the day and I had had it. We thought we were heading home, but Father asked for one more duty. I rolled my eyes and looked disgusted.

As soon as Father walked away, Terry grabbed my shoulder and said, "Don't you ever do that again. If Father wants us to work all night, we're going to do it."

So yeah, Mom was a disciplinarian, and it came in many forms.

49

VIRGIE AND SID

Told by Linda #3

Virgie and Sid continued to live in Texas until Sid's oil lease job played out. The lease owner allowed them to continue living in their tiny house, even after all the pumps were converted to electric power. He told them they could stay as long as oil production made a profit. That arrangement suited them to a T—they liked that life was uncomplicated out there in the middle of not much. They saw people at church services on Wednesday evening and twice on Sunday. That was good enough for them.

The lease was shut down in 1958. Velva found Virgie and Sid a house in Joplin. They moved there in June. Though they were now close, we saw little of them other than on Thanksgiving Day. They were joined by Aunt Velva and Uncle Harold, Uncle Nathan and his new wife Rita and Virgie and Sid. Dad's family was boring compared to Mom's, except for Aunt Velva. She was dynamite in high heels and made the day fun all on her own. Mom said she could raise the dead if she set her mind to it.

Year after year, Sid remained notorious for his slow gait, hunched over profile and the narrow line of chewing tobacco stains issuing from the corners of his mouth. He spoke as little as a man could, short of saying nothing. I often wondered what he and Virgie talked about. Maybe his silence gave her more time to pray. She viewed life through a religious lens, and a very narrow one at that. She believed her denomination was the only true religion. You had to believe as they did or you were doomed to hell. She continued to harbor a particular hostility toward Catholics. We knew that from the fit she threw when Dad considered joining the church years earlier. I believe she loved us in an offhanded way; something required, but unembraced.

Seeing Virgie once a year was about right for Mom, though there were exceptions. On rare occasions, Dad would pile a few of us into the car for a drive to Joplin and a quick visit. On one occasion, Carol babysat the youngest back home, while I looked after the kids who made the trip. Dad spoke little in nearly every circumstance, but on those drives he sank even deeper within himself and only surfaced when we got there.

As we approached their one story, white frame house, Virgie and Sid were standing on the sidewalk out front. Virgie's hair, now sea-salt white, was still cut short and curled tight against her head. I wondered how long they had been standing there, and why they didn't just wait in the house. They appeared pleased to see us, though I may have been imagining that—assuming a grandmother would be happy to see her son and grandkids. I found Virgie impossible to read. There was a negative undercurrent when she was around—like a furious riptide hidden beneath a rolling ocean surface.

We lined up, youngest to oldest, and hugged Virgie and Sid. Mom was close behind. Her warmth and loving embrace were like an antidote to Virgie's cold nature. Dad was next. He shook Grandpa's hand and said, "Hello Mr. Snead." And then he leaned forward and placed his face against Virgie's. They both appeared stiff and only casually committed. I wondered if he would ever call her "mother". He didn't.

We were never invited into Virgie's house, and that trip was no different. She gave each of us a nickel and told us to go to the small neighborhood grocery store a few blocks away. "Buy some candy," she said. "And you can play here in the front yard when you get back." She enjoyed an uncanny sense of timing, knowing Dad was unlikely to stay very long. And that's exactly how it went. We had barely finished our treats before Mom and Dad came out of the house and we headed home.

Virgie, died of a stroke in 1967. Despite the mayhem Virgie caused, Mom cried when she found out—I think more for how she knew Dad would feel than that it caused her any personal pain. And she was right. Dad felt abandoned all over again. He wished he had been able to see her just one more time before she died. It's hard to imagine what he might have said.

Dad cried at the funeral. It was unnerving for most of us and some cried only because he was wiping his eyes. I remember seeing his tears just three times in my life; once, when Carol left for the Peace Corp, again, when Stan left for Viet Nam and finally, at Virgie's funeral when the preacher spoke of her commitment to God and her religion. He talked about her dedication to the church, what a good mother she had been and how she would be missed by Sid and her children. Mom squirmed in her seat when he said that, though I'm sure the preacher was unaware that Virgie left Dad when he was just ten years old.

Grandpa Snead was in shock. His sister, a banker in Texas, said that he and Virgie had been together every day since they married in 1930. She hated the idea of him wasting away in a nursing home and begged Mom and Dad to take him in. She contended that, after losing Virgie, he was unlikely to live a year. Her hole card was an offer to pay a monthly stipend for his care. I felt sorry for Sid. He had lost his wife and now the rest of his life was being negotiated at the gravesite where she had just been buried. Mom would have welcomed him regardless, though the extra income had to be appealing. She invited Sid into our home immediately. He was thrilled.

Mom cleared out a large bedroom across the hall from the kitchen and adjoining the bathroom. Grandpa's bed, his favorite chair and a TV were delivered within days. He settled in and seemed happy. The kids gave him more attention than he had ever had. Some watched TV with him and all of us brought him anything he needed. I think he enjoyed our company, though he was accustomed to the quiet of *alone* and courted it most of the time.

Grandpa suffered with a hiatal hernia for much of his life. The same type of snake oil salesman who convinced him to buy a sheet of tinted plastic to create a color TV, sold him useless devices to cure his acid reflux. He swore the latest gizmo was working until the power of suggestion wore off, and then a new charlatan would show up. One of the boxes delivered with the meager trappings of his life, gave testament to how often he fell for their nonsense. When Mom opened it, she found contraptions made of leather, metal and cloth. Grandpa showed her how they worked; or didn't in this case. She listened patiently and smiled or frowned when he did. When his stories ended, she said, "Let's go see a doctor tomorrow and see what he has to say." Grandpa agreed.

The doctor examined him carefully and concluded that, given his age, corrective surgery was too dangerous. He recommended a bland diet and only two meals per day. "And a beer a day might be good for him too," the doctor said. Grandpa was elated. If he ever drank liquor, it was thirty years ago and prior to Virgie. Given his reaction, I'd say he had—and he missed it.

A new routine evolved. Mom prepared breakfast for the kids as usual. After putting the kitchen back in order, she made a special breakfast for Grandpa at 10:00 a.m. While he was eating, she began making lunch for the kids. After they finished and headed back to school, she did the dishes, cleaned the kitchen and by 2:00 p.m. she had Grandpa's lunch ready. He typically ate, went back to his room for a nap and returned at 3:00 p.m. for his one beer. Mom always had it sitting on the table in the kitchen. It was fun watching him drink it; 'chug' it would be more accurate. He downed the entire contents in two mighty swigs.

Grandpa lived for just over a year and a half after Grandma died. His life had never been fuller. He ate well and he was able to drink a beer every day. He died of natural causes in 1968 and was buried next to Virgie.

PART VI

MURALS ON CAROUSELS

Our lives play out like paintings on a mural
Mounted on a carousel
Inching away through time.

50

THE MIDDLE YEARS

Told by Mary and Ginger

Mary #7

By 1968 we were fully conditioned to Dad's new schedule. He left Coffeyville at 6:00 a.m. each Monday morning. After working all week in Topeka, he drove back to Coffeyville around mid-day on Saturday.

Linda and I helped out by traveling to small towns along Dad's route back home. On arrival in a new community, we went door-to-door trying to schedule hearing test appointments. Elderly folks, impressed with our good manners and diligent work ethic, often invited us in for cookies or cake. It might take a stop or two, but early on, someone would offer the use of their phone to make calls instead of knocking on doors. In larger towns, we might return for three or four weeks in a row. To show her appreciation, Mom baked bread the day before we left and sent it with us as a special thanks. Our new friends were typically disappointed when we finished going through the phone book. Maybe they were going to miss our sparkling personalities, but I think it was all about Mom's bread.

Saturday afternoons hummed with the whispered question, "Is he in a good mood?" The older brothers and sisters laughed at that. They told us that same question circulated for twelve years' worth of weekends on the farm.

And just like them, for a day and a half, our lives centered around trying to keep Dad happy. That was a task easier wished than done.

I believe Mom resented the new arrangement. She was a romantic. Her vision of marriage included a full-time husband, and she had recently had one, but for only three years. She wanted someone around to share her life, even if that someone was more an observer than a participant. She longed for the comfort of Dad lying next to her in bed at night—the body of a man she had loved since a teenager—the body of a man who gave her thirteen children. She craved the kiss they exchanged before going to sleep each night and upon waking up each morning.

Mom's resentment steeled her nerve. She was constantly strapped for money and began asking Dad for a larger allowance. Their exchanges typically became tense. Though the negotiations happened before we got up in the morning, or after we went to bed at night, we overheard more than a few of them. Mom was still trying to get by on $600 a month. With that, she had to pay utility bills, home, health and car insurance, food costs and incidentals that invariably cropped up while raising so many of us. Eventually, he increased her allowance to $700.

～

Stan joined the Army that year. It turned out that 1968 was one of the most dangerous periods possible to sign up. The war had become a constant in our lives by then. The nightly news consistently led with a recap of events unfolding in Vietnam and always ended with the number of American deaths reported that day. In late January, North Vietnam launched the Tet offensive which resulted in significant losses for the U.S. and South Vietnam. Though the allies survived the attack, it marked a turning point in sentiment about the War. The hippies, unlike the beatniks, had a cause to rally around: END THE WAR!

Kelly was back from Korea and working at the Induction Center in Kansas City, Missouri. He was safe and I think Mom and Dad believed Stan would be too. They continued to believe it until the day he was assigned to Vietnam. On the morning he left, Mom said goodbye through tears and sobs.

She went to the kitchen, unable to watch him leave. Dad, clearly shaken, walked him to the street where a friend waited to drive him to Ft. Leonard Wood. When Dad returned to the house, sick with worry, he laid down on the sofa and stayed there for two days.

Stan spent twelve months in Vietnam before completing his enlistment in Washington, DC at Walter Reed Hospital.

He made it through.

Ginger #8

1968 marked a turning point in our lives.

That year, Martin Luther King and Bobby Kennedy were assassinated. Women burned their bras, young men burned their draft cards, African American athletes staged protests at the Olympics, civil rights issues were resonant, class differences provoked anger and students across the nation rallied against the Viet Nam war. The planet shrank into our living rooms as news coverage expanded with greater candor, and *now* was happening *in the moment* to everyone— everywhere.

The world was in transition, and so was our family. The five oldest were now on their own. They left behind the lessons Mom and Dad taught them, and that they taught us. The bump system was alive and well and Hal was its new king. Mom was smart about leadership changes. She automatically began to depend more and more on the oldest, often deferring to him, or her, on mundane decisions. It sent a signal—in her absence, the first in line, called the shots.

All of us had jobs and were making money one way or another. At the same time, we fielded baseball players, a wrestler, a competitive swimmer and two varsity tennis players. There were scholastic heavyweights, Queen candidates for most of the organized sports teams including Basketball and Homecoming Queen. We were active in the Catholic Youth Organization and members of student council. All of it was possible because Mom knew how to raise kids. She encouraged without pushing. She celebrated our wins and chalked up losses to experience. There was always a next time, and she taught us to embrace it.

Dad continued a practice of, *if you can't go to all of their events, don't go to any of them*. We all knew the rules, so disappointment was out of the question. It went to extremes sometimes, like when our neighbor, Pete Stover, agreed to escort Mary and I to a dad-daughter date night. I gave it little notice at the time—it's just the way our lives worked, but I wonder what others thought of the arrangement. We had a dad. Where was he?

If it sounds like Dad was uncaring, I've given the wrong impression. He loved the kids with every fiber of his being. While I doubt anyone can remember any meaningful hugs, his cuddling days having ended well before their long-term memories kicked in, he was 'super dad' when it came to a crisis. It was then he morphed into a different being altogether.

The evidence was pure and dramatic. For instance: During Carol's Peace Corp service in Ecuador, she began passing out for no definable reason. Peace Corp personnel called Mom and told her Carol would be flown to Walter Reed Army hospital in Bethesda, MD. Mom was terrified. She called Dad. He drove home from Topeka that evening.

"How long before she'll be in the U.S.," Dad asked as he entered the house four hours later.

"They said it would take a day to make arrangements," Mom answered. "The guy who called said around forty-eight hours."

Without hesitation, Dad declared, "I'm going out there."

Dad was deathly afraid of flying. A plane trip was out of the question. His only option was to drive. He took a southern route to avoid a moisture packed weather system dumping snow on every state between Missouri and Washington, DC. Eventually, he had to head north and directly into the heart of the storm. When roads became impassable with deep snow, he found a way to work around them. A drive that should have taken sixteen hours, took twenty-three. He stopped only for gas, to use the bathroom or to buy food he could eat while driving.

Snowfall sometimes blinded him and he had to stop to let it clear. Cars were abandoned on both sides of the road. Just outside of Washington, a car in front of him began spinning from one side of the road to the other. *It has to be black ice*, Dad thought. If he touched the brakes, his car would spin out of control too. He decided to let the moment play out on its own terms. The spiraling car appeared to be in slow motion, its chaotic direction fueled by a frantic driver. Dad sat calmly. Within seconds, he would either hit the spinning car, or watch it spiral off the road. After one more pass in front of him, the other car careened headfirst into a ditch on the left. There was nothing he could do. He would call the Highway Patrol at his next stop. He collected himself and drove on as if nothing had happened.

Dad was waiting at the hospital when Carol arrived.

He consulted with her doctors, who discovered she had an arrhythmia. It could be controlled with medication. He called Mom to tell her the news, spent time with Carol, got a motel room and ate his first real meal in two days. After a good night's sleep, a visit to say good bye to Carol and one more talk with her doctor, he was on the road and heading back home.

He became the same steady champion when Kelly was put in the hospital with a blood infection during basic training or when Linda suffered a poisonous spider bite and was moved to a hospital in Tulsa.

When his presence really mattered, he was there.

51

THE CENTER OF THE UNIVERSE

Told by Pat, Terry & Tim

Dale Barbara

Mike | Carol | Linda | Kelly | Stan | Hal | Mary | Ginger | Pat | Terry | Tim | Teresa | Al

---

Pat #9

The Swinging Sixties went out rocking. Woodstock, the largest, most talent filled, most talked about concert in American history showed that decade the door. The Beatles sang their swan song on the roof of Apple Records Corporation. And the first human visitor to the moon left his footprints on its face.

The era of the 'farm' kids also ended by 1969. Our first five brothers and sisters were either working full time jobs, had joined the military or were off attending college. Most would consider that number, 5 kids, a family in itself, but Mom and Dad still had eight at home. Written about earlier, Mom had passed through the 'heartbreak' stage of sending kids off to school. She had sailed through the 'dutiful' stage and had 'drop kicked' the last two out the door. In fact, on Al's first day of school, in her bathrobe, she chased him out of the house, down the sidewalk and across the street.

The 1970s, unimpressed with the multiple personalities of the '60s—peace, love and rock and roll—entered the world on a glittering disco ball. In short order, the decade's first three years produced an anti-war march on Washington, President Nixon opened talks with China, conservative America embraced populism and family values, bombings intensified in Viet Nam, Watergate became synonymous with scandal, McDonalds introduced the Egg McMuffin, HBO began operations, *The Godfather* set box office records, Nixon signed the Paris Peace Accord taking the US out of the Viet Nam conflict, Roe v Wade became the law of the land and Billy Jean King defeated Bobby Riggs to usher in the age of 'girl power'.

That was the big picture. In our world, we were just trying to get through school, work hard, earn money and have as much fun as possible. That last goal was easy at our place. All eight of us had our own friends; a countless number of people, but we crossed paths with uncanny efficiency. Our home vibrated with living. It really *was* the center of the universe for a lot of kids. It was interesting to watch how people behaved in our house. They were more considerate there than in any other setting I had seen them. I think it was because Mom was a mother figure to all of them. She enjoyed a status of unique distinction. It's a mystery how she did it, but people wanted to be better around her. A couple of girls I knew even said they wanted to marry a Wilson just to be part of the family.

On weekdays, summer or winter, the house filled up like a roller coaster at the county fair. Then, on Saturday, the ride stopped and everyone got off. Dad was home for the weekend. Now, don't get me wrong, he was friendly, but only five words friendly. Beyond that, especially when we were younger, he expected us to be invisible. We knew it, our friends knew it—even the dog knew it.

As mentioned earlier, Dad believed someone had to be in charge, and there was never a question about who that was. Though his methods were tough, it was difficult to deny their effectiveness. He was a clever man and seemed to know how much discipline we needed at every stage of our lives. When we were little, he was a dictator who demanded absolute obedience. As teenagers, and after we got our first real jobs, he loosened the reins and became a thoughtful ruler. Eventually, whether we left home for school, a job, or to get married, he became a 'first' among equals. At each stage, for only one individual at a time, a door opened and you stepped into a new world; the world of a familiar, but changed father.

Dad was comfortable navigating between roles if events provoked it. One day, he caught Hal going into the bus station to play pinball games. The 'thoughtful ruler' he had become with Hal, might have waited until they both got home, and then asked a question, like, "Do you think it's a good idea to be throwing your money away on those games?" He might have, but he didn't. Instead, he followed him into the bus station, became the 'dictator' and said, "get out of here and never come back to this place." He never brought it up again.

Contrast that with how Dad responded when Stan returned from the Army. Keep in mind, this was a guy who had served in Viet Nam, a guy who, while eating breakfast, had to speculate whether artillery barrages were incoming or outgoing. He had witnessed the carnage of war. When his camp was bombed, he spent hours in dug out shelters lined with sand bags. While on guard duty, he walked the perimeter carrying an M14. Now, living at home and working toward an Associate's degree from Coffeyville Junior College, he announced his plan to buy a motorcycle.

Dad listened, and with practiced calm, the 'first among equals' he had become with Stan, asked, "Where do you plan to live with your new motorcycle?" Stan paused, then realized it was not a question at all. It was, at that moment, a new rule – *You can live in my house as long as you want. But you and a motorcycle will not be staying here at the same time.* The "thoughtful ruler" had spoken.

Terry #10

It seemed that everyone in Coffeyville knew us. We could walk into any store in town and someone would say, "You're a Wilson. Aren't you?"

As a little kid, I remember thinking, *I'd better be good because they all know who I am.* It eventually sunk in that I was number ten in a long line of brothers and sisters who created standards we all lived by. I was known by the reputation *they* created, and my path was cleared long before I stepped onto it. Teachers expected me to get good grades. Neighbors expected me to be considerate. Coaches expected me to be dedicated. Employers expected me to work hard, and friends knew they could depend on me. There was a lot to live up to.

Our home life was different from most others. Boyfriends, girlfriends, just friends and friends of friends were welcome there. During the summer, it seemed that someone, often more than one of our buddies, spent the night. There were window air conditioners downstairs, but the only break from the heat upstairs came from an attic sized fan mounted on wheels and placed in the doorway of the rec room. It was designed to pull in air from open windows. Everyone jockeyed for a position on the floor in front of the fan, and there we spent the night.

A number of us had paper routes and needed to get up early to throw them. One morning, Mom came upstairs and woke us up one-by-one. She came to a Mexican friend of ours who had spent the night. Tongue in cheek, she said, "I know I had a lot of kids, but I'm sure I didn't have a Mexican." He laughed harder than any of us.

Mom always had breakfast ready when we came downstairs. Friends who spent the night were as welcome as the family. The same was true at lunch. I'm guessing some of them ate their healthiest meals at our house. When we toasted Mom's homemade bread, our friends got in line and made theirs too. When she baked cinnamon rolls with caramel icing, they peeled off a couple for themselves. They also enjoyed their share of her cookies, pies or cakes. They loved Mom.

Our friends saw Mom at sporting events where we competed. They watched her cheer for them just like she did her own kids. Well, not *exactly* like her own. I was a wrestler. In one of my early matches, I won by pinning my opponent. Mom clapped so hard she broke blood vessels in her hands. After the match, I think my friends were cheering as much for Mom as me.

Tim #11

Moms rarely get the credit they deserve, and ours was no exception. In our defense, it's impossible to know about everything they do? We were aware of obvious things, like lending a hand with paper routes, taking us swimming, helping with homework, cooking, cleaning, baking. Those things happened in plain sight; we were part of it. But much of her life was lived in late nights and early mornings. Long after we went to bed, she made clothes for the girls and mended them for everyone else. She paid bills after waking us up and preparing breakfast. I know, because one morning I saw her balancing her checkbook while I ate my first four pieces of toast and finished my eggs.

Our laundry room was in the basement. We tossed our dirty clothes down the steep, narrow stairwell. If you were doing your part, your items landed at the bottom, past the last step. Somehow, we pretended we were being thoughtful by giving Mom a clear path down the wooden planks. I wonder how many times a day she descended those steps, gathered up the once soaring dirty clothes piled up in her path, hauled them to the table next to the washer and dryer, separated colors from whites, emptied the dryer and folded its contents, placed those that needed pressing into a basket and moved them next to the ironing board, unloaded the washer and refilled the dryer, then ironed what she had time to finish before heading back upstairs to cook the next meal?

~

I was on the high school swim team. As busy as Mom was, she came to every meet possible. She even agreed to drive a carload of swimmers to a few out-of-town events. Since I trained all year long, my work hours had to be cut short. If I needed money, as strapped as she was for cash, Mom found a way to help me. I know she did the same for all the other kids and learned only later in life what sacrifices she made to do it.

Mom treated the boys different from the girls. Once the boys were teenagers and working, she let us come and go pretty much as we pleased. Mary, the official worrier of the family, tended to fret about us staying out too late. On more than a few occasions, she woke Mom after midnight and reported, "Mom, the boys aren't home yet."

"Just go to bed," Mom would say, "they'll be fine."

One summer weekend a couple of older friends and I decided to go fishing for a few days. It was a spur-of-the-moment decision and our fishing hole was out of town. I asked Teresa to let Mom know where I was going. As it turned out, Teresa forgot. Two days later, I walked into the house and said, "Mom, I'm home, wait till you see the fish I caught for you."

"Home," she said, "I didn't know you were gone."

~

Trust is an interesting gift. It's earned through experience and reinforced by consistency. Mom trusted us based on what she knew and how we responded. When I was sixteen years old, I found out a friend of mine had a car he would sell for $200. At the time, I had a steady income running two paper routes, but was short the up-front charge.

I rode my bike to a bank where one of our neighbors was the bank's president. I told the receptionist I wanted to borrow $200 and would pay it back in six months. She excused herself and a few minutes later returned with the president. He took me to his office and listened to my plan.

"Give me time to consider your offer and I'll see if I can get approval," he allowed. "We'll get back with you when I know."

Later that afternoon, the president called and said they would lend me the money. I rode my bike back to the bank, signed any paperwork they put in front of me and collected the $200. Too excited to go home first, I rode directly to my friend's house, paid the $200, tossed my bike into the trunk and never rode it again. I owned a car.

Eventually, with age and banking experience, I realized no bank on earth would loan money to a sixteen-year-old kid. I stopped by the president's office one day and asked him how he pulled that off.

"I called your mom," he admitted. "I told her I would make the loan if she would co-sign it. She did, and she kept it to herself and told me to do the same."

"Why didn't she tell me?" I asked.

"She didn't say," he answered, "but I'd guess she wanted you to gain confidence from it."

I did. And that was how she could go a couple of days without knowing what I was doing. She was sure it was the right thing and her trust was well placed.

At the same time, she generally kept track of the girls…in theory at least. I'm guessing Mary did exactly what she was supposed to do, and I'm equally sure Ginger was up to whatever struck her fancy at the moment. Either way, they were home at curfew or risked being grounded for a minimum of one week. I know Mom trusted the girls just as much as the guys; she just considered them more vulnerable.

In addition to our regular jobs (some of us worked two at a time), Terry and I mowed the Parish lawns, trimmed bushes, raked leaves and took care of whatever Father O'Hare asked us to do. Al joined us when he became big enough. All of us were altar boys until we went to the seventh-grade center, Jr. High or High School. In fact, Al served 8:00 a.m. mass every day for one full summer. It was impressive to see a little kid give up his opportunity to sleep in, even if for a worthy cause.

If I've given the impression all we did was work, the opposite was true. We had more fun than we deserved, and Mom and the older brothers and sisters made sure of it. Mom took us to the city pool or a local lake many times a week. Carol paid for Mary and Ginger to take dance lessons. Linda picked us up regularly and took us to the skating rink, the zoo or to spend a week at her house in Parsons. Stan and Hal bought me, Pat and Terry a Shetland pony and took us to the Fairgrounds to ride him whenever we wanted. Terry bought Teresa a Chris Everett tennis racquet. When Al played baseball, Hal practiced with him at the Holy Name playground.

On top of work and play, there were the inevitable disagreements that led to scuffles. Once, Hal had Pat in a headlock, demanding that he say "uncle". Pat refused. The fight went on so long that Mary ran to the neighbor's house and asked Pete Stover to intervene. He came over right away and broke them up. Pat never said "uncle".

Our center of the universe was complex, challenging, filled with laughter, love and accomplishment. Through all of its diversity, we were prepared for whatever the future had to offer.

52

STORM CLOUDS GATHER

Told by Mary and Ginger

Dale   Barbara

Mike | Carol | Linda | Kelly | Stan | Hal | Mary | Ginger | Pat | Terry | Tim | Teresa | Al

---

GINGER #8

One of the happiest days of our family's life was the moment Mary announced her engagement to Terry Downing. They represented goodness times two.

Aunt Madeline, by the most rigorous standards of the day, was a master seamstress. She offered to make Mary any wedding dress she wanted. Mary spent hours scouring bride's magazines until she found *the* one. It was elegant, intricate and stunning—so intricate, I feared Aunt Madeline might reconsider her offer and suggest an alternative. Instead, she took the picture and began a yearlong effort to bring the image to life.

She constructed a succession of patterns; each pass a refinement of her original vision. Early on, the dress was merely dots and dashes expressed on thin pattern paper and draped over a mannequin. Eventually, its structure began to take shape and we caught glimpses of the flawless nature of Aunt Madeline's creation. The dress would not only be similar to the picture—it would be better.

Aunt Madeline encouraged Mary to help her select the most complimentary fabrics and accessories. Next, they began a series of fittings that took place over many months. Every pearl, every sequin was hand sewn onto the dress and veil. Satin and lace, coaxed into perfect accord, streamed down the wedding aisle on Mary's special day. Over the years, the same dress graced the figures of seven women— sisters, sisters-in-law and nieces.

The dress served many, including Mom when she cleverly used it to make her wishes known. Terry's girlfriend, Laurie, was visiting Coffeyville for only the second time since they began dating five months earlier. Mom, a bit tipsy, excused herself from a conversation with the young couple. She returned moments later *the* wedding dress draped over her arm.

"This is the dress you're going to marry my son in," Mom declared.

Laurie laughed. Terry smiled and said, "Well, I guess it's decided then, we need to look for rings."

Laurie was married in the dress.

∽

It was 1973. Mike, Carol, Linda, Stan and Mary were married and working, Kelly was living in Denver while Hal was in college at Pittsburg State. I had started my first year at Coffeyville Junior College and was the new "bump master" at the house. The Coffeyville family had shrunk to six kids. Al, the youngest, finally enjoyed the status that came with age in our family. He still couldn't bump anyone, but there were fewer around who could bump him, so he generally found a chair available.

We were enjoying the confidence of consistency that life serves up most of the time. We could count on Mom being home, that she would have lunch on the table at noon, that our laundry would be done and that Dad would be home on weekends. We went to school and then to our jobs every day. All of that was about to change.

One afternoon, Mom asked me to look at a swelling on her neck. I was immediately apprehensive. She rarely complained about any health issues. In fact, she was hardly ever sick. Even when she came down with something, she continued to work as if nothing was wrong.

She led me to the bathroom and stood in front of the sink.

"The light is better here," she said, while pointing to a spot on her neck. "I think you can feel it."

To my regret, feeling it was unnecessary. I could see it.

"I'm going to call Mary," I said. "You need to see a doctor. It's probably nothing, but we shouldn't take any chances."

MARY #7

Ginger's call was scary. She tried to downplay it, but I knew she was worried. I told her to call Mom's doctor immediately. I was working at a local bank in Tulsa. I knew they would let me off and volunteered to come home if Ginger needed support. Ginger said she would be fine and we hung up.

I began thinking of all the kids at home and prayed nothing serious would be found. I knew Mom was in trouble.

GINGER

I took Mom to see her doctor the next day. He ordered blood tests, then began feeling her neck. I tried to detect any change in his expression as his fingers stroked both sides of her throat. Nothing. He finished the physical exam and then said he was going to order a biopsy.

"We'll call as soon as we know anything," he said.

Mom was unusually quiet on the way home. She stared out the side window, lost in thoughts I could only imagine. Twice, she said, "It's probably nothing."

The doctor called the next day and told Mom he was sending her to a specialist in Tulsa. His staff would arrange the appointment.

"What kind of specialist," Mom asked.

"A diagnostician," he answered.

"Is it serious?"

"That's what the specialist will tell us," he said.

MARY

Ginger's call laid waste to the adage, "No news is good news." I was hoping to hear it was just some temporary swelling and didn't amount to anything. Though nothing was confirmed, *No* news in this case sounded very ominous. If she needed to see a specialist, something was wrong. Mom called Dad and he headed home to take her to Tulsa. She promised to stop by my house after they saw the doctor.

They arrived early to the Doctor's office. Mom offered every detail of the meeting:

> We sat in a waiting room lined with straight backed, metal framed chairs. They felt cold against my back. While I filled out the paperwork, Dale pretended to read magazines fanned out on wooden end tables. He would glance through one, set it back down and pick up another. I know he was nervous.
>
> I finished the last form, took it to the receptionist and returned to sit by Dale. He took my hand. After all our years together, his touch made me feel safer.
>
> A young nurse stepped into the room, looked at me and said, "Please follow me, Mrs. Wilson." I wanted to cry.
>
> The specialist, a dignified man, probably in his forties, met us in a room half way down a wide hallway. He was thoughtful and engaging. My Coffeyville Doctor must have offered some details, because he knew about our family. He told us some tests would be run and after he had time to study the results, we would meet again. Between the tests, Dale and I sat in the exam room holding hands.
>
> It felt like we waited for hours, and then, as soon as the doctored returned, more like seconds. He moved into the room softly, like someone bearing bad news might do.
>
> "Your doctor in Coffeyville took a biopsy of the lymph nodes in your neck. I just spoke with our Pathologist who confirms that

it is Non-Hodgkin's Lymphoma. The other tests we did today confirms the diagnosis."

The words stunned me. Dale recoiled before recovering enough to sit military stiff in his chair. The rest was a blur. I know the doctor mentioned grading it, though my mind was racing too fast to take it all in. I depended on Dale to fill me in later. The one thing I do remember Dale saying was, "Don't tell the kids how bad it is."

Dad and Mom came back to my house before heading home. When they told me the results, I was shocked. The words battered me. I had convinced myself such a thing could never happen, especially to Mom. She still had six kids to raise.

It turned out to be in Stage IV. There were concentrated amounts in her neck, stomach and probably a number of other areas they would discover later. He said they would design a plan and together, we would do everything we could to beat it.

Mom said she would call Ginger. We were to keep it to ourselves for now.

GINGER

I was caught off guard when Mom called. The room closed in around me and I felt light headed. Such horrible news made no sense. How could someone like Mom have cancer? I guessed that's how every child in the same situation feels—their lives suddenly awash in danger.

"Don't tell the kids," Mom said.

At that very moment, I saw Al rush out the front door. He had picked up the office phone and heard our conversation.

"Too late for that," I said. "Al was listening. He knows."

"Well," Mom said, "go ahead and tell the others. They'll find out soon enough anyway."

Minutes after hanging up with Mom, Mary called. She told me everything I already knew. We spent a few minutes convincing one another Mom would beat cancer, that God would protect her. In her everyday life, Mary trusted in a compassionate Redeemer—but in that moment, I knew doubt and faith were battling for her emotions. I knew it, because I was going through the same struggle. It was then, in a situation steeped in the unknown, I realized how doubt and faith go hand in hand. Doubt exposes the danger—faith assures that God is greater than any threat.

"Don't tell the kids," Mary cautioned.

"It's too late for that," I told her, "Al was listening in when Mom called."

MARY

"Crap!" I said, "if he knows, the others will find out soon enough."

Ginger cut in "Mom told me to go ahead and tell everyone."

"Oh, good," I said. "I'll call Al as soon as I can."

I finally reached him about an hour later. I thought he would need consoling. To my surprise, it was *he* who helped *me*. He told me he ran to the church the minute he heard about Mom. This is what he said happened:

> The church sat empty but for silent statues and the figure of Christ hanging from a wooden cross suspended over the altar. I stood in the center isle and vented my anguish. How could you do this? I shouted at God. How could you let this happen?
>
> Just then, a retired priest, Father Dillon, walked into view. He was a gentle soul, small and unassuming. His days of leading a congregation were now far behind him. He walked down the aisle to stand near me. 'What's troubling you, son?' he asked.
>
> I told him about Mom. I said it was impossible to understand how God could have let such a thing happen.
>
> He talked for maybe ten minutes. All of it was important, but if I had to put it in just a few words, it was something like this: You won't find God in the creation of this illness. He will be found in the miracle that follows. He will be known by healing your mother. Pray about that.

Al said those words made all the difference and that he had a whole new perspective. I think he was trying to lead me to whatever peace he found through Father Dillon's counsel. It worked. While still anxious and afraid, I knew what to do next. My faith reasserted itself and I believed we could pray Mom back to good health. The battle had begun.

A few days later, Mom's doctors laid out their plans. They would remove any of the tumors they could access without doing damage to the surrounding tissue. Mom would receive radiation every day for six weeks and then she would go on oral chemotherapy for what turned out to be two years. For the next month and a half, she lived at our house during the week and went home on weekends.

Ginger and I traded information daily.

GINGER

Father O'Hare had an entire congregation praying for Mom—she was remembered at every mass, every day. Neighbors and friends, even people we had never met, brought food and drink to the house. The dining room table overflowed with the generosity and concern of an entire community.

I noticed Mom's energy waning with each trip home. Her radiation treatments were reduced to every-other day due to burns on her skin. Beyond that, her attitude remained upbeat and she worked like she always had. She often visited sick folks in the hospital and expected us to do the same. Mary said she became an active cheerleader for patients taking radiation in Tulsa. She was establishing the "cancer" wing of her army of friends.

Dad was home more often during Mom's treatments. He drove some of the kids to Tulsa to see her in the hospital and generally tried to spend more time with us. Pat said it was because he realized he might be raising us himself and needed to find out who we were. We all laughed at that. In an odd way, I think there was some truth to it. Dad typically maintained a guarded distance from everyone, and 'everyone' included us.

To be fair, he knew *who* we were, he was just trying to find out *where* we were—what we were up against at that stage in our lives? He became curious about how we spent our time, and who we spent it with.

Dad was trying to transform himself, and I loved him for that. He had always been above the fray, issuing edicts from on high. Now, if his fears came to pass and Mom lost her battle, he would have to walk among us. He was preparing.

That's when I realized things were worse than we were being told. *Mom might not make it*. I shared my thoughts with Mary and she admitted having the same grim feelings. We talked about the changes in Dad.

"Do you think he believes she might die?" Mary asked.

"I'm not sure," I answered. I hesitated; considering information I had kept to myself until that moment. I decided Mary had a right to know.

"I think you should hear something Teresa told me," I said.

"About Dad?"

"Yes," I answered. "It happened one morning when she and Dad were sitting at the dining room table. They were alone, she was eating cereal for breakfast, while Dad drank coffee and read the paper. She thought she heard him sniffle and it caused her to stiffen. Just as she decided it couldn't be, he dropped the paper onto the table, never looked her way, and took out a handkerchief to dab his eyes. He was fighting tears. After he slid the handkerchief back into his pocket, he picked up the paper and began reading again as if nothing had happened."

The story broke our hearts. Like us, he was struggling to imagine what he would do without Mom.

~

The Coffeyville kids pulled together as best we could. We were going to school and all of us had jobs—some were working two of them. We thought we were keeping up pretty well until one day three weeks into Mom's chemotherapy treatments. I was away that day—going to college full time and working for an insurance company in the afternoons.

This is how Terry said our attitude adjustment took place:

> Mary stopped by one afternoon to see how we were doing. She was a worrier and neither time nor experience could change that. She needed to *know* we were ok. We loved Mary like no other. Her visit was welcome and appreciated—a small relief from Ginger's Drill Sergeant tactics. After a few minutes of chit chat, she began walking through the house to see if anything needed to be done before Mom came home that weekend.
>
> We followed her from one room to the next—pleased she hadn't found anything worth commenting about. And then, after leaving the kitchen, she stepped into the hallway and faced the door to the basement. I braced myself. She was going to turn on the light. None of us ever did that before chucking our dirty clothes into the dark of the waiting abyss—the results of our efforts to be determined later by the laundry gods. We rarely went down there and it was anyone's guess what Mary would find. I rolled my eyes at the kids standing around me.
>
> Mary switched on the light. There, at the bottom of the staircase, laid a heap of soiled laundry, each item once airborne on their way to the pile. Various items were strewn over steps half way down the narrow passage, the thrower having missed their mark by miscalculation or hurried delivery.
>
> Mary turned and glared at us. Typically, the personification of calm and love, her reaction caught us off guard. "You kids need to show more consideration for Mom," she said, as she eased down the stairwell, picking up clothes from every step beginning half way down the flight. "I can't believe you would leave all of this for her to do on the weekends. What's wrong with you kids?"
>
> Having reached the basement floor, she bent over and filled her arms from the pile of clothes at her feet. "Get down here and help me," she demanded. And on it went, a little berating, gather laundry—more berating—more gathering. "Don't you kids realize how sick she is?"

Mary, with our help, washed, dried and folded clothes the rest of the day.

All of a sudden, we were doing less well than I thought.

In our defense, that amount of laundry was no more than a day and a half worth of clothes; two days at most.

∼

After six weeks of radiation, Mom came home. She was placed on oral chemotherapy for an indeterminant period. The drugs made her weak and she felt sick much of the time. Some days were worse than others. After evenings of unusually intense pain, Al slept at her bedside in case she needed help during the night.

We were living with a human time bomb—never sure if she was getting better or worse. Through it all, she worked harder than ever. I wondered if she was trying to pack as much into each day as possible, unsure how many more she had left to fill up.

Dad helped as never before. He was sensitive to her needs and took her out to dinner every weekend. He was more anxious than anyone. He tried to hide it, but we all saw it on his face; his stern exterior was fading under the pressure.

53

HONORARY MOTHER OF THE YEAR

Told by Teresa #12

By late 1974, Mom was a year into her treatments. Though slowed by chemotherapy, she was doing most of what she always had. There were now a few moments we could forget about how sick Mom was and pretend that cancer had let her go. We all knew better, but I think we needed to believe otherwise. How else could we bear the pain that came with thoughts of losing her? No, it was best to believe she had already won the battle.

Sometime in October of that year, Mary Jane Vowell, one of Mom's best friends and admirers, began to organize an effort to nominate her for Mother of the Year for the state of Kansas. The Knights of Columbus from Holy Name church were eager to sponsor her. The odds against receiving the award were daunting, as the rules required that all of the nominee's children had to be over fifteen. Al and I were younger than that.

Mary Jane pushed on anyway. She became the official chairwoman for the local effort. Her group's evidence included pictures of Mom, organizations she belonged to, letters from prominent local dignitaries and even a letter from Senator Bob Dole who would later represent the Republican party in the Presidential election of 1996. Mary Jane was counting on the selection committee making an exception considering that Mom could pass before meeting the criteria. She believed the body of proof she assembled would be enough to sway their decision.

The nomination document began with Mom's contributions to numerous organizations over many years. To name just a few:

- PTA Member from Mike's first year in school in 1947 through 1974 and beyond. Mom was an active PTA member at every school her children attended. The list included Holy Name, Garfield Elementary, McKinley Middle School, Roosevelt Jr. High and Field Kindley High School; often, most of them at the same time.
- School Board Member
- Home room mother for many of her children's classes
- Assistant Girl Scout leader
- Boy Scout Den Mother
- Church Circle Chairwoman
- County Election Board
- Vice President of the Altar Society
- Kansas Federation of Republican Women
- Sen. Bob Dole's re-election campaign

The first recommendation letter came from the Grand Knight of the Knights of Columbus at Holy Name parish. His final paragraph stated: "No one could put in five hundred words what a woman like Mrs. Wilson has done over many years. If she does not win, it will be because true greatness can rarely be captured in words or pictures. Greatness such as hers is undefinable – it is a glorious second in endless time which can be felt by the many who are touched, but can hardly be explained. If her calling in life was to raise children, then we can only say that God must be very proud to have made such a fine choice."

Next was a letter from Father O'Hare, Pastor of Holy Name Church and school. Here are just a few excerpts:

> "She is, undoubtedly, a veritable endless source of inspiration and edification to all of us who are privileged to know her—and I have known Barbara for twenty years."

> "She is, without exception, the most marvelous, most wonderful and most Christ-like of human beings. True to character, her depth of faith, deep devotion, and dedicated loyalty to God is so devoid of ostentation that it could almost escape being noticed."

High school teachers, Dorothy Brophy and Dorothea Fahler wrote:

> "A mother gives warmth to the world—roots to the family—dividends to schools and courage that brings gentleness to nations. She's God's greatest invention—she's a mother—She is MRS. BARBARA WILSON."

Senator Bob Dole's letter included:

> "Most of those who know her, confess to often wondering where Mrs. Wilson finds the time for her civic activities with the many demands of raising so large a family. The answer appears to be that she has always found the time to work on what she believes in and it is apparent that *people* are what she believes in most strongly."

A manager with The Coffeyville Journal, a daily newspaper, submitted an impressive letter. In it, he pointed out that the typical newspaper carrier lasts from six months to one year.

> "A child will lose interest in a relatively short time without the active support of his or her parents," he wrote. He went on to say, "However, there are exceptions, and the Coffeyville Journal is most fortunate to have a family of this nature.

> Barbara Wilson has encouraged and guided not one, but five of her children in the business of route management." He wrote that Hal served 23 months…Pat, 24 months, Terry 21 months, Tim 36 months and Al, the youngest, had taken over the route

in June of 1973 and was still managing it. "All have been exceptional carriers; providing prompt, dependable service to their customers each day. Exceptional children to be sure, but without the support and encouragement of Barbara Wilson, the opportunity to learn about responsibility and its importance in business would not have been possible."

I would add that most of the brothers also had a second route for morning papers like, the Wichita Eagle, the Tulsa World or the Kansas City Star.

The President of First National Bank wrote about Mom bringing his family homemade bread to welcome them to the neighborhood. He also spoke of the maturity of her children and how they had, "…shown the effects of strong religious, moral and close-knit family relationships."

Those recommendations were followed by letters from each of the kids detailing their education, work histories and general thoughts about what made Mom great. The overriding message of their presentations centered on the fact that Mom was "always there". Each of us felt her presence in every aspect of our daily lives. She represented safety, comfort, encouragement and love.

In the end, the national American Mothers Committee decided, regardless of special circumstances, the rules must be followed. The Kansas Mother of the Year committee, however, made an exception. Mom was the only woman in Kansas history to be chosen Honorary Merit Mother of the Year.

The award was presented by the Governor at his mansion in Topeka.

54

A NEW ERA

Told by Al #13

Mom was improving. Her doctor maintained that her blood work looked good and they could find no new tumors. The ones they treated were shrinking. The waiting to *know* continued.

In an odd twist of fate, Mom's gall bladder had to be removed two years after her cancer therapy began. We contacted Mom's oncologist, a gentle man with quiet confidence. He had handled her cancer treatments from the beginning. He told us they would get a close look at areas radiated in the beginning. Everyone was anxious about what they might find.

On the day of the operation, we gathered in a large waiting area at the hospital. The surgery took longer than expected. The room felt smaller with each passing moment. No one said much. Most were praying, others pacing. Cautious smiles were exchanged and we instinctively touched one another for reassurance.

Mary, standing in the doorway leading to the hall, saw the doctor first. "He's coming," she said. He entered the room in his scrubs, a surgical mask still dangling from his neck. His neutral expression disguised any results.

He finally stated, "Everything went fine."

We held our breath for what was next.

"And there was no sign of cancer."

The doctor was as happy as the rest of us.

"It's a miracle," someone claimed.

"It's as close as any of us are going to get to one," the surgeon said.

We were delivered the miracle Father Dillon had forecast.

∼

Mom's illness exposed the flaws in their health insurance coverage. Their policy paid only a portion of her hospital stay, surgery, and ongoing therapy. The deficit was so large that Dad had to make payments over many years to pay it off. Mom resolved they would never be in that position again. She would find a job with health insurance. I admired her for it. I accepted she needed to do it, but it was hard to think of her working outside the home.

For her part, Mom simply set aside the life she had been living and started a new one. Her options were limited. She had been a telephone operator, organized the logistics of moving her family too many times to count, managed a farm operation, which included selling eggs, milk, apples, horses and cattle, raised thirteen productive children, worked within a crushingly tight budget, was a chef and a seamstress, counseled her own kids and hundreds of others and was an officer in a number of charitable organizations. And what was her first job? Washing dishes at the local hospital.

I hated the idea of it.

On her first day, I called the hospital and asked for Mrs. Wilson. The operator connected me with the kitchen supervisor, who reluctantly passed the phone to Mom.

"Why are you calling," she asked.

"You have to come home," I answered. "We need you here."

"I'm working," she said, "don't call unless it's an emergency."

In time, she left the hospital and began delivering orders for an auto parts store. Next, she was a clerk at Mary and Terry's insurance office; no health insurance. She then worked in the fabric department at Walmart.

Finally, she found a job she loved at the County Health Department. They provided great health care coverage and even retirement benefits.

Being the youngest in the family was a curse and a blessing. The curse: Chairs were a mystery to me. If I ever got to sit in one, it lasted only until someone else entered the room and said, "Up. You're getting bumped." And everyone who entered the room was older than me. A possible benefit? I stayed fit through all the ups and downs.

I was a momma's boy, so naturally everyone called me a brat. Until I was five years old, I thought my name *was* 'Brat'. Anyone could give me an order, "Get me this," or "Get me that." I was expected to follow through and it was only with Mom's intervention, that I was saved from satisfying unreasonable demands.

That's about the extent of the curse. There may have been more, but it was dwarfed by all the blessings. First, I knew early on I was privileged. I may have been on the bottom rung of the ladder, but I got to see everyone else climb it above me. I saw the benefits of a good education to whatever degree you chose to pursue it. I saw that advanced degrees could be earned in universities or in life, and either could lead to meaningful success. I saw that working hard paid off in more ways than money. I learned the value of good manners, a respectful attitude toward adults, the importance of community service and so much more. I got to watch them engage with life—fill it up with their own visions. They knew great success and crushing defeat. But the most amazing thing about my brothers and sisters was that neither outcome stopped them from taking the next step.

Uncle Al and Aunt Madeline continued to visit often. They were like a second set of parents, always willing to help when we needed it. If our lives were a box of Cracker Jax, they were the free toy inside.

Everything changed when Uncle Al's mother died in 1978. We called her Aunt Mae, though we were unrelated. We treated her like any other member of the family and loved her dearly. She often came to visit with Aunt and Uncle and lived with us when her husband, Joe, was placed in a nursing home in Parsons. According to Mom, she could outwork any woman she had ever met.

Her loss was devastating to Uncle Al. He was an only child and now, even surrounded by our family and Aunt Madeline, he felt alone. He began taking trips to Pittsburg, Kansas to stay in the house where he had grown up. He claimed he needed to keep the place in good condition to sell it. Aunt Madeline knew better. He wanted to be near the trappings of his mother. It was as close as he could get to her.

～

Back home, Mom was working at the health department and all the kids, except Teresa and I, were starting their own lives. Dad was still living in Topeka during the week and coming home on weekends. I call that period, "The Golden Age" because the older kids came home often and they brought with them husbands, wives, new babies and friends. The house vibrated when we were all together. I loved those times.

Mom prepared for the weekend by baking bread, cinnamon rolls, pies or cakes— sometimes two of those treats— often, all of them. On Saturday, she cooked a huge pot of soup, beef stew or chicken and noodles. After eight o'clock mass on Sunday morning, she made her signature breakfast of bacon, eggs, biscuits and gravy. It was like the old days, just livelier.

Dad had mellowed. He once gave us spankings for jumping on the bed or making too much noise. Now, he welcomed the crashing sounds of people careening off the rec room walls during ping pong matches. He stayed up all hours of the night playing poker with the brothers and their friends. When they tired of poker, he brought out the dice. The pock marks on the dining room's wooden wainscoting were evidence of the hundreds of dice thrown against it.

Dad laughed easily in those days. During one poker session, a friend of Pat's was on a losing streak. The cards were dealt, bets were made and finally the players revealed their hands. During a succession of losses, Pat's friend said, "Well, there go my new rims." Next hand turned over, "Well, there go my tires." After another loss, "Now I can't even afford air." Dad laughed so hard tears were streaming down his face.

On another occasion, Dad scoped my ear canals and found that I had impacted wax. He told me to go to a doctor and have them irrigated.

When I got back home, he was eager to know what happened.

"What did they find?" he asked.

"They found Jimmy Hoffa," I said.

I've never seen him laugh so hard. And that made me happy.

The family was growing with each new marriage or baby's arrival. Dad had trouble keeping track of all the names. I'm guessing he gave up soon after the tenth grandchild. He did his best to stay on top of it, but there were just too many and they were coming too fast.

TERRY #10

Uncle Al died in 1981. I could describe how sad everyone was. I could paint a picture of the somber funeral, or tell about the people who cried during the priest's moving eulogy. It would all be true. And it would miss the mark pitifully. No attempt to recount his importance could do justice to his value in our lives. Despite his faults, he mattered more than he offended.

~

Not long after Uncle Al died, and after everyone had moved out, Dad called to say he needed help. He was moving home and wanted Tim and I to haul his belongings back to Coffeyville. We met him in Topeka on a Saturday morning. I expected to move much more than we found that day. I probably could have handled most of it myself, but I was glad Tim was there. It just seemed there should have been more fanfare, more celebration—just more. It did after all, represent the end of a sixteen-year chapter of his life. Whatever else it contained, those years included his support of thirteen kids. In my mind, that was worth some recognition. Instead, we now stood before a pickup truck whose bed, only three quarters full, held the entire evidence of his efforts.

I think he sensed my melancholy and decided the moment needed lightening. As if on cue, he spread his arms out wide and declared, "My empire!"

Back to AL #13

The 80's were a continuation of the new era. Dad was home for good. He opened a hearing instrument office to work in Coffeyville and surrounding areas. Mom was still loving her job at the Health Department. Aunt Madeline had grown lonely in Kansas City and decided to relocate to Coffeyville. She moved to an apartment on Ninth Street. All thirteen kids were now out of the house, though they continued to come home on weekends whenever possible.

You see, we were and are, one another's best friends. We enjoy time together. It is the soundest truth I know. In celebration, every two years since 1968, over 100 people travel from as far away as California, North Carolina, Minnesota, Alabama and Texas for a family reunion. It lasts four days and three nights. The latest marriages are applauded, new babies are pampered and passed from one mother to another for fitting awe and approval, (Some men hold them too, but they pass them along quickly, pretending to smell something and claiming they need changed), and always, the air is thick with happiness to be together.

Mom loved the reunions. No matter where she was during those four days, someone was at her side, generally, both sides. Her ever-present smile was proof enough that those were the happiest days of her life. She was walking within the evidence of her existence—testament to a life well lived.

A tradition was born at those reunions. The adults consistently hug one another and often kiss hello and goodbye. It is so commonplace that the next generation, and the one after that, consider the gesture essential. It is heartwarming to watch toddlers smile and run toward one another to embrace.

54 A NEW ERA

I started an insurance agency from scratch. The company I represented rewarded their top producers with an annual, all-expenses paid trip to glamorous locations across the globe. The first trip I won was to Rio in 1988. We were allowed one guest. I felt no one deserved to take that trip more than Mom. When I asked her, she had trouble imagining getting to do something so special.

I doubt that any human being enjoyed their time on a vacation more than Mom did in Rio. She was a hit with the agents and their husbands and wives. She went to the beach with the other ladies and at sixty-six, in her one-piece, black bathing suit, her dark hair cut short and stylish, she looked as fit and toned as any of them. It would have been tough to decide which woman had borne thirteen children. She was as happy as I had ever seen her.

55

UNPREPARED

Told by Kelly #4

In late June, 1989, Mom and Dad came to visit Jerry, Hal and I on the acreage we owned in Collinsville, OK. Mom and Hal went to fish the pond. I stayed with Dad, who had decided to take a nap. As he lay sleeping on the couch, I remember thinking: *The difference between him lying there asleep, and him in a coffin, is slight.* His color had taken on a gray tinge and he appeared to have aged unusually fast over the last couple of months.

We suggested he go to my doctor, a prominent diagnostician in Tulsa, and have a general checkup. To our surprise, he agreed. Stan was living in Tulsa at the time, so we met at his condo. Dad drove Mom, Stan and I to his appointment.

After filling out the required paperwork, X-rays were ordered and we were asked to have a seat in the waiting room. Wilsons could typically overcome somber occasions, like on that day, with clever joking around about one thing or another. But this moment was different—no one even tried to lighten the mood. Time slowed and our anxiety grew. Mom wrapped her arm inside Dad's and leaned heavy against his body.

In a moment of relief and dread, a young nurse called Dad's name. She led us to an office, which seemed odd. Why not a typical exam room? In a quick succession of events, Mom and Dad took the two chairs in front of the grey, metal desk—Stan and I moved to stand behind them—the doctor entered the room. He laid out a folder. His collected manner proved he had been in this moment before.

After introducing himself, he said, "It's not good news, Mr. Wilson." A beat. "You have an advanced case of lung cancer. Another beat. "If anyone would like to see the x-rays, I can show you what we're dealing with."

"I'd like to see them," I said. Stan agreed. Dad decided to wait and Mom wanted to stay with him.

The doctor led Stan and I into another room. It was dark except for the light from an x-ray viewer.

"Here's the problem," the doctor said. He traced streaks of light running in every direction in Dad's lungs.

"Is there anything that can be done," I asked.

"Nothing that would change the outcome," he answered.

"How much time does he have?"

"Thirty to sixty days would be my best guess," he said, "but no one can know for sure."

We returned to the office. The doctor sat down and began speaking matter-of-factly to Dad and Mom. He explained the results and made clear there were no good options. Dad nodded his head; neither of them asked questions. That surprised me. I thought the shock of such news would cause intense wonder.

Dad stood, helped Mom to her feet, thanked the doctor and we left.

We drove back to Stan's condo. On the way, I asked Dad if he wanted to know anything about timing. He returned an emphatic, "No!"

Dad and Mom stayed in the car while we loaded their bags into the trunk. We said our goodbyes without any mention of what had just happened. Horrible news needs to be heard only once. Stan and I went inside and I stood at a large window overlooking the parking area. I watched them drive away. It was sad. Dad, a giant of a man in our world, looked painfully small behind the steering wheel as they rounded out of sight. I felt disconnected. It's the only way I know to explain it. There was a finality about the whole thing—a realization that irreversible events take on a life of their own. From that point forward, we would merely be managing Dad's death.

I resolved to spend as much time as possible in Coffeyville. Within a week, Dad decided he wanted two things in particular. He wanted to be baptized a Catholic and he asked if we could take a road trip. He wanted to see the Gulf of Mexico, and on the way, visit the oil lease where he stayed with Virgie as a kid. Both things were going to happen.

The next day, Mom explained the situation to our Pastor and Dad was baptized immediately. Two days later, Dad, Mom, Mary and I loaded the car and we were off.

Dad rarely said much in the best of times. Nothing about our trip changed that. He played word games with us and politely nodded his head when Mom pointed out roadside features, he likely found completely irrelevant. He seemed there, but not. That all changed when we topped a particular hill in Texas—his hill. It was there he sat up taller and became animated. We were getting close to Virgie's old place.

"Look, Daddy," Mom pointed out, "it's still there." She knew what mattered to him—it was the little brown building with a hitching post in front. In that very spot, summer after summer, Virgie and Sid waited for Dad's bus to stop. I wondered if he was picturing them standing in front of the oil-stained truck, waving hello and eager to see him?

As we neared the building, I slowed the car. "Do you want me to stop?"

He paused, but apparently had already relived his memories. "No," he said. "Let's find the lease."

He directed me down a country road. After a few turns and a short backtrack, I wondered if he remembered where it was. Just then, he said, "Right there!"

I stopped, unsure of where I should go. "Pull in right here," Dad said. That's when I saw what must have been the old driveway entrance. I moved the car within inches of a paint chipped metal gate. The shallow space left just enough room to get the car off the road. It was hot outside, so I left the car running and cranked up the air conditioner.

The land Dad began to survey was sand covered and desolate. "That's where they lived," he said. I remembered being there as a little kid; Stan and I chasing lizards willing to give up a tail if caught. Virgie and Sid's tiny house had disappeared as if swallowed by the sand hills all around us. The oil well horse-heads had disappeared, and now, only the dirt mounds they once straddled offered evidence of their existence. One had tubing collars strewn around its base. Spent sucker rods rusted in a small stack near another.

Mom, Mary and I remained quiet, giving Dad time to say goodbye to his past. He looked to the left, stopping momentarily to study some aspect in his view. After a moment's reflection, he scanned the deep horizon, pausing here and there to consider another memory, his vision hard with knowing.

I pretended to reflect with him, even though the scene lacked any meaning beyond its benefit to Dad. I glanced his way occasionally. In place of a dying man, I saw the young kid who needed his mother, and who had longed to call this barren piece of earth his home.

"Let's go," he said.

~

Throughout the trip, Dad asked me to travel the back roads of Texas. He wanted to see smaller towns where folks were still in touch with their roots. He wanted to see people living.

Corpus Christi was our next stop, but too far to reach that day. We drove to Fredericksburg, a unique town originally settled by Germans. They carried on the traditions of their heritage and that day were having a festival of some sort. After spending the night, we rose early Sunday morning and attended Mass at the nearest Catholic church. It was the first time I watched Dad take Holy Communion. I'm unsure what I expected, but it moved me and I was thankful I was able to see it.

Our next stop was San Antonio. Remember, Dad fantasized about cowboy life and one of the most thrilling moments in Texas history happened at the Alamo. The physical character of the fort and its surroundings were less impressive than Dad expected. He tired easily, though he stayed with our tour group and seemed to enjoy everything the guide had to offer. That afternoon, we took Dad to an I-Max theatre that presented a continuous version of the Alamo story. He was impressed with the huge screen, though he knew the story as well as it was told.

When we reached Corpus Christi, we checked into a beach front hotel and made sure Dad and Mom had an ocean view. I think he felt a certain awe about the waves and the magnitude of so much water. We offered to walk with him to the beach. He declined. One day and one night satisfied him.

We drove to Shreveport, Louisiana the next day. The thoroughbreds were running at Louisiana Downs. I reserved a table for four in a restaurant overlooking the track. It was all new to Dad, though I'm sure he was beyond being impressed. I just kept wondering what he was thinking; how it was all coming in to him. Nothing about his demeanor or conversation revealed what that might be.

We left for Coffeyville after one night in Shreveport. It had been a full week of travel and the rest of us were ready to get home. Looking back, I realize Dad felt differently about it. I think he saw it more as the end—period. All that was left was dying, and he knew it. He would have preferred it happen on the road.

We were driving toward his greatest dread; the drama that precedes the end of life. He would now have to endure a procession of children and friends pretending to encourage him, but who were actually there to say goodbye, their faces registering the pain his passing was causing them, their tears slipping out and triggering his own sadness, the well-intentioned words that would come up short of the moment, the offers of prayers that could only satisfy the prayer, the well-intentioned best wishes and finally, the last look. He would have to summon the courage to brave all of it.

Three weeks after the diagnosis, Dad made it clear he wanted to be left alone. He decided it was the least he could do for himself. Death had announced its claim, but he would control how it played out. All of the brothers and sisters who could make it, had come and gone. Now, Mom, Mary and I fell into an unwritten routine. One of us stayed with him whenever he was awake.

One afternoon, I was sitting in Mom's recliner, Dad in his, when he dropped the newspaper he was reading and said, "You know what?"

"What?" I answered.

The wry smile that typically preceded some witty pronouncement now animated his face. He looked directly at me and smiled. I wanted to hold on to that moment, but had to let it go so I could listen.

"I've always said I wanted to be the first to go," he said. "Now, I'm not so sure."

We both laughed.

Dad made clear we should keep him out of the hospital. He wanted to die in his own bed and among his own people. We arranged for Hospice care in the home. He began spending most of his time on the sofa. I stayed up with him at night. Mom and Mary attended him during the day. Many of the other kids came and went through the back door. They were there to do whatever they could.

I put cool washcloths on his forehead, kept a cup full of ice chips on the table next to him and rubbed his feet as long as he seemed to enjoy it. At one point, he said, "It's like the flu." And then asked, "When is he going to take me?" It was more a request than a question.

Mom commented often about how strong he was; how he was facing this final challenge with courage and dignity. She sat next to him and rubbed his back whenever he sat up.

I was angry with myself for missing the clues about when he would pass. In my mind, it could be a week or a day—probably closer to a week. The first clue had to do with the two rings Dad owned. One was gold with a tiny diamond at its center. He had worn it for as long as any of us could remember. It became part of his identity. He gave that ring to Stan. The other, he had purchased a few years earlier. The setting contained three substantial diamonds, the type ring he dreamed of owning most of his life. The night before he died, lying on the sofa, he slid that ring from his finger and held it out to me.

"Take this," he said.

I should have known.

The next morning, he decided to go to his own bed.

I should have known.

He refused to take his medications.

I should have known.

I thought he just needed to sleep so I used the time to drive home for some fresh clothes. I told him goodbye and that I'd be back in the evening. I kissed his forehead and left.

I was back before sundown. Mom told me our Priest had been there earlier to give Dad the last rites, more as insurance than prediction. He had been asleep ever since. A number of brothers and sisters stopped by, as they had every day since we returned from the trip. A few of us were sitting at the kitchen table around nine that night. We were talking about nothing important, when Mom appeared at the hallway door.

"I think he just died," she said.

Stan and I hurried to the bedroom. Dad was on his back, his arms at his sides. I placed my open hand on his still chest—I wanted to be sure. I felt so many things at that moment. I was happy for Dad, he got what he wanted, though it seemed odd to think about dying as winning a battle. And then I considered Mom and the brothers and sisters. I felt sad for all of us. The most dynamic force any of us had ever known was gone. I remembered what Velva said about losing their own dad; "Who would we now please?"

I had kissed his forehead before leaving that morning and now I kissed it again, for the last time. Stan took a moment to stand over him. We left the room and closed the door.

The funeral director arrived within an hour. Dad had lasted for a little more than a month since the diagnosis.

∼

The funeral took place on August 4, 1989. It was an unusually cool day for that time of year, more like spring than summer. Linda was the Administrative Assistant to the Chief of Police. Out of respect for her, a number of police officers formed an honor guard leading up the church steps. They added a ceremonial dignity to the cheerless affair.

Mom, along with the thirteen brothers and sisters, their wives, husbands and children took up nearly half of one side of the church. Aunt Madeline, Mom's brothers and some of their families sat just behind us. Friends of Mom and the brothers and sisters spread out on both sides of the wide center aisle. Most of them barely knew Dad. Some had never even met him. But they were there, testaments to the value of our friendships.

During our drive to the cemetery, I remember thinking, *look how the world goes on as if nothing has happened. And here we are, consumed by sorrow. Shouldn't everything stop for just a moment?*

57

AFTER DAD

Told by the Brothers and Sisters

AL # 13

Mom handled Dad's passing different than I expected. I was surprised by how little she mourned. Maybe she had exhausted her sorrow during the emotional month leading up to the end—the predicted event having squandered its power to depress her. It's more likely the reaction was simply consistent with her nature— she just refused to yield. Regardless, she set about reorganizing her life; absent Dad.

She began water aerobics with some of her friends, became more active in community service organizations, took bank sponsored bus trips and generally did more socializing than ever before. Aunt Madeline stopped by every evening and the two of them enjoyed a cocktail before dinner. I was happy they had one another.

Mom and I had taken the company sponsored Rio trip in 1988. In 1989 we went to Bermuda, in 1990 Acapulco, followed by Hawaii, the big island, in 1991. Those trips were great and Mom was in her element traveling the world. She was a hit with my friends at every venue. She stood out. Her upbeat attitude was infectious and people tended to gravitate to her. I think it was because she gave each of them individual attention. She was expert at spreading her kindness, honed to a fine edge through mothering thirteen kids, their friends, her friends, neighbors and anyone else who needed her.

I've heard people say, "I need to start thinking of myself. I've lived too much for others." In Mom's case, taking care of others was the fuel that powered her. She thrived on bringing pleasure to another person's life. Instead of diminishing her, it lifted her up and made her more complete. Giving and getting were the same thing.

MARY # 7

Though I missed Dad, I was happy for Mom. I think she enjoyed her independence for the first few years after he died. She had lived with someone for over sixty-seven years; first, the Kelly family, and then Dad and all of us kids. Being responsible for only herself must have felt liberating.

In 1992 Mom invited two exchange students from Nicaragua to live with her. They stayed for one school year and became friends with the whole family.

The out-of-town kids came home on many weekends, so things remained pretty much the same. Mom was happiest when surrounded by her children. I write that knowing she found joy in nearly everything she did. She developed a habit of claiming that every visit, every new meal, every trip was *the best* she had ever had. What a blessing—each day destined to be *the best* of an already wonderful life.

Aunt Madeline moved to a two-bedroom apartment across the street from Holy Name. She joined a quilting club and took part in other activities at the church. All-in-all, I believe she was content.

Uncle Pat, the Silver Star recipient, was in his 80s. He came to visit Mom and enjoyed himself so much he stayed for months. He joined Mom's water aerobics group every day. An avid golfer, Coffeyville provided many potential playing partners; Stan, Terry Downing, Pat and other locals he met on the course. He also loved fishing and visited Pat's farm pond regularly.

In 1993 he decided to have his knee replaced so he could continue playing golf. During the operation he had a heart attack. Shortly after moving him to a hospital in Kansas City, he died. He was buried near Dad's grave.

Mom felt horrible about it, but in her unshakable way, she recovered quickly and moved on.

LINDA #3

The house on Fifth Street became too much for Mom to manage. Utilities and insurance were expensive and she was tired of rambling around that huge house alone. In 1997, she decided to sell it. The notion upset some of the kids. That was where we all gathered. It was the only home many of them had ever known. I guess we all believed she would keep it until the end. We thought she was too sentimental to ever let it go. In the process, we lost track of just how tough and practical Mom could be. She had no interest in holding on to the past. In her world, yesterday held memories, today was for living and tomorrow was full of possibilities. A house was just a house and she refused to be shackled by its meaning to other people.

A few days before Mom moved to a new apartment, the thirteen kids were home for a family reunion. Mom decided to cook her famous breakfast one more time when we were all together. In order to accommodate fourteen people, we joined two long tables together and brought in extra chairs from the kitchen. Some of us set the table with plates and silverware. Others poured orange juice, added jelly and honey to both ends of the table, or placed napkins on each plate. Mom prepared homemade biscuits. She fried ham, bacon and fresh side. As the biscuits baked, she fried twenty-four sunny side up eggs.

Mom took Dad's chair at the head of the table. After thirty-four years, it was the last time we were together in that house.

CAROL # 2

My family and I lived in Montana and later in Nevada. I saw Mom most often when I came home for family reunions every two years. It was a chance to catch up with everyone else and get some idea of how Mom was doing. She was in her element at those reunions; the matriarch of a happy, prosperous family.

One evening, she and I were sitting together in the building where everyone gathered. We watched a parade of people coming and going. The little kids, now many of them her great-grandchildren, were having a water balloon fight. Older kids were playing at the cornhole toss. Many were gathered at tables, both inside and out, trading stories. Conversation and laughter spilled out from all directions. Individuals flowed from one group to another, fitting into each new cluster like a puzzle piece. The entire room was one body.

Mom wrapped her arm inside mine and said, "Can you believe how lucky we are?"

I knew it was more a comment than a question. I squeezed her hand and said, "It all starts with you, Mom. We are who you made us."

As people came and went, I began pointing out how many of us had lived with one another from time to time:

Kelly lived with my husband Bill and I between jobs.

Bill lived with Ginger's family during a construction project near her home in Indiana.

Kelly and Jerry lived with Mary and Terry when they first moved to Tulsa.

Hal lived with Kelly and Jerry after graduating from college.

Terry lived with Kelly and Jerry and worked for Jerry painting houses over two summers.

Ginger lived with Kelly and Jerry during a summer break from college.

Pat lived with Mary and Terry for a short time.

Al lived with Stan when he thought about moving to Tulsa.

There were probably others, but those were the ones I could remember at the time. Mom beamed. "I hope you're always close," she said. "I want these reunions to go on forever. I want that to be my legacy, and I'm leaving whatever money I have to make it possible."

Mom came to Las Vegas a number of times after Dad died, including in 1992. I told her that Aunt Velva was living with her daughter Colleen's family in a local suburb. She asked me to invite them over for dinner. It had been years since she and Velva were together, and she was excited to see her again.

I have witnessed many touching moments as a school teacher, administrator, sister and mother. The most unique among them fill you up—make you proud to be human.

That was how I felt when Mom and Aunt Velva saw one another after too many years. As soon as Velva entered the room, they each cried out the other's name and fell into one another's arms. Through sobs and kisses, they held tight. In time, hand-in-hand, they moved to the sofa and sat down as one. They talked about Dad, the kids, Virgie, Harold and each other. They recaptured some of the memories that shaped them, their histories coming to life through rarely told stories. They laughed and cried again—their joy filled the room and made us all smile.

Mom told me later that Velva's twangy voice was like music to her ears and her hearty laugh a forgotten treasure.

That was the last time they saw one another. Velva died in 1994 and was laid to rest next to Harold in Carthage, Missouri.

STAN # 5

Mom had been on her own for a few years, when she met a man she liked and dated for a time. He was Dad's opposite in nearly every regard—talkative, outgoing, close minded and uninspiring. He held only one ace; he was a romantic. We were happy for Mom, and thankful she had someone to enjoy time with. He died not long after they met.

Aunt Madeline began to fail a few years after Mom sold the house and moved to an apartment. She refused to go to an assisted living facility. Short of that, she finally agreed to move in with Linda, who was good enough to welcome her. Eventually, she needed more care than Linda could give. Aunt was having trouble remembering from one minute to the next; her 'now' existing in ever shorter windows. We decided to use that deficit to our advantage.

Arrangements were made for her to enter an assisted living facility in Coffeyville. One day, after a doctor's appointment, instead of taking her back to Linda's, we drove to Windsor Place, a Senior Living Facility. The staff met us at the front door and led Aunt Madeline to a large room near the front of the building. Her personal belongings were waiting for her. She laid her purse on the dresser she had owned for over 50 years, inspected her hair in its oblong mirror and thanked us for our trouble. She was home.

As we were leaving, Aunt followed us into the lobby. With a certain flair and a sweep of her hand, she said, "I own all of this building."

What a magical illusion, I thought. *Good for her.*

PAT # 9

Shortly after Aunt Madeline moved to Linda's, Mom rented her former apartment across the street from Holy Name church. The long, one-story, multi-unit building stretched away from the sidewalk toward the mid-block alleyway. Mom's unit was on the near end, closest to the church's front doors. I know she felt lucky to make that her home.

Mom was a fixture at nearly every activity the grandkids competed in, volunteered for, acted in or chose to join. They knew she would be there to support them. She was the loudest fan at sporting events and the longest applauder at school plays.

She had cooked lunch for most of them, just as she had her own kids. She expected them to mind her, exacted punishment when it was deserved, but consistently showered them with affection. She helped them with homework and gave advice whether they asked for it or not. Hers was a second home to the grandkids. In return, they loved everything about her. They were part of her.

While Mom flourished, Aunt Madeline became less aware with each passing month. Her memory, merely slipping for a time, had fallen off a cliff.

I represented a food service company. One of my accounts included the Senior Care facility where Aunt Madeline was living. I typically visited the kitchen staff first, took their order and then stopped by to see Aunt. The proof of her decline was literally on her face. She had been meticulous about her makeup from the day she began wearing it. Her routine was reliable. She spent thirty minutes each morning creating her "new face" as she called it. Then, just before bed, she removed all of it with a generous application of Noxzema and a soft cloth.

She continued that practice until the very end, though her wavering attention to detail became obvious. It was most noticeable by the expanding application of her lipstick. I knew where her lips were supposed to be, but based on the ever-changing spread of that deep red paste, it was anybody's guess where they might end.

I typically escorted her to the couches in the community living area where we sat and talked. One day, I asked her if she remembered much about Uncle Al, her husband of over fifty years.

She paused to think about it. Her penciled-on eyebrows furled. "Who is that?" she finally asked.

I let it drop.

Aunt Madeline was living in a collapsing present; her memories measured in minutes. I wondered if there might be some benefit to that existence. If the past were forgotten, chances are the future was equally unexplored in her featureless mind.

Aunt Madeline died in 2002.

58

UNTIL LATER

Told by Kelly #4

Dale	Barbara

Mike · Carol · Linda · Kelly · Stan · Hal · Mary · Ginger · Pat · Terry · Tim · Teresa · Al

In 2008 and 2009, Mom fell a few times for unexplained reasons. Her first tumble happened during a walk in her neighborhood. While unsure, she thought she had tripped over an uneven break in the sidewalk. The result was a swollen black eye and extensive bruising on her face. She took it in stride, even laughing at herself for being clumsy. We worried, but hoped it was just a one-off event. And then she fell in her apartment twice, once in the shower.

Through Linda's encouragement, Mom decided to move to her house that summer. Things were going well, though Mom suffered from aching joints and general body discomfort. Regardless, she continued to find joy in nearly everything she did. She was the star at family gatherings, sat in her lawn chair at the grandkid's football or soccer games, visited friends, attended church every Sunday and enjoyed a group breakfast afterward. On days when her aches and pains were particularly difficult, all we had to do was ask if she wanted to go to the casino and she came to life like a sudden gust of wind.

Linda was secretary to the head counselor at the Coffeyville Middle School. She worked all day and then came home and prepared a three-course meal. One evening, Mom told Linda she worked too hard all day to be making a dinner for the two of them.

"I should be in there helping you," Mom said.

Linda stepped into the living room and answered, "You raised thirteen kids. It's our turn to take care of you. So, you just relax. I've got this."

"I didn't say I was coming in there," Mom said. "I just said I *should* be helping."

In early September, she fell in the shower again. She complained that her back hurt, so we took her to the doctor. He found a small crack in one of the bones on her spine. He decided they could correct the problem with a minor procedure, but it would require two nights in the hospital. Mom was fine with that. Going back to her week-long stays while delivering a baby, the hospital was like a luxury resort in her world. Her satisfaction was often measured by the quality of food. And like so many other "best ever" recent moments in her life, she typically found the fare outstanding.

Many of the kids and their families visited over those two days. The last few were there when I called at 8:30 on the evening of September 10, 2009. Mom sounded fine, though her thoughts were disconnected at times. I figured the medication she had been taking over the previous two days might be having an effect.

"You're not making much sense, Mom" I said, "put one of the kids on the phone and I'll call you in the morning."

She handed the phone to Mary. She said Mom was doing great, and the doctor believed they would release her the following day. Mary told me she planned to stay the night. I learned later that Mom would have none of that. "I'm doing fine," she told Mary. "You go home."

The visitors drifted away throughout the evening. Mary was the last one in the room until she left around 9 pm.

In less than an hour, hospital staff called Mary and Linda and told them Mom had been moved to Intensive Care. When they arrived at the hospital, they learned that her vitals had crashed, she had coded and they were doing everything they could to revive her. Eventually, the attending physician came to the waiting room and said there was no hope. She was gone.

∼

Before the funeral, we gathered in the parking lot across the street from our former family home. The mood was predominately sorrowful, though joy sometimes asserted itself. Those moments centered around the affection shared between brothers and sisters, nieces and nephews, and cousins, along with neighbors and friends. Beyond the competing emotions of sorrow and joy, a second contrast became apparent: As depressing as the moment was, we were there to honor the most passionately optimistic person most of us would ever know.

It was time to enter the church. We filed in, oldest to youngest, each Wilson accompanied by their spouse and surrounded by their own children. A typical funeral required reserving from two to five pews on the right side of the church for family members. For an 87-year-old woman, one, maybe two rows would be more than enough. In our case, Father reserved over half of one side of the church. We filled those pews and more.

A friend of mine commented: "I was on the left side of the church, maybe half way back. Row after row was already filled up and I began to wonder how many of them, like me, had been touched by Barbara. How many loaves of homemade bread, how many sheets of cinnamon rolls, how many meals had she served this loving crowd?

And then your family began walking in and it seemed like the line would never end. I tried to hold it back, but I began crying before the service even began."

Songs were sung and mass was started. At the appointed moment, Father O'Hare, who had driven from Wichita just for this purpose, moved to the pulpit to deliver a eulogy. He began with: "Barbara prepared two messages she wanted to leave her family. She asked me to read them at this event. Both were in her own hand, the penmanship still beautiful and flowing. She acknowledged that the first letter was borrowed from an article she found in the Catholic Digest. She felt it expressed her feelings perfectly."

A letter to my beautiful family with all my love.

> If I had a choice to give you worldly goods or character, I would give you character. With character you will get worldly goods,

because character is loyalty, honesty, ability and, I hope, a sense of humor.

All the wealth on earth is not equal to a good name. Be kind to everybody. Do charity to all, especially members of the family. In our family, love and peace have reigned, and I pray that the same will continue

My blessing I bestow upon you now. Find favor in the eyes of God and humanity in joy and full contentment.

As for me, just shed a respectful tear if you think I merit it, but I am sure that you are intelligent enough not to weep all over the place.

Just remember, when I shove off for greener pastures, that I do so joyfully and unafraid, and if you must know, a little curious.

Lovingly,

Mother

The next passage is all her own. She wrote it the night before a surgery:

Dear Ones:

I'm writing this because I'm a little apprehensive about tomorrow. I want you to know that if I don't make it – it will be fine. I've had a wonderful life (mainly because of all you wonderful kids) - - and I don't particularly want to get a lot older. I know you will all be okay. You have each other and I'm so glad you're all so close. Please always stay close. Have a reunion every year and I'll be watching.

Thank you for being what you are.

I love you!!!

Mom

The mass lasted for roughly 30 minutes, at its heart was the taking of communion. The family led a procession of people to the waiting priest, host in hand—gently administering the evidence of God's grace.

The cemetery was only a few miles away. The line of cars following the hearse stretched out-of-sight behind us. The graveside service was short and unremarkable—except for the body that prompted it. Mom's casket rested on a bier in front of her and Dad's headstone. A few of the brothers and sisters touched it before walking away.

I held back, standing next to the coffin and trying to find words worthy of the moment. How can the essence of such a valuable life be captured? How can an appropriate end be fashioned?

And then I remembered life's mural on a moving carousel. I pictured Mom stepping into the painting next to Dad.

They were smiling.

PICTURES

Mom (Barbara) Dad (Dale)

PICTURES

High School Graduation Pictures

PART VI   MURALS ON CAROUSELS

1963

1978

Family Pictures

PICTURES

2016

2018

Family Reunion Pictures

PART VI   MURALS ON CAROUSELS

The Dress

THE FAMILY

Dale Wilson
Barbara Wilson
Mike Wilson
Carol (Wilson) Lark
Linda (Wilson) Ryburn
Kelly Wilson
Stan Wilson
Hal Wilson
Mary (Wilson) Downing
Ginger (Wilson) Krueger
Pat Wilson
Terry Wilson
Tim Wilson
Teresa (Wilson) Lee
Al Wilson

Mike
Angie Wilson
Rebecca Peronteaux
Brance Wilson
Nicolas Mockus
Ian Wilson
Ashley Drietz
Devin Drietz
Lincoln Drietz
Ramsey Drietz

Carol (Wilson) Lark
Bill Lark
Troy Lark
Jeanette (Hinchey) Lark
Travis Lark
Allison (Levy) Lark
Taylor Lark
Cade Lark

Linda (Wilson) Ryburn
Carol (Underwood) Thomison
Krystan (Caldwell) Smith
Grady Smith
Karter Koehn
Emma Koehn
Max Caldwell
Nicole (Woods) Caldwell
Oliver Caldwell
Sawyer Caldwell
Archer Caldwell
Joe Underwood
Mark Weatherby
Kelli (Underwood) George
Shane George
Zach George
Rodney Close

Tanner Close-George
Ashley George
Miranda George
Kavery George
Kameila George
(Baby boy due in March)
Karla (Ryburn) Bauer
Paul Bauer
Autumn Bauer
Lenny Sparks
Logan Sparks
Mackenzie (Bauer) Kirkpatrick
David Kirkpatrick
Jaden Bauer
Malone Escavido
Brycen Bauer

Kelly Wilson
Jerry Malach

Stan Wilson
Corrina (Shipman) Wilson
Clark Wilson
Kelli (Crabtree) Wilson
Juliette Wilson

Hal Wilson
Holly (Tackett) Wilson
Chelsea Wilson
Audrey Wilson
Brianna Wilson

Mary (Wilson) Downing
Terry Downing
Tara (Downing) Mann
Will Mann

Molly Mann
Maggie Mann
Sarah (Downing) Bromley
Kwin Bromley
Braylee Bromley
Lindsey (Downing) Schroeder
Caleb Schroeder
Lincoln Schroeder
Layne Schroeder

Ginger (Wilson) Krueger
Patrick Krueger
Ryan Krueger
Nicole (Perez) Krueger
Liam Krueger
Brooklyn Krueger
Matthew Krueger
Alissa (Gothard) Krueger
Isla Krueger
Veda Krueger
Otto Krueger
Liv Krueger
Brendan Krueger
Jill (Terdy) Krueger
Ella Rose Krueger
Owen Krueger
Arabelle Krueger
Jack Krueger
Elizabeth (Krueger) Bild
James Bild
Lucy Bild
Madeline Bild
Annie Bild
Patrick Bild

Charlie Bild
Oliver Bild
Thomas Krueger

Pat Wilson
Cheryl (Nellis) Wilson
Kyle Wilson
Monica (Conklin) Wilson
Lilly Wilson
Logan Wilson
Keith Wilson
Jacquelyn (Shoemake) Wilson
Delaney Wilson
Collin Wilson
Kevin Wilson
Melanie (Lay) Wilson
Cole Wilson
(Baby due in June)

Terry Wilson
Laurie Wilson
Erica (Wilson) Martin
Kyle Martin
Natalie Martin
Haylie Martin
Rebecca (Wilson) Marure
Matt Marure
Hudson Marure
Eloise Marure

Farrah Marure
(Baby due in January)
Robert Wilson

Tim Wilson
AnnaMarie (Scaletta) Wilson
Seth Wilson
Rebecca Wilson
Samantha Wilson
Sloane Strobietto
Tony Scaletta
Ashley (Wilson) Smith
Graham Smith
Alexis Wilson

Teresa (Wilson) Lee
Mike Lee
David Lee
Tony Lee
Jen (Evans) Lee
Hannah (Lee) Duethman
Nik Duethman
Gabe Duethman
Adaline Duethman
Harry Duethman

Al Wilson
Paul Werner

LONG MARRIAGES

Carol (Wilson) and Bill Lark	53 years
Kelly Wilson and Jerry Malach	51 years
Stan and Corrina (Shipman) Wilson	31 years
Hal and Holly (Tackett) Wilson	36 years
Mary (Wilson) and Terry Downing	51 years
Ginger (Wilson) and Patrick Krueger	45 years
Pat and Cheryl (Nellis) Wilson	47 years
Terry and Laurie (Speigel) Wilson	40 years
Tim and AnnaMarie (Scaletta) Wilson	28 years
Teresa (Wilson) and Mike Lee	41 years
Al Wilson and Paul Werner	33 years

OCCUPATIONS

First and Second Generation (Including Spouses)

Accounting Supervisor
Accounts Manager – Insurance
Actor
Assistant Dean of Students - University
Assistant to the Chief of Police
Attorney (4)
Business Owner/Entrepreneur (6)
Buyer/Seller on Internet Platform
CEO of Top Twenty Mortgage Bank
Chemical Engineer/Sales Management
Chief of Police
City Maintenance
City Services Manager
Claims Manager - Insurance
COO – Education Program for Koch Industries
Corporate Event Manager
CPA
Draftsman
VP - Executive level placement
Financial Analyst
High School Principal (3)
Home School Teacher
Homemaker (5)
Home-School Teacher
Hospital Receptionist
International Teacher Program
Judge
Lawyer (4)
Legal Assistant
Manager of Commercial Underwriting – Insurance
Management – Corporate Development and Strategy
Mechanical and Civil Engineer
Mechanical Engineer
Medical Billing Specialist
Medical Equipment Sales Representative
Neurosurgeon
Nurse (3)
Nurse Practitioner
Nurse Supervisor
Orthopedic Surgeon

Paraprofessional - Education
Personal Fitness Trainer
Physical Therapist
President of Several Operating Companies – Real-estate
Project Manager – Fermi Labs
Property Management
Publicist
Purchasing Department Supervisor
Race Horse Handicapper
Real-estate Lender Representative
Realtor
Sales Director – Tech Industry
Sales Management – Oil and Gas
Secretary
Senior Living Caregiver
Speech Therapist
Superintendent of Schools (2)
Teacher (7)
Truck Driver
Union Electrician
University Development (2)
University Development Representative
Venture Capital – Medical
Writer

AUTHOR BIOGRAPHY

Kelly D. Wilson is a U.S. Army veteran, college graduate, former Sales Manager for an oilfield products manufacturing company, a race horse handicapper and writer. His most important skills involve observing and remembering—qualities that turned the expression of a life journey into the essence of "You're Getting Bumped."